Challenging Borders

Challenging Borders

Contingencies and Consequences

Edited by Paul McKenzie-Jones, Sheila McManus, and Julie Young

AU PRESS

Published by AU Press, Athabasca University
1 University Drive, Athabasca, AB T9S 3A3

https://doi.org/10.15215/aupress/9781771994019.01

Cover design by Natalie Olsen, kisscutdesign.com
Cover image *Border Disruptions* (2019) by Heather Parrish and Leslie Gross-Wyrtzen
Printed and bound in Canada

Library and Archives Canada Cataloguing in Publication

Title: Challenging borders : contingencies and consequences / edited by Paul
    McKenzie-Jones, Sheila McManus, and Julie Young.
Names: McKenzie-Jones, Paul R., 1970– editor | McManus, Sheila, editor | Young,
    Julie E. E., 1978– editor
Description: Includes bibliographical references.
Identifiers: Canadiana (print) 20240483936 | Canadiana (ebook) 20240484983 |
    ISBN 9781771994019 (softcover) | ISBN 9781771994033 (EPUB) |
    ISBN 9781771994026 (PDF)
Subjects: LCSH: Borderlands—Social aspects. | LCSH: Borderlands—Political
    aspects. | LCSH: National characteristics. | LCSH: Sovereignty. | LCSH: Freedom
    of movement.
Classification: LCC JC323 .C43 2025 | DDC 320.1/2—dc23

We acknowledge the financial support of the Government of Canada through the
Canada Book Fund (CBF) for our publishing activities and the assistance provided
by the Government of Alberta through the Alberta Media Fund.

Canadä   Alberta
              Government

This collection is for nations, communities, and individuals who have been and are being harmed by border regimes around the world.

Contents

Acknowledgements

In June 2019, a group of people assembled in Lethbridge, Canada, for a conference titled "The Line Crossed Us: New Directions in Critical Border Studies." Many were based in the United States, and several more had travelled from overseas. Little could any of us have known that less than a year later, governments around the world would abruptly close their borders in response to a global pandemic, one that put an indefinite end to face-to-face gatherings of the sort from which this volume evolved. Seldom had the power of borders to separate been thrown into such high relief.

The conference that would soon seem so impossible originated in an email that Sheila had sent to Julie and Paul the previous year, welcoming two new border researchers to the University of Lethbridge and inviting us for coffee and a chat. We bonded around a sense that the broader field of critical border studies was ready for more transnational and transdisciplinary comparisons and collaborations where artists, activists, and academics work together to challenge border regimes. The Lethbridge Border Studies Group was born.

The conference that brought together the researchers in this collection was supported by individual research funds, including support from Julie's Canada Research Chair in Critical Border Studies, and institutional support from the University of Lethbridge's Faculty of Arts and Sciences, School of Graduate Studies, Office of Research and Innovation Services, Communications (especially Catharine Reader), Information Technology, and the facilities department. We also give our heartfelt thanks to the invaluable contributions of students Sydney Cabanas, Madeline Mendoza, and Seanna Uglem to organizing the 2019 conference and to Stephanie Laine Hamilton for her indispensable help in compiling this manuscript.

Challenging Borders

Introduction: Pushing Boundaries

"We didn't cross the line; the line crossed us" is at once a recognition and a refusal: a statement of fact that the drawing of settler-colonial boundary lines tried to erase and rewrite existing relationships to land and territory and a rejection of the authority and claims symbolized by those lines. It is both a geographic argument and an expression of struggles over land, belonging, and identity. The phrase is most often attributed to Mexican communities crossed by the boundary line when the United States pushed its boundary south in the 1840s and 1850s. Whatever its origins, however, "We didn't cross the border; the border crossed us" has become a rallying cry of Indigenous nations and migrant justice organizers across North America and around the world.[1]

"The Line Crossed Us" was also the name of the 2019 conference where the chapters collected here were first presented. The gathering sparked conversations between some of the academic disciplines that ask questions about borders and between academics and the artists and activists who are contesting and reimagining borders and their meanings. The wider field of critical border studies has always encompassed a variety of disciplines and approaches, but the academic scholarship has tended to remain within disciplinary silos while academics, artists, and activists rarely see one another's work. The conference brought Indigenous and migration politics into conversation while also historicizing contemporary border issues and "crises," and the chapters here challenge the sense of permanence that often characterizes how borders and nationalism have been built and framed, politically and historically. Rather than accept the inevitability of how nation-states and their borders are understood in material reality, these authors unsettle those teleological assumptions to explore new and different ways of understanding competing and overlapping sovereignties, jurisdictions, and authorities. They invite us to think across disciplines about what it means to "do" border studies.

Fostering an ability to see and make connections across these traditional divides is increasingly important because borders remain unshakably central to the identities, functions, and policies of modern nation-states and the international refugee regime. The chapters here are grouped thematically rather than by discipline, geography, or chronology, already refusing some of the rigid binaries that North American and European borders try to produce. The authors include activists, artists, and filmmakers, as well as scholars from fields as diverse as geography, history, Indigenous studies, migration and refugee studies, and political science, creating a multivocal conversation across and between disciplines. In these eight chapters, we can see the push and pull of nationhood versus migration, freedom of movement versus restrictions of travel, contested claims of sovereignty replete with contradictions and compromises of multiple peoples claiming the same spaces as their own, and the inherent disjunction of borders being both a source of hope for those seeking sanctuary and a method of protection against those same people.

Part 1, "Visualizing Borders," includes four chapters that invite us to see, think about, and produce knowledge about borders and their consequences in different ways. In the first two chapters, two very different creative and political projects invite us to see borderlines and borderlands differently. In "Toward a Decolonial Archive: A Reflection on the Operationalization Process of Critical Transborder Documentary Production Practice," Ramón Resendiz and Rosalva Resendiz discuss their collaborations with key partners as they developed the archival documentary film *El Muro | The Wall* (2017). The film explores the contested space and history of South Texas / Northern Mexico and foregrounds how Indigenous resistance to colonial, imperial, and postcolonial dispossessions continues to shape the landscape of this region. The collaborators engaged in a critical documentary filmmaking process and envisioned the end product as a decolonial didactic tool that would refuse the erasures foundational to settler-colonial mythologies of place and consider the generative potentialities of such work. In "Working the Border: Interdisciplinary Encounters Across Intellectual, Material, and Political Boundaries," political geographer Leslie Gross-Wyrtzen and visual artist Heather Parrish situate themselves in the forests of the Spanish-Moroccan borderlands to demonstrate that art can trouble perceptions of borders as fixed and settled, exposing instead their dynamism and permeability. A crucial element of their contribution is the way it invites viewers of the art installation and readers of the chapter to engage in discussions of the multiplicity, contingency, and contradiction inherent in conceptualizations and practices of boundaries, borders, and barriers. Their collaboration also offers insights into the possibilities and limitations of collaborative and multidisciplinary encounters that seek to bridge theoretical, methodological, and political boundaries.

The next two chapters in the first part push the metaphor of seeing borders differently in other thought-provoking directions, exploring in one instance the links between a nation's borders and the "national body" and asking us in the other to move beyond what have become stale binaries in traditional perceptions of borders as fixed and settled. In "Remapping the Geo-body of a Nation: How Young People in Finland Understand Shifting Borders," geographer Chloe Wells explores how teenagers in Finland imagine and give meaning to their nation's borderlines in the context of the country's loss of roughly 10 percent of its territory during World War II. Growing up some seven decades later, at a time when the Finland-Russia border was relatively open and cross-border traffic had increased, her young respondents had internalized the postwar map of Finland and were remote from both the events and the emotions of the war. Yet they still mentally referenced the prewar "geo-body" to make sense of prevailing national discourses that continue to reflect inherited narratives of loss and pain. In the final chapter of this part, "From Lines in the Sand to the Wave/Particle Duality: A Quantum Imaginary for Critical Border Studies," political scientist Michael Murphy embraces the models provided by the groundbreaking work of scholars ranging from Gloria Anzaldúa to Karen Barad to propose a way out of what he sees as a common impasse in the field of border studies, where researchers are engaged in either macroscopic analyses that focus on overarching concepts like sovereignty and territory or microscopic studies of localized, lived experiences of borders. He suggests instead a "quantum imaginary," applying the wave/particle duality in quantum theory to argue that if we see borders as dual rather than binary, we can better capture the nature of borders as multiple, complex, and paradoxical.

By linking chapters about a film, an art installation, young people's drawings, and theoretical physics, part 1 generates conversations about creative and theoretical perspectives on borderlines beyond lines on a map or a specific location. The mobility and multiplicity set out in Murphy's quantum imaginary, for example, finds an immediate case study in Gross-Wyrtzen and Parrish's disassembled, layered images, while the ways a borderline leads to grief and disconnection are embodied in both *El Muro | The Wall* and the way Finnish youth come to terms with a national discourse of "losing a limb." There is a resonance here with Anzaldúa's characterization of the US-Mexico border as "una herida abierta"—an open wound—and Salter's theorization of the border as "suture" to describe the "world-creating function" of borders. Reading these chapters in connection to one another offers a nuanced visualization of the violences enacted through bordering practices while also opening different ways of engaging with the work that borders do, in ways that are both mundane and brutal.[2]

The complexity of North America's border regimes, new and old, is explored in part 2, "Cuttings and Crossings." The act of crossing any border is fraught with hope and uncertainty, ambition and fear, and these authors examine the ways in which border crossings—and the manner of those crossings—have different meanings and consequences depending on the identities of those crossing the border. The first two chapters in this part focus on the Indigenous borderlands of the western Canada-US boundary line. In "Border Crossed: Sinixt Identity, Place, and Belonging in the Canada-US Borderlands," anthropologist Lori Barkley, matriarch Marilyn James, and activist Lou Stone trace some of the effects that the 1846 decision to run the border west of the Rockies along the forty-ninth parallel had on the Sinixt. After 1846 roughly two-thirds of their traditional territory (*təmxʷúlaʔxʷ*) was now north of the line in British Columbia, and the remaining third was south of the line in Washington State, dividing people between the Confederated Tribes of the Colville Reservation in Washington in 1872 and a small reserve in British Columbia in 1902. After the Canadian government declared the Sinixt "extinct" in 1956, their *təmxʷúlaʔxʷ* began to disappear from maps, and other Indigenous nations began to extend their territorial claims in the area. The Sinixt thus "exist in" and have to make space for themselves in "multiple borderlands." Historian Ryan Hall argues in "Last Refuge: Indigenous Refugees and the Making of Canada's Numbered Treaties" (chap. 6 of this volume) that we must understand the political motivations of Canada's Numbered Treaties, especially Treaty 7 in southern Alberta, within a framework of Indigenous peoples being displaced within their own homelands and forced to cross a settler-imposed border within them. Rather than the popular framing of the United States and Canada as intrinsically different nations in their societal and political makeup—even in the ways they self-represent their relationships with Indigenous peoples—these two chapters reinforce that the two nations are forever entwined rather than separated by their border because of the ways they have used it to restrict and police Indigenous movements and bisect Indigenous homelands.

The last two chapters in this part examine the deliberate dehumanization that underpins present-day US border control practices. Interdisciplinary feminist scholar Claudia Donoso's "Keeping Them Vulnerable: Female Applicants and the Biopolitics of Asylum in Texas" discusses how biopower operates within border policies that regulate, criminalize, and dehumanize the bodies of female asylum seekers from Central America. Marking the distinction between refugees and asylum seekers, Donoso shows how crossing the border prior to seeking asylum, as is the right of the asylum seeker, has been turned into a criminal act by the flexing of biopower within US border policy. In the last chapter of this part, "Experiences at the New Canadian-American Frontier: 'I just assume that no laws exist . . . ,'" Evan Light, a scholar of communications and surveillance, political scientist Sarah Naumes, and sociologist Aliya Amarshi note that the policing of immigrants has entered the digital era, as the United States' border-crossing norms now include insisting on the right to investigate travellers' social media. The chapter discusses one research project that uses personal experiences of border crossers to better understand Canadian border policies and a second project that exposes the myriad ways in which the border is now a complex system of surveillance and documentation that informs decisions on who can and cannot cross. Ultimately, the authors argue that the border needs to be rehumanized and processes of dehumanization dismantled.

Grouping analyses of how Indigenous nations have had to confront and resist settler-colonial boundaries with contemporary policies used to constrain and surveil some border crossers while allowing others to move more freely exposes some of the commonalities between the strategies North America's nation-states have used for centuries to dehumanize anyone who challenged their border regimes. By focusing on a common thread of displacement in the past and present, this part also refutes the presumed gap between studies of Indigenous histories of border encounters and present-day migration and refugees.

Anne McNevin's afterword, "On Being Unsettled: Discomfort and Noninnocence in Border Studies," is informed by her plenary talk at the conference. She notes that this collection, an anthology that represents a particular kind of

Western academic enterprise, is "the outcome of a conference that was uncomfortable" and needed to be so. Every effort to disrupt disciplinary boundaries and conventions inevitably also reinscribed certain kinds of borders and certain kinds of knowledge about borders. Each presenter shared their knowledge while speaking in a place they were not from and to an audience that did not necessarily share their disciplinary or cultural perspective. The academics outnumbered the artists and community activists, generating rich conversations that, nevertheless, were not and never can be "innocent endeavors" and did not move as far as we might have hoped away from academic perspectives. As McNevin observes, this anthology then came together against the backdrop of the global COVID-19 pandemic, which "focused the attention of those slow to acknowledge all manner of global interdependencies" at the same time as it "precipitated a defensive mobilization of national borders, both materially and symbolically, almost as a reflex response." Borders rarely matter so little, and so much, as during a global crisis, staying "stuck on enduring cuts of difference hiding in plain sight" like the "global colour line." McNevin concludes that what this collection can add to the broader field of critical border studies are "helpful orientations for critical inquiry" and a model for inter- and cross-disciplinary conversations.

This collection thus sits at the intersection of, and speaks back to, several broad areas of border studies scholarship that are themselves usually conversations held in isolation. For example, there is an enormous amount of scholarship about the histories of Indigenous peoples in what became North America's borderlands and the many different ways those nations encountered and resisted the imposition of those lines.[3] Similarly, historians, geographers, political scientists, and others have spent a great deal of time and attention on the histories of migrants and refugees encountering those borderlines for the first time. The chapters by Barkley, James, and Stone; Hall; Donoso; and Light, Naumes, and Amarshi are therefore valuable contributions to the existing scholarship but also push it in useful new directions by challenging the ways the border is too often reified by scholarly disciplines that still use settler-colonial nation-states to organize their research and blurring the too-common scholarly divide in which studies of Indigenous peoples in what are now borderlands regions are often written as if they are completely disconnected from the experiences of migrants and refugees.[4] There are a few exceptions to that pattern, and the chapters here will contribute to bridging that gap.[5] More broadly, the chapters by Wells and Murphy speak to a deliberate fluidity of identity and duality within borderlands that de-emphasizes and challenges their static nature within assertions of nationhood and border management.

However rich these existing fields of scholarship are, their isolation from one another and from the artists and activists doing their own work to challenge border regimes does more than just impoverish each field; it limits our ability to challenge the power of borders. A question that reappears throughout this collection is whether it is possible to "decolonize" border studies in the context of settler-colonial states and whether "decolonization" is an appropriate lens, since it can tend to recentre the settler-colonial nation-state.[6] At the same time, however, decolonization can be a useful lens when examining immigration and refugee policies in those same settler states. North America's borders both are a legacy of and contribute to the ongoing patterns of settler colonialism; as such, they are regularly resisted, ignored, and refused by Indigenous communities and nations as well as by migrants and residents of border communities.[7] For Indigenous communities in what is now referred to as North America, the imposition of settler borders over traditional territories means that displacement is not only a foundational event but an ongoing experience.

Questions of displacement and borders, therefore, remain intensely salient in the current North American context and beyond, but to build on McNevin's intervention, efforts to "decolonize" border studies risk reinscribing the power of normative views of what borders are and what they do. In a country like Canada, which claims an identity as a nation of immigrants, the colonial context and inescapability of settler-colonial assumptions bear closer analysis in the fields of migration, refugee, and critical border studies. There have been nascent attempts to link struggles for migrants' rights with Indigenous organizing as noted, but very little scholarship and academic networking have been carried out in this area in recent years. The chapters here by Resendiz and Resendiz, Gross-Wyrtzen and Parrish, and Barkley et al. demonstrate how collaborative and creative work can challenge border regimes more directly and rethink border studies in the context of Canada and settler-colonial states.

The broader field of critical border studies is ready for more transnational and multidisciplinary comparisons and collaborations where artists, activists, and academics work together to challenge border regimes. This collection is a step in that direction by choosing to cross the lines that have separated our disciplines, fields of inquiry, and multiple strategies of resistance and refusal. The authors here connect thematically and contradict the ways that examinations of borders have too often highlighted processes of separation, distinction, and even isolation. Taken together, we challenge our colleagues in the wider field of border studies to look at similar issues from different angles and create a more composite picture of borders, migration, and Indigenous belonging across borderlands than has previously been offered elsewhere. These chapters ask us to think about borders differently, and in this way "doing" border studies can move us closer to undoing the harm that border regimes have caused and continue to cause.

Notes

1. See, for example, J. D. Cisneros, *The Border Crossed Us: Rhetorics of Borders, Citizenship, and Latina/o Identity*; Craig Fortier, "No One Is Illegal, Canada Is Illegal! Negotiating the Relationships between Settler Colonialism and Border Imperialism through Political Slogans"; and Karl Jacoby, *Shadows at Dawn: An Apache Massacre and the Violence of History*.
2. Gloria Anzaldúa. *Borderlands / La Frontera: The New Mestiza*, 24–25.; Mark B. Salter, "Theory of the /: The Suture and Critical Border Studies," 734–55.
3. See, for example, Clarissa Confer, Andrae Marak, and Laura Tuennerman, eds., *Transnational Indians in the North American West*; Michel Hogue, *Metis and the Medicine Line: Creating a Border and Dividing a People*; Benjamin Hoy, *A Line of Blood and Dirt: Creating the Canada-United States Border Across Indigenous Lands*; Kino-nda-niimi Collective, *The Winter We Danced: Voices from the Past, the Future, and the Idle No More Movement*; Jane Merritt, *At the Crossroad: Indians and Empires on a Mid-Atlantic Frontier, 1700–1763*; Evelyn Meyer, *Narrating Northern Borderlands: Thomas King, Howard F. Mosher, and Jim Lynch*; Joshua Reid, *The Sea Is My Country: The Maritime World of the Makahs*; Brendan Rensink, *Native but Foreign: Indigenous Immigrants and Refugees in the North American Borderlands*; Audra Simpson, *Mohawk Interruptus: Political Life Across the Borders of Settler States*; Alan Taylor, *The Divided Ground: Indians, Settlers, and the Northern Borderland of the American Revolution*; and Richard White, *The Middle Ground: Indians, Empires, and Republics in the Great Lakes Region, 1650–1815*.
4. See, for example, Kelly Lytle Hernández, *Migra! A History of the U.S. Border Patrol*; Miguel Antonio Levario, *Militarizing the Border: When Mexicans Became the Enemy*; Deborah Kang, *The INS on the Line: Making Immigration Law on the US-Mexico Border, 1917–1954*; Julian Lim, *Porous Borders: Multiracial Migrations and the Law in the U.S.-Mexico Borderlands*; D. J. Mattingly and E. R. Hansen, *Women and Change at the US-Mexico Border:*

Mobility, Labour, and Activism; Sheila McManus, *Both Sides Now: Writing the Edges of the North American West*; Julie E. E. Young, "Seeing like a Border City: Refugee Politics at the Borders of City and Nation-State," 407–23; and Julie E. E. Young, Luann Good Gingrich, Adrienne Wiebe, and Miriam Harder, "Tactical Borderwork: Central American Migrant Women Negotiating the Southern Border of Mexico," 200–221.

5. See, for example, Harald Bauder, "Closing the Immigration-Aboriginal Parallax Gap," 517–19; K. Conway and T. Pasch, *Beyond the Border: Tensions Across the Forty-Ninth Parallel in the Great Plains and Prairies*; Craig Fortier, "Decolonizing Borders: No One Is Illegal Movements in Canada and the Negotiation of Counter-national and Anti-colonial Struggles from within the Nation-State," 274–90; Kino-nda-niimi Collective, *Winter We Danced*; Jarett Martineau, "Rhythms of Change: Mobilizing Decolonial Consciousness, Indigenous Resurgence and the Idle No More Movement," 229–53; Walter Mignolo, *Local Histories/Global Designs: Coloniality, Subaltern Knowledges, and Border Thinking*; Heather N. Nicol, "From Territory to Rights: New Foundations for Conceptualising Indigenous Sovereignty," 794–814; Simpson, *Mohawk Interruptus*; Anna Stanley, Sedef Arat-Koç, Laurie K. Bertram, and Hayden King, "Intervention: Addressing the Indigenous-Immigration 'Parallax Gap'"; and Harsha Walia, *Undoing Border Imperialism*.

6. Eve Tuck and K. Wayne Yang, "Decolonization Is Not a Metaphor," 1–40.

7. Adam Gaudry and D. Lorenz, "Indigenization as Inclusion, Reconciliation, and Decolonization: Navigating the Different Visions for Indigenizing the Canadian Academy," 218–27; Kino-nda-niimi Collective, *Winter We Danced*; Martineau, "Rhythms of Change"; Nicol, "From Territory to Rights"; Anna Pratt, "The Canada-US Shiprider Program, Jurisdiction and the Crime-Security Nexus," 249–72; Patrick Wolfe, "Settler Colonialism and the Elimination of the Native," 387–409.

Bibliography

Anzaldúa, Gloria. *Borderlands / La Frontera: The New Mestiza*. 3rd ed. San Francisco, CA: Aunt Lute Books, 2007.

Bauder, Harald. "Closing the Immigration-Aboriginal Parallax Gap," *Geoforum* 42 (2011): 517–19.

Cisneros, J. D. *The Border Crossed Us: Rhetorics of Borders, Citizenship, and Latina/o Identity*. Tuscaloosa: University of Alabama Press, 2013.

Confer, Clarissa, Andrae Marak, and Laura Tuennerman, eds. *Transnational Indians in the North American West*. College Station, TX: Texas A&M University Press, 2015.

Conway, K., and T. Pasch. *Beyond the Border: Tensions Across the Forty-Ninth Parallel in the Great Plains and Prairies.* Montréal and Kingston: McGill-Queen's University Press, 2013.

Fortier, Craig. "Decolonizing Borders: No One Is Illegal Movements in Canada and the Negotiation of Counter-national and Anti-colonial Struggles from within the Nation-State." In *Producing and Negotiating Non-Citizenship: Precarious Legal Status in Canada,* edited by Luin Goldring and Patricia Landolt, 274–90. Toronto: University of Toronto Press, 2013.

Fortier, Craig. "No One Is Illegal, Canada Is Illegal! Negotiating the Relationships between Settler Colonialism and Border Imperialism through Political Slogans." *Decolonization: Indigeneity, Education & Society,* September 21, 2015. https://decolonization.wordpress.com/2015/09/21/no-one-is-illegal-canada-is-illegal-negotiating-the-relationships-between-settler-colonialism-and-border-imperialism-through-political-slogans/.

Gaudry, Adam, and D. Lorenz. "Indigenization as Inclusion, Reconciliation, and Decolonization: Navigating the Different Visions for Indigenizing the Canadian Academy." *AlterNative* 14, no. 3 (2018): 218–27.

Hernández, Kelly Lytle. *Migra! A History of the U.S. Border Patrol.* Berkeley: University of California Press, 2010.

Hogue, Michel. *Metis and the Medicine Line: Creating a Border and Dividing a People.* Chapel Hill: University of North Carolina Press, 2015.

Hoy, Benjamin. *A Line of Blood and Dirt: Creating the Canada-United States Border Across Indigenous Lands.* Oxford: Oxford University Press, 2021.

Jacoby, Karl. *Shadows at Dawn: An Apache Massacre and the Violence of History.* New York: Penguin, 2008.

Kang, Deborah. *The INS on the Line: Making Immigration Law on the US-Mexico Border, 1917–1954.* Oxford: Oxford University Press, 2017.

Kino-nda-niimi Collective. *The Winter We Danced: Voices from the Past, the Future, and the Idle No More Movement.* Winnipeg, MB: ARP Books, 2014.

Levario, Miguel Antonio. *Militarizing the Border: When Mexicans Became the Enemy.* College Station: Texas A&M University Press, 2012.

Lim, Julian. *Porous Borders: Multiracial Migrations and the Law in the U.S.-Mexico Borderlands.* Chapel Hill: University of North Carolina Press, 2017.

Martineau, Jarett. "Rhythms of Change: Mobilizing Decolonial Consciousness, Indigenous Resurgence and the Idle No More Movement." In *More Will Sing Their Way to Freedom: Indigenous Resistance and Resurgence,* edited by E. Coburn, 229–53. Halifax, NS: Fernwood, 2015.

Mattingly D. J., and E. R. Hansen. *Women and Change at the US-Mexico Border: Mobility, Labour, and Activism.* Tucson: University of Arizona Press, 2006.

McManus, Sheila. *Both Sides Now: Writing the Edges of the North American West.* College Station: Texas A&M University Press, 2022.

Merritt, Jane. *At the Crossroad: Indians and Empires on a Mid-Atlantic Frontier, 1700–1763.* Chapel Hill: University of North Carolina Press, 2003.

Meyer, Evelyn. *Narrating Northern Borderlands: Thomas King, Howard F. Mosher, and Jim Lynch.* New York: Peter Lang GmbH, Internationaler Verlag der Wissenschaften, 2016.

Mignolo, Walter. *Local Histories/Global Designs: Coloniality, Subaltern Knowledges, and Border Thinking.* Princeton, NJ: Princeton University Press, 2000.

Nicol, Heather N. "From Territory to Rights: New Foundations for Conceptualising Indigenous Sovereignty." *Geopolitics* 22, no. 4 (2017): 794–814.

Pratt, Anna. "The Canada-US Shiprider Program, Jurisdiction and the Crime-Security Nexus." In *National Security, Surveillance, and Emergencies: Canadian and Australian Sovereignty Compared,* edited by K. Walby, R. K. Lippert, I. Warren, and D. Palmer, 249–72. Montréal and Kingston: McGill-Queen's University Press, 2016.

Reid, Joshua. *The Sea Is My Country: The Maritime World of the Makahs.* New Haven, CT: Yale University Press, 2015.

Rensink, Brendan. *Native but Foreign: Indigenous Immigrants and Refugees in the North American Borderlands.* College Station: Texas A&M University Press, 2018.

Salter. "Theory of the /: The Suture and Critical Border Studies." *Geopolitics* 17, no. 4 (2012): 734–55.

Simpson, Audra. *Mohawk Interruptus: Political Life Across the Borders of Settler States.* Durham, NC: Duke University Press, 2014.

Stanley, Anna, Sedef Arat-Koç, Laurie K. Bertram, and Hayden King. "Intervention: Addressing the Indigenous-Immigration 'Parallax Gap.'" *Antipode,* June 18, 2014. https://antipodefoundation.org/2014/06/18/addressing-the-indigenous-immigration-parallax-gap/.

Taylor, Alan. *The Divided Ground: Indians, Settlers, and the Northern Borderland of the American Revolution.* Visalia, CA: Vintage, 2007.

Tuck, Eve, and K. Wayne Yang. "Decolonization Is Not a Metaphor." *Decolonization: Indigeneity, Education & Society* 1, no. 1 (2012): 1–40.

Walia, Harsha. *Undoing Border Imperialism.* Washington, DC: AK Press / Institute for Anarchist Studies, 2013.

White, Richard. *The Middle Ground: Indians, Empires, and Republics in the Great Lakes Region, 1650–1815.* Cambridge: Cambridge University Press, 1991.

Wolfe, Patrick. "Settler Colonialism and the Elimination of the Native." *Journal of Genocide Research* 8, no. 4 (2006): 387–409.

Young, Julie E. E. "Seeing like a Border City: Refugee Politics at the Borders of City and Nation-State." *Environment and Planning C: Politics and Space* 37, no. 3 (2018): 407–23.

Young, Julie E. E., Luann Good Gingrich, Adrienne Wiebe, and Miriam Harder. "Tactical Borderwork: Central American Migrant Women Negotiating the Southern Border of Mexico." In *Transnational Social Policy: Social Support in a World on the Move 2017*, edited by Luann Good Gingrich and Stefan Köngeter, 200–221. New York: Routledge, 2017.

Part 1
Visualizing Borders

1 Toward a Decolonial Archive

A Reflection on the Operationalization Process of Critical Transborder Documentary Production Practice

Ramón Resendiz and Rosalva Resendiz

On May 20, 2016, we entered production for the archival documentary film *El Muro | The Wall* (2017), which entailed a collaborative methodological process with Eloisa G. Tamez, Margo Tamez, and the Lipan Apache Band of Texas Tribal Board.[1] Months of preproduction work and research had gone into the theoretical and methodological framework leading up to this day, and the footage would go through many more months of editing and consultation before its debut as a feature-length documentary film, which took place at the Native Voices Film Festival in Seattle, Washington, on November 17, 2017. In what follows, we elucidate some of the key methodological approaches and processes of mediation between researchers/filmmakers and participants as well as what has been the life of the film since Ramón began writing the conceptual framework in the winter of 2014. Our purpose here is to reflect on the generative potentialities created at the intersection of media activism, collaborative research, storytelling, and the field of critical documentary filmmaking toward the disavowal of the colonial erasures necessary for the creation of modern settler-colonial imaginaries. A minor note to the reader: due to the collaborative nature of this project, we draw on the Chicanx feminist testimony tradition and shift between the plural (we) and the singular (I/me) perspective to underscore the hybrid nature of producing a collective documentary film that bridges research and practice. The instances in which we employ "I/me" in this text refer to Ramón's experiences, as these sections chronologically present his ethnographic reflections and fieldnotes in the production of this project.

Framing the Border

In 2005, the US Congress began enacting legislation for the purpose of building a physical fence along its southern border with Mexico. The proposed "border wall" sought to fence a total of 700 out of the 1,954 miles of the international boundary between Mexico and the United States. Construction of the border fence had been deemed complete in January 2010 by the United States Department of Homeland Security (DHS) at least four years before we began working on the film. The result was a seemingly arbitrary barrier spanning some 651 miles along the US side of the US-Mexico border at a taxpayer cost of roughly $2.8 million per mile.[2] The metrics for its success were vastly psychological and symbolic, with little data demonstrating it had met its intended purpose of slowing down illegal immigration, drug trafficking, or organized crime.

Largely omitted in the process of constructing the border wall were the coercive means through which the human rights and freedoms of local landowners and border inhabitants were forfeited for the purposes of a "secure border." This became evident at the legislative level in 2005 when the US Congress passed the bipartisan REAL ID Act, which allowed the US government to erect the wall without consulting local affected communities. This entailed a discriminatory disregard of Indigenous peoples' ancestral land claims, including Spanish land grant protection provisions provided by the 1848 Treaty of Guadalupe Hidalgo. An array of state, federal, and international laws were violated for homeland security purposes emblematic of what Giorgio Agamben has termed "a state of exception."[3] These violations became "legal" in 2006 with the congressional passing of the Secure Fence Act, which allowed the DHS to waive any state and federal laws that might have interfered with the building of physical barriers along the border—thirty-six in total.[4]

Whereas the US-Mexico border has regained hypervisibility in contemporary mass media portrayals, at the time of the border wall's completion in January 2010, it almost seemed as though US Americans had forgotten about its historically cyclical militaristic deployment. This changed in the summer of 2014, when news media outlets began reporting on a surge of asylum-seeking unaccompanied minors, leading to a recentring of the border as a key rhetorical point for the upcoming 2016 US presidential election.[5] Henceforth the border would become a mobilization tool for nationalist right-wing amnesia, as has been evident since Donald Trump's first press conference in which he called for the building of a border wall.[6]

Here, then, six months before Trump called for the building of a wall, our journey began toward the making of an archival documentary film that sought to foreground the "forgotten" and purposely "erased" histories of settler-colonial violence against the presence of Indigenous peoples in Texas and the US-Mexico borderlands. These processes of deliberate historic erasure are best summarized by what Brian Delay has termed the "Texas Creation Myth."[7] Following the Texas Revolution, this myth was reproduced across the United States, claiming that prior to Anglo colonization, Texas was a wasteland ravaged by wild Indians whom the Mexicans were unable to "tame." Anglo settlers created a myth of heroism and triumph over nature, yet the real political reasons remained hidden. Delay's concept informs some of the key theoretical and material stakes present in the context of the settler-colonial state of Texas and by extension the United States, both of which intrinsically depend on the constitutive redeployment of nationalistic rebordering practices.

El Muro | *The Wall* was produced for the purpose of disavowing settler-colonial imaginings of terra nullius (a no one's land), of which the "Texas Creation Myth" is emblematic. The collaborative project envisioned the production of a decolonial didactic tool by foregrounding the history of south Texas / northern Mexico—prior to its annexation by the United States, before the Texas Revolution, before Mexico called the region Coahuila y Tejas, and before the Spanish came to call the region Nuevo Santander or even El Seno Mexicano (the Mexican womb).

The documentary demonstrates that contested space has been a social and historical fact. The shaping of this region has been imagined and reimagined by Aboriginal, colonial, and imperial agents. Doreen Massey notes that the identities of places are not static; they are dynamic and ever changing due to their nature, constructed from social relations. As such, Massey views places as processes with multiple, layered identities and numerous internal conflicts. bell hooks further argues that the meaning of home "has been very different for those who have been colonized, and that it can change with the experiences of decolonization and of radicalization."[8]

Chicana feminists have led the way in contesting "the terms of capitalist spatial formation" and the narratives used "to naturalize violent racial, gender, sexual, and class ideologies."[9] It is through narratives that spaces and subjectivity are produced. Narratives form and conceptualize traditions, myths, and definitions onto spaces, and it is through narratives that nation-states reproduce their claims to their borders. Mary Pat Brady points out that there has to be "border amnesia" in order to maintain the nation-state, strategically and violently "erasing cultures, identities, and differences, while simultaneously producing subjectivities."[10] It was our goal to show that contested space continues to play an important role in a postcolonial era in which an imperialist paradigm continues to impose—or attempts to impose—its will on the region.

Thus, *El Muro | The Wall* foregrounds the shaping of the landscape by the continued resistance of Indigenous inhabitants, such as the Lipan Apache, who have lived, and continue to live, on their traditional land, despite colonial, imperial, and postcolonial efforts to dispossess them of it. The focal point is the struggle of Eloisa G. Tamez against the DHS, which implemented eminent domain to seize a portion of her ancestral land in El Calaboz Rancheria. This portion of the San Pedro de Carricitos Land Grant of 1786 was granted by the Spanish Crown, which began with Jose de Escandon's entrance into the area in 1745 with the settling of Nuevo Santander.[11] The film foregrounds purposely forgotten aspects of history: colonial records explicitly acknowledge the Lipan Apache ownership of the land in Texas before the United States existed as an entity.

The film makes use of what Leela Gandhi has termed the "forgotten archive of the colonial encounter," "[which] narrates multiple stories of contestation and its discomfiting other complicity" for the purposes of questioning the deployment of nationalistic postcolonial dichotomies.[12] The unjust seizure of their land by the DHS impacts Lipan Apache cultural traditions and their way of life, since their lives are intrinsically tied to the land and river, to which they no longer have access—a breach of the *United Nations Declaration on the Rights of Indigenous Peoples*.

Beginnings: *Operación Ocelote*

I first met Eloisa G. Tamez on January 3, 2015, after having read about her case in an article in the *Texas Observer Magazine* titled "Holes in the Wall," by Melissa del Bosque, published on February 22, 2008. Del Bosque's article was the first to critically look at the US border fence in south Texas, which was the last place to be seized by the DHS, as it had devoted its first efforts to fencing sectors along the US states of Arizona, California, and New Mexico. In the article, del Bosque notes the ongoing process of land seizures by the DHS, which started in the autumn of 2007, and she was the first journalist to seriously investigate what had determined the placement of the US border fence. She was also the first to report on the coercive methods employed by Customs and Border Protection (CBP) and the DHS in acquiring land via eminent domain lawsuits and threats. One-third of the 320 condemnation suits filed against landowners in 2007 were still pending more than a decade later, mainly due to the lack of funding to pursue litigation on behalf of the federal government during Barack Obama's second term.[13] Del Bosque would later become one of the film's participants at Margo Tamez's suggestion, as she had been crucial in chronicling the building of the Border Wall and the broader social impacts created by its construction.

As of early 2017, the Trump administration began sending out condemnation letters to landowners whose property was in the planned construction site of the US border fence.[14] This was followed by a thirty-five-day government shutdown starting on December 22, 2018, due to congressional gridlock between the then Democrat-controlled House of Representatives and Trump's demand for $5.6 billion to build new sections of border fencing.[15] In January 2020, US CBP announced it had identified $11 billion to add 576 new miles of fencing at an average taxpayer cost of $20 million per mile.[16] And on February 13, 2020, the Trump administration informed Congress it planned to divert an additional $3.8 billion of Pentagon funding for the purposes of building the wall.[17] On the ground, CBP intensified its aggressive eminent domain landgrab on private and Indigenous lands, including proposals to cut across historic cemeteries, wildlife refuges, and the Organ Pipe Cactus National Monument, a sacred burial ground to the Tohono O'odham Nation and a UNESCO biosphere reserve.[18]

At the time in 2015, I was searching for an environmental justice story on which to base a film that foregrounded histories of resistance against US-Anglo imperialism and racism that also incorporated the importance of the Rio Grande River not as a border/barrier or line of demarcation but as a generative nexus of the relationship between humans and the environment. I had grown up in Brownsville, Texas, visiting distant relatives in northern Mexico as well as the river and its ecotone at the mouth of the Gulf of Mexico. In every respect, the moment was personally ripe to engage in a political documentary that questioned the production and legitimacy of the border narratives and practices, especially given the fact that for generations, our families found themselves on various sides of these borders. The key juncture here was the legitimacy from which the modern nation-state has/had continued to draw its power—that is, law, memory, and the colonial archive.

My first meeting with Eloisa Tamez was at an IHOP in Brownsville, Texas, in 2015. In preparation for the project, I studied the history of dispossession and conflict that followed the takeover of the Southwest by the United States, from the Texas Revolution in 1835 to El Plan de San Diego in 1915, a plan for sedition that inspired the last uprising in south Texas and called for a union of Mexican mestizos, Indigenous peoples, Asians, and Black people.[19] The uprising was led by Aniceto Pizaña and Luis de la Rosa and resulted in failure and a reign of terror by the Texas Rangers, who indiscriminately slaughtered innocent ethnic Mexican mestizos and Indigenous peoples by labeling them bandits.[20] This roughly eighty-year period had been rife with the armed persecution of "Mexicans," land grant owners and heirs, and "Indians" by armed militias (including the Texas Rangers) for the purposes of stealing land and eradicating its people for Anglo occupation.[21]

I had emailed Eloisa two weeks before at the behest of my professors, Irene J. Klaver and Brian C. O'Connor, both of whom would be crucial to the overall creation of the film. The meeting itself was brief, under thirty minutes, and I was quite nervous. I was just a twenty-one-year-old master's student speaking with the first "ordinary" citizen who sued the DHS when they attempted to seize her ancestral land and whose case had made it to a hearing at the Inter-American Commission on Human Rights held by the Organization for American States (OAS) and the United Nations Committee on Ending Racial Discrimination (UNCERD).

Eloisa was full of fire. She was a citizen and Tribal Elder of the Lipan Apache Band of Texas and served over twenty years in the US Army Medical Corps, retiring as a full colonel. She held a master of science in nursing from the UT Health Sciences Center at San Antonio, had graduated with her PhD in health education from the University of Texas at Austin, and was now a full professor and the director of the graduate nursing program at the University of Texas Rio Grande Valley (UTRGV).

I arrived a few minutes before she did and anxiously awaited her arrival over a cup of coffee. I don't recall her attire, but I do remember recognizing her from some of her previous media appearances. I stood up and greeted and thanked her for her time and for meeting on such short notice. She had just returned from Canada, where she had visited her daughter, Margo Tamez, who had been pivotal in the organizing and mobilization efforts against the wall in the autumn of 2007, leading up to the federal court case in 2009, and taking her case to the OAS and the UNCERD. These two latter instances would involve the help of the UT–Austin School of Law Human Rights and Immigration Clinic and especially the work of Denise Gilman and Ariel Dulitzky, who are also featured in the film.

I pitched Eloisa my initial idea to produce an environmental justice film that foregrounded historical resistance movements against colonial erasures and problematized space, memory, and history. In essence, I sought to produce an intersectional, counterhegemonic, decolonial document/ary, which talked about the multiple times "Mexicans" and Indigenous peoples had fought back against genocidal persecution by the Texas Rangers.

We talked about the history of the area, and I shared that I had grown up in a *colonia* and that my aunt (Rosalva) was also a member of the faculty at UTRGV. She told me that she had spoken to many journalists over the years and that she would be willing to participate in the project, provided she was heard on her own terms. She advised that I speak with her daughter in the future as well. I think there was an air of uncertainty as to whether I was capable of producing a film of this type, and it was admittedly premature on my end to be talking about a film of this nature. I told her I would be in touch in the near future with a proposal. I tried to get the bill; she told me she would get it, and I awkwardly obliged. I thanked her for her time again and exited the restaurant, feeling unsure as to what making "a decolonial documentary" might entail and lacking an overall sense of confidence in my own abilities as a documentarian.

Following our initial meeting, I returned to Seattle for the winter and spring academic quarters and did not touch base with Eloisa again until my return to south Texas in June of the same year. This was a brief email exchange to determine whether she was still interested in participating in the film, which had started taking conceptual shape during the spring as part of my graduate coursework. Her response was brief but reaffirming; she replied that she was always willing to speak out about this injustice.

During this same period in the drafting of the original conceptual framework for the film proposal, I began to understand the complexity that such a topic truly entailed, and after consulting with my professors, I proceeded to ask my aunt, Rosalva "Rosy" Resendiz, to help me codirect and produce the film, given my relatively young age and lack of experience. Rosy graciously obliged; she would later be of critical importance in the execution of the negotiation and production process. This was also the week before Trump announced his bid for the US presidency, which neither one of us then imagined would be remotely within the realm of possibility.

Methodological Interventions: Toward a Decolonizing Production

In developing the theoretical and methodological framework that would direct the production of the film, most of the key provisions were derived from the theoretical interventions set forth by Linda Tuhiwai Smith's *Decolonizing Methodologies* (1999), Jay Ruby's *Picturing Culture* (2000), Fatimah Tobing Rony's *The Third Eye* (1998), and Philip Deloria's *Indians in Unexpected Places* (2004), as well as some of the filmmaking conventions pioneered by John Marshall and Timothy Asch. Chief among these were the following:

1. Operating on an ongoing procedural basis of constant free, prior, and informed consent (FPIC) before, during, and after the production process, which contained an inherent provision by all participants involved in the project to withdraw participation at any point in the process. If exercised, this clause would entail deleting all footage gathered from our hard drives and backups.

2. Ongoing editing consultations with all participants over their respective portrayals as well as with the key participants and tribal citizens. The participants were to receive a chance to review every edited cut of the film, provide feedback, and gather additional archival materials they thought pertinent to the integrity of the film.

3. Only after consulting with all involved participants and after receiving their approval could the film be disseminated in public screenings.

4. Free mass and public dissemination of the final film, as its political intent was and continues to be in circulation for didactic

purposes, to raise awareness of the ongoing issues along the US-Mexico border and about Eloisa G. Tamez's fight.

5. Co-ownership of the final product between the filmmakers and the key participant, Eloisa G. Tamez, which would require the consent of all participants to sell the film in a for-profit capacity (though selling was never the intended goal).

6. Inherent reciprocity, which included providing the Emilio Institute for Indigenous and Human Rights (operated by Eloisa G. Tamez and the Lipan Apache Band of Texas) with a hard drive including all of the unedited footage gathered throughout the production of the film to contribute to their ongoing efforts to create an archive of their own.

7. Finally, and this was inspired by a larger epistemic and imaginative political perspective, to openly acknowledge the co-construction entailed by the project at all times. This spoke directly against the stereotypical legacy of the portrayal of Indigenous peoples as not contemporaneous in post/modernity.[22]

This last point specifically returns to the visual culture created by "salvage ethnography." Ethnographers such as Robert Flaherty, Franz Boas, and Margaret Mead perpetrated the myth of "the vanishing Indian." Salvage ethnography was a movement to document the lives of Indigenous peoples because ethnographers believed "Indians" would vanish/disappear due to an inability to survive colonization and modernity.[23] Fatimah Tobing Rony terms this an impulse of ethnographic *taxidermy*, in which "Indigenous peoples were assumed to be already dying if not dead, [in which] the ethnographic 'taxidermist' turned to artifice, seeking an image more true to the posited original."[24] Addressing and redressing this taxidermic process was of critical importance in the making of the documentary and informed the archival and aesthetic nature of the film in three key ways:

1. To honour our agreement and do justice to Eloisa's story and history of Indigenous resistance.

2. To utilize the same colonial archive (maps, documents, architecture) to disavow the "Texas Creation Myth," drawing attention to "the forgotten archive of the colonial encounter."[25]

3.   To create a decolonizing document that would *write back* against the colonial erasures perpetrated by both ethnographic documentary and the misrepresentation of Indigenous peoples in cinematic film (i.e., the western genre, in which Indigenous peoples of the American Southwest were portrayed as vanishing with the arrival of Anglo settlers devoid of the historic context of the violence exercised by settlers against these Indigenous communities).[26]

In addition to the aforementioned methodological procedures, the film's participants were also to be vetted for participation in the project by the Tamez family and the Lipan Apache Band of Texas Tribal Board, given the fact that the film centred predominantly around her story, and we sought only to give a platform to those who had been deemed allies or had aided in the case against the continued US assault on Indigenous lands and human rights. In working toward this end, no agent aligned with or sympathetic to the colonial/imperial goals of CBP or the DHS was to receive any face time, especially since the political intent of the film was to redress asymmetric colonial injustices. To provide a space for the colonizer would have been a breach of trust on our end and would have also been counterintuitive to our decolonial goals.

Tribal Board Review of *Operación Ocelote*

In August 2015, I met with Eloisa again, this time in her office at UTRGV. It had been a few months since we had touched base. I had prepared a rough draft of the proposal for the film, which I handed to her. She looked at the first page and told me she would get back to me with comments. She asked if I had any questions at that time, and I expressed some apprehension in asking about whether it would be possible to employ the Rio Grande as one of the key storytellers of the film. She beamed and said that would be wonderful, because the river was the source of life. Later in the film, Margo would address the sacredness of the river.

The proposal in its then-current state contained an expansive theorization regarding the role of boundaries, borders, and the river, along with some of the environmental considerations inherent to discussions of the border and border habitats. The working title of the film was *Operación Ocelote*, a reference to the now critically endangered indigenous feline that once freely roamed the walled area. In addition to the key methodological procedures for the film, the proposal contained an expansive appendix with some of the major historical figures that the colonial archive has sought to forget and that have been villainously framed in the realm of the popular imagination. Many of our border heroes, such as Gregorio Cortez, were labeled outlaws but were remembered in our oral history as people who stood up against injustice.

Americo Paredes was the first folklorist/ethnographer to bring to light these counterstories of resistance.[27] In *With His Pistol in His Hand: A Border Ballad and Its Hero* (1958), Paredes analyses the multiple narratives surrounding the legend and hero worship of Gregorio Cortez, who was wrongly accused of theft and, in an act of self-defence, killed a lawman, resulting in an unjust persecution by the Texas Rangers. Along the Texas-Mexico border, the Texas Rangers were the villains, yet they have been memorialized as righteous lawmen. The people recorded their abuses in *corridos*/ballads, leaving an oral history of remembered injustice and trauma. From Paredes's work, heroes such as Cortez entered the decolonial discourse in print and film. (In 1982, Edward James Olmos starred in *The Ballad of Gregorio Cortez*). Hero worship of "outlaws" is intrinsic to the contestation of border spaces and border narratives and demonstrates the tension between the nation-state and its subjects.

Our meeting ended on a positive note, and I asked Eloisa if at that point we could contact her daughter, Margo. Eloisa advised me to do so, as feedback from Margo would be of critical importance in being able to responsibly produce the film (especially since her doctoral dissertation had been about the border wall and the violent erasures it entailed to the lives of the Lipan Apache).[28]

I received a reply from Margo, who greeted me warmly but informed me that I was in violation of the proper protocols to engage in conversation with members of the Lipan Apache Band of Texas. We arranged for a Skype meeting the following week, and she provided me with a set of community guidelines to abide by: "Nde.' Guidelines and Principles for Respectful Partnerships with Government, Law (Advocacy), Energy, Environment, Policy, Academia (Advocacy)."[29]

Fortunately, the working proposal was already largely in compliance with the stipulated guidelines. The key element that the guidelines helped us address in the proposal was to name the Emilio Institute for Indigenous and Human Rights as the entity to whom we would provide all of the raw materials gathered from the production process rather than just the individual participants.

The meeting with Margo proved fruitful and promising, and she mentioned that her mother held great hopes for the film. We went through the proposal together, and at the time there were no additional attached stipulations to the proposal in order for it to be submitted to the full tribal board for review. The only condition was that we conduct all inquiries and communication pertaining to the film and any/all potential Lipan Apache participants through her; she would act as our liaison until the tribal board's Committee on the Protection of the Nde' (Lipan Apache) Knowledge and Cultural Property finished their review of the proposed project.

Following our conversation, I returned to Seattle to complete my final quarter of coursework, and in November 2015, I received an email from Margo. She was in south Texas and wanted to meet with Rosy regarding the direction of the film. The three of them (Eloisa, Margo, and Rosy) met on a Friday morning in November and exchanged gifts. From that point forward, Rosy and Margo's labour was pivotal for the completion of the project. Around this same time, I also received some funding for the film from the Department of Gender, Women, and Sexuality Studies at the University of Washington by Shirley Yee, who also provided some critical feedback and showed great confidence in the project. This was the only time we received any funds to make the film; everything else would be independently funded by us and our family.

The review itself lasted roughly over six and a half months, during which time I completed my coursework, went on leave from the university, and returned to Texas in January to hopefully make a thesis film. I emailed Margo because I would be in south Texas and wanted to know if I could receive permission to visit Eloisa for further consultation on the film. My request was approved, and I was granted a brief meeting with Eloisa, who expressed her approval of the film project. However, it would not be until March 16, 2016, that the full Committee on the Protection of the Nde' (Lipan Apache) Knowledge and Cultural Property approved the project, ultimately with no stipulations other than that we continue to remain respectful.

Post/Production and *El Muro | The Wall*

Whereas the preproduction and review process entailed a substantial amount of time, the production process was rather streamlined in comparison. This was largely due to Margo's aid following the review process, helping us identify pertinent participants from our initial potential list. In the end the film featured seven participants, three of whom were members of the Lipan Apache Band of Texas, one from the Lipan Apache Tribe of Texas, and three additional individuals who had critically helped raise awareness of the issues posed by the border wall. Four additional participants whom we interviewed would not make it to the final cut, but we remain eternally grateful for their time, and their interviews remain archived by the Emilio Institute for Indigenous and Human Rights.

During the production process, I acted as the singular technical crewmember, and Rosy was the main interviewer (up until her departure abroad, during which time other family members crewed for me while I conducted the interviews). After our first interview with Eloisa on May 20, 2016, the film remained in production through July 29, 2016, with the final interview taking place in front of the Alamo with Lipan Apache Tribal Chairman and Chief Daniel Castro Romero. The other participants in the film included Melissa del Bosque (journalist for the *Texas Observer Magazine*), Margo Tamez (tribal liaison and associate professor at UBC Okanagan), Denise Gilman (director of the UT–Austin School of Law Immigration Clinic), and Ariel Dulitzky (director of the UT–Austin School of Law Human Rights Clinic). An additional interview was conducted in the spring of 2017 with Ashley Leal (an anthropologist and member of the Lipan Apache Tribe of Texas).

Following the production process, I relocated to North Texas to begin editing the film at the University of North Texas while I worked at Texas Woman's University. During this time, I produced the first cut, which I defended as my master's thesis on November 28, 2016, at the University of Washington. By then the political relevance and urgency of the film had become painfully obvious to all of the participants involved in the production, as Trump had won the 2016 US presidential election. However, it would be nearly a year before it would premiere in its final form on November 17, 2017.

During the time between the first and final cuts, additional consultations took place with the participants, and we allowed a six-month period for additional general comments after the first cut was done. Brian O'Connor and Irene Klaver, along with Margo, were of great importance in the conceptual and aesthetic archival editing of the footage.

Prior to its official premiere in November, Rosy also organized a public community screening at the UTRGV Edinburg, Texas, campus to present the film to the local community for comment and additional feedback. Eloisa and Margo, along with many other members of the Lipan Apache Band of Texas, were in attendance, as well as members from our neighbouring country down south in Mexico.

We also procured the voluntary help of Adrian Flores and Brandon Odom from Finest Roar Productions, who composed and performed the musical score for the film free of charge, both of which we are very thankful for. The film was well received and would make its way back to the community in an official premiere capacity on Thursday, February 15, 2018, at the Historic Cine El Rey Theater in McAllen, Texas.

Thoughts and Discussion

In the end, the film led us to travel the majority of the Mexico-Texas border as well as to visit the unceded Okanagan Territory of the Okanagan Valley in British Columbia, Canada. This would itself become a small distance compared to the circulation of the film, which has been publicly screened on three continents, at various film festivals, and at many academic conferences. And as stipulated by our original proposed methodology, the film is also available for public viewing online, subtitled in English and Spanish.

In reflecting on the production of the film, we would like to revisit the key parts of the theoretical framework regarding the "production of a counterhegemonic didactic decolonial tool," given that the film has taken on a different significance since the original proposal for the film was initially drafted. Since then we have seen a sharp rise in xenophobic ethno-nationalism in the United States, which right-wing politicians have seized upon and utilized through the rhetorical deployment of the US-Mexico border and the continuous call for the building of a border wall. To return to these central issues, we employ Kate Crehan's observations in "Gramsci's Concept of Common Sense: A Useful Concept for Anthropologists?" (2011) because it very well bridges some of the larger theoretical concepts embedded in *El Muro | The Wall* and that it attempted to theoretically address. Crehan problematizes dominant notions of cultures and their relation to the formation of the nation-state. She notes, "Actual nation-states may be quite recent creations in historical terms and their boundaries in reality far from fixed, but nations themselves—those imagined communities, as Benedict Anderson termed them, underpinning the concept of the nation-state—seem almost to inhabit a realm outside time. They both 'loom out of an immemorial past" and "glide into a limitless future."[30] In bringing attention to the modern creation of both nation-states and the boundaries entailed in their creation, as well as the role played by historicity, futurity, and memory, Crehan brings us back to the amnesiac processes intrinsic to the construction of the settler-colonial state and settler mythologies such as the "Texas Creation Myth."

Though *El Muro | The Wall* only presents a singular instance of the coercive power of the nation-state and historic colonial erasures, it presents a case study in the creation of a historical document that talks back against the material and imaginative archive necessary for the stability of the colonial bordering processes of settler colonialism. We say this to bring to mind the fact that the film itself addresses the continued assault on Indigenous peoples, who are an unsettling reminder of Anglo settlers' illegitimate occupation of the Americas and their continued dispossession of Indigenous peoples through coercive, legal, and extralegal means. The landscape continues to reflect these attempts as an archive of violence and resistance. Regarding the action of "writing back," as expounded upon by Linda Smith's *Decolonizing Methodologies*, it has been our hope that by producing a film of this kind to act as a decolonial document in itself for the purposes of telling stories back, we may begin to ameliorate the violence enacted by colonial mythologies. Margo says in the film, "As long as the people remain of a consciousness, the stories are going to stick," and we hope that in its circulation, Eloisa's story of resistance sticks.

Notes

1. Ramón Resendiz and Rosalva Resendiz, *El Muro | The Wall.*
2. Michelle Guzman and Zachary Hurwitz, *Violations on the Part of the United States Government of Indigenous Rights Held by Members of the Lipan Apache, Kickapoo, and Ysleta del Sur Tigua Tribes of the Texas-Mexico Border*, 2–4.
3. Giorgio Agamben, *State of Exception.*
4. Nicole Miller, "How Property Rights Are Affected by the Texas-Mexico Border Fence: A Failure Due to Insufficient Procedure," 631–32.
5. Sural Shah, "The Crisis in Our Own Backyard: United States Response to Unaccompanied Minor Children from Central America."
6. Jose A. DelReal, "Donald Trump Announces a Presidential Bid."
7. Brian Delay, "Independent Indians and the U.S.-Mexican War," 49–50.

8. hooks quoted in Doreen Massey, *Space, Place, and Gender*, 166.

9. Mary Pat Brady, *Extinct Lands, Temporal Geographies: Chicano Literature and the Urgency of Space*, 6.

10. Brady, *Extinct Lands*, 60.

11. Hubert J. Miller, *Jose De Escandon: Colonizer of Nuevo Santander*.

12. Leela Gandhi, *Postcolonial Theory: A Critical Introduction*, 4–5.

13. Melissa del Bosque, "Over the Wall."

14. Melissa del Bosque, "Texans Receive First Notices of Land Condemnation for Trump's Border Wall."

15. Jessica Taylor, "Trump Signs Short-Term Bill to End Government Shutdown, but Border Fight Still Looms."

16. John Burnett, "$11 Billion and Counting: Trump's Border Wall Would Be the World's Most Costly."

17. Brakkton Booker, "Trump Administration Diverts $3.8 Billion in Pentagon Funding to Border Wall."

18. Eric Ortiz, "Ancient Native American Burial Site Blasted for Trump Border Wall Construction."

19. Americo Paredes, *A Texas-Mexican Cancionero: Folksongs of the Lower Border*.

20. Paredes, *Texas-Mexican Cancionero*.

21. Monica Munoz Martinez, *The Injustice Never Leaves You: Anti-Mexican Violence in Texas*.

22. Philip Joseph Deloria, *Indians in Unexpected Places*; Fatimah Tobing Rony, *The Third Eye: Race, Cinema, and Ethnographic Spectacle*; Linda Tuhiwai Smith, *Decolonizing Methodologies*.

23. Deloria, *Indians*.

24. Rony, *Third Eye*, 102.

25. Delay, "Independent Indians"; Gandhi, *Postcolonial Theory*.

26. Philip Joseph Deloria, *Playing Indian*; Smith, *Decolonizing Methodologies*.

27. Americo Paredes, *With His Pistol in His Hand: A Border Ballad and Its Hero*; Paredes, *Texas-Mexican Cancionero*.

28. Margo Tamez, "Returning Lipan Apache Women's Laws, Lands, and Strength in El Caseriboz Rancheria at the Texas-Mexico Border."

29. Margo Tamez et al., "Nde' Guidelines and Principles for Respectful Partnerships with Government, Law (Advocacy), Energy, Environment, Policy, Academia (Advocacy)."

30. Kate Crehan, "Gramsci's Concept of Common Sense: A Useful Concept for Anthropologists?" 274.

Bibliography

Agamben, Giorgio. *State of Exception*. Chicago: University of Chicago Press, 2005.

Anderson, Benedict. *Imagined Communities: Reflections on the Origin and Spread of Nationalism*. London: Verso, 2006.

Booker, Brakkton. "Trump Administration Diverts $3.8 Billion in Pentagon Funding to Border Wall." National Public Radio, February 13, 2020. https://www .npr.org/2020/02/13/805796618/trump-administration-diverts-3-8-billion-in -pentagon-funding-to-border-wall.

Brady, Mary Pat. *Extinct Lands, Temporal Geographies: Chicano Literature and the Urgency of Space*. Durham, NC: Duke University Press, 2002.

Burnett, John. "$11 Billion and Counting: Trump's Border Wall Would Be the World's Most Costly." National Public Radio, January 29, 2020. https://www.npr .org/2020/01/19/797319968/-11-billion-and-counting-trumps-border-wall-would -be-the-world-s-most-costly.

Crehan, Kate. "Gramsci's Concept of Common Sense: A Useful Concept for Anthropologists?" *Journal of Modern Italian Studies* 16, no. 2 (2011): 273–87.

Delay, Brian. "Independent Indians and the U.S.-Mexican War." *American Historical Review* 112, no. 1 (February 2007): 35–68.

del Bosque, Melissa. "Holes in the Wall." *Texas Observer Magazine*, February 22, 2008. https://www.texasobserver.org/2688-holes-in-the-wall/.

del Bosque, Melissa. "Over the Wall." *Texas Observer Magazine*, June 27, 2017. https://www.texasobserver.org/over-the-wall/.

del Bosque, Melissa. "Texans Receive First Notices of Land Condemnation for Trump's Border Wall." *Texas Observer Magazine*, March 14, 2017. https://www .texasobserver.org/texas-border-wall-mexico-condemnation-letter/.

Deloria, Philip Joseph. *Indians in Unexpected Places*. Lawrence: University Press of Kansas, 2004.

Deloria, Philip Joseph. *Playing Indian*. New Haven, CT: Yale University Press, 1998.

DelReal, Jose A. "Donald Trump Announces a Presidential Bid." *Washington Post*, June 16, 2015. https://www.washingtonpost.com/news/post-politics/wp/2015/06/ 16/donald-trump-to-announce-his-presidential-plans-today/.

Gandhi, Leela. *Postcolonial Theory: A Critical Introduction*. 2nd ed. New York: Columbia University Press, 2019.

Guzman, Michelle, and Zachary Hurwitz. *Violations on the Part of the United States Government of Indigenous Rights Held by Members of the Lipan Apache, Kickapoo, and Ysleta del Sur Tigua Tribes of the Texas-Mexico Border*. The Working Group on Human Rights and the Border Wall. University of Texas at Austin, June 2008.

Martinez, Monica Munoz. *The Injustice Never Leaves You: Anti-Mexican Violence in Texas*. Cambridge, MA: Harvard University Press, 2018.

Massey, Doreen. *Space, Place, and Gender*. Minneapolis: University of Minnesota Press, 1994.

Miller, Hubert J. *Jose De Escandon: Colonizer of Nuevo Santander*. Edinburg, TX: New Santander Press, 1980.

Miller, Nicole. "How Property Rights Are Affected by the Texas-Mexico Border Fence: A Failure Due to Insufficient Procedure." *Texas International Law Journal* 45, no. 3 (2010): 631–54.

Ortiz, Eric. "Ancient Native American Burial Site Blasted for Trump Border Wall Construction." NBC News, February 12, 2020. https://www.nbcnews.com/news/us-news/ancient-native-american-burial-site-blasted-trump-border-wall-construction-n1135906.

Paredes, Americo. *A Texas-Mexican Cancionero: Folksongs of the Lower Border*. Austin: University of Texas Press, 1976.

Paredes, Americo. *With His Pistol in His Hand: A Border Ballad and Its Hero*. Austin: University of Texas Press, 1958.

Resendiz, Ramón, and Rosalva Resendiz, directors. *El Muro | The Wall*. Documentary Worlds, 2017. Runtime 1:13:06. https://vimeo.com/261423435.

Rony, Fatimah Tobing. *The Third Eye: Race, Cinema, and Ethnographic Spectacle*. Durham, NC: Duke University Press, 1996.

Ruby, Jay. *Picturing Culture: Explorations of Film & Anthropology*. Chicago: University of Chicago Press, 2000.

Shah, Sural. "The Crisis in Our Own Backyard: United States Response to Unaccompanied Minor Children from Central America." *Harvard Public Health Review* 9 (2016). https://bcphr.org/tag/central-america/.

Smith, Linda Tuhiwai. *Decolonizing Methodologies*. 1st ed. London: Zed Books, 1999.

Tamez, Margo. "Returning Lipan Apache Women's Laws, Lands, and Strength in El Calaboz Rancheria at the Texas-Mexico Border." PhD diss., Program in American Studies, Washington State University, Pullman, WA, 2010.

Tamez, Margo, Carmelita Lamb, Daniel Castro Romero, and Eloisa García Tamez. "Nde' Guidelines and Principles for Respectful Partnerships with Government, Law (Advocacy), Energy, Environment, Policy, Academia (Advocacy)." Emilio Institute for Indigenous and Human Rights, El Calaboz, TX. Unpublished manuscript, 2013.

Taylor, Jessica. "Trump Signs Short-Term Bill to End Government Shutdown, but Border Fight Still Looms." National Public Radio, January 25, 2019. https://www.npr.org/2019/01/25/688414503/watch-live-trump-addresses-shutdown-from-white-house-rose-garden.

2 Working the Border

Interdisciplinary Encounters Across Intellectual, Material, and Political Boundaries

Heather Parrish and Leslie Gross-Wyrtzen

For more than two decades, thousands of West and Central African migrants have traversed Morocco each year en route from their home countries toward Europe. Militarized border enforcement along Morocco's northern coast has made it increasingly difficult and dangerous to cross into Europe via the Mediterranean Sea, causing many migrants to opt for the land-based route instead. Also fraught with peril and violence, the borders of the two Spanish enclaves contiguous with Moroccan territory are rigorously guarded and surrounded by six-metre-high fences. Migrants camp in forests adjacent to the border fences, hidden by the trees, before attempting a treacherous climb. While the forest provides cover, it is also a space of exposure. In the forest, migrants lack proper shelter and access to food and drinking water; they are vulnerable to nightly raids by border police and internal deportations to more southern locations in Morocco. Spaces of both danger and refuge for humans, these same forests are also integral to a biodiverse ecoregion that spans Moroccan territory, the Mediterranean Sea, and parts of Spain's southern coastline. This ecologically rich transborder environment is the sole natural habitat for a significant number of species.[1] State administration of these territories juggles awkwardly between border enforcement and ecological management.

In the summer of 2018, the authors met in this borderland region while on respective research trips. Leslie, a political geographer, was conducting interviews in central Morocco while studying the impacts of European border policies on the lives and well-being of West and Central African migrants. Heather, a visual artist, was on the southern coast of Spain preparing for an exhibition that explored the dynamic shoreline where ocean and land encounter and shape each other. With a common focus on boundaries and a mutual interest in each other's work, our attention converged on this forested borderland that spanned the middle ground between our two sites.

With Leslie's research centring the multiple violences of political borders and Heather's interest in environmental boundaries as lively inhabitations of interconnectivity, this forest held something for us both. We wondered how to make sense of our different approaches to this space—one grounded in social and political realities and the other in activating material and imaginative potentialities. Could art and social science together, in reciprocity, expand our capacity to understand and express the complexities held in such a border space?[2]

The invitation issued by "The Line Crossed Us: New Directions in Critical Border Studies" conference, from which this volume emerges, provided the grounds toward which our collaboration could begin. What has emerged is an iterative, ongoing practice—*Border Work*—exploring the politics and aesthetics of borders through the languages and methodologies of visual art, critical theory, and political geography. The art installation *Border Disruptions*, presented at the conference, was the first instantiation of this evolving work. In evoking a border wall in scale and form yet composed of free-hanging strips of luminous, illusive imagery, it embodied our initial effort to generatively "trouble borders." This chapter, into which ideas, questions, and images (fragmented, fracturing, and reincarnated) have migrated, is another. Through each "cut" we hold the central question: How can our collaboration, in both subject and practice, disrupt prevailing hegemonic binaries around borders—such as included/excluded, mobile/immobile, art/science, citizen/alien—and open capacity for new imaginings of liberatory (antire-pressive, antiviolent, antiracist) possibilities? And can a practice of expansive relationality create alternative understandings of "us" and "them" within and beyond borders?

Placing (Our) Border Work

In this work, and underlying it, we recognize our positionality with respect to borders of control, benefitting from the relative mobility that our citizenship, economic, and institutional resources afford us. At the same time, we recog-nize a corresponding responsibility, the "ability to respond," that underlies our situatedness.[3] Holding to the words of feminist scholar and physicist Karen Barad, "Responsibility is not an obligation that the subject chooses" or a "cal-culation to be performed" but rather an incarnate "relation always already integral to the world's ongoing intra-active becoming and not-becoming . . . through the iterative reworking of im/possibility, an ongoing rupturing, a cross-cutting of topological reconfiguring of the space of response-ability."[4]

We embark on this work with the particular tools of a research scholar and a visual artist and a desire to centre relationalities of respect and to practice (even as we *learn* to practice) ethics of care in our responses to social and political problems that loom large in contemporary society.

As we write this chapter, there is much public debate about the work of political borders in the world today. In the United States, where both authors reside as citizens, asylum-seeking children are separated from their fam-ilies in contravention of international law; detained border crossers sleep in for-profit detention facilities on concrete floors in overcrowded *hieleras* (iceboxes); across the Mediterranean Sea, African and Middle Eastern asylum seekers risk death to traverse turbulent waters in pursuit of livelihood and safety in Europe. The violence of border policing, defended as a fundamental responsibility of the modern nation-state, occludes the still-contested status of settler-state territory by Indigenous nations. The chapters in this volume document the various ways that the drawing of lines has displaced or sought to erase Indigenous people (Hall, chap. 6; Barkley, James, and Stone, chap. 5), have shaped people's sense of place and belonging even generations after the fact (Wells, chap. 3), and continue to impact the ability to move, access health care, or preserve their homes (Donoso, chap. 7; Light, Naumes, and Amarshi, chap. 8).[5] These chapters also document struggles not included in the official archive that come in the form of legal battles (Resendiz and Resendiz, chap. 1), refusal of recognition, and thinking relationally rather than linearly (Murphy, chap. 4).[6] In chorus with these contributions, this chapter explores how working the boundaries between political geography and visual art can cultivate a multidimensional conceptualization of borders that conveys their capacity to ascribe both belonging and division.

In political geography, borders are not just physical structures delineating space and access but also invisible structures of inclusion and exclusion, sedimented by history, policy, memory, and interrelations.[7] Visual art can bring invisible border structures into view, offering opportunities for critical reconsideration and, where necessary, resistance. Through material and imaginative constructions, art can complicate popular perceptions of borders as fixed, question their function as exclusive, and expose their permeability.[8] When power is conceptualized as the "control of the flows of information," Renée Marlin-Benet identifies "art power"—the unique quality of power enacted by artwork—at and across borders. Art manifests its power in communicating "sensory data" and "emotional sensation," both forms of information. Facing the restrictions structured into political borders, artwork's ability to engage ambiguity (having multiple meanings) and indeterminacy (having unspecified, unknown meanings) can be especially potent to open space for the creative flow of ideas and imagination, to disrupt and renegotiate hardened barriers, to imagine *otherwise*, and to possibly enable new/other realities.[9] For us, the work of political geography offers grounding to our artistic inquiry, a physical place contextualized by social-scientific research and situated in lived experience, while artwork provides the materiality for imaginative reconceptions. The border forests in Morocco, understood through binocular lenses of political geography and visual art, became the generative place for our work to come into focus.

Collaborative Practice

The forested borderland prompted us to examine the ways our thinking and expressions are shaped (and contained) by our respective disciplines and practices. Leslie's work uses ethnographic methodologies to explain political borders as technologies of racial violence and exclusion even as they condition possibilities for new forms of belonging. Heather's art practice explores the dynamic potentialities of boundaries as porous and productive sites of exchange. Considering light and water as subject and medium, she works to unsettle simple binaries and "unfix" exclusionary conceptions of (metaphorical, biological, societal, historical) boundaries. As scholars concerned with complicating and denaturalizing borders, it was important for us to challenge the givenness of our own disciplinary boundaries—to step "out of bounds"—to practice a border crossing of our own through interdisciplinary collaboration. "Working the border" means venturing beyond our individual work into "interstitial space," inhabiting the "between" as a prevailing rather than transitory state.[10] T/here we bring together our multiple border ontologies and methods, moving beyond a transactional relationship and into a "rhythmically interwoven, expansive relationship"—the necessary condition for "geographies of freedom."[11]

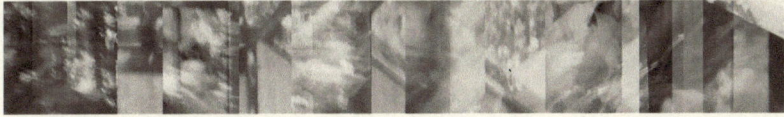

In its most liberatory forms, interdisciplinarity is not simply a method of arriving at a more creative, ethical, effective solution to a social problem but itself a critical practice that aims to disrupt the boundaries that separate us along ideological or identitarian lines often folded into disciplined ways of knowing.[12] As a range of subjects and approaches are brought into the same space, new horizons of possibilities come into view.[13] Indeed, one of the goals of interdisciplinarity is to challenge the "common sense" of a problem that is often driven by one particular subject position or epistemological orientation. It holds the potential to make knowledge more relevant, balance incommensurable claims and perspectives, and raise questions concerning the nature and viability of expertise.[14] Natalie Loveless writes specifically about the strengths of bringing art into the research process (what she calls "research creation"), arguing that it "mobilizes the artistic as a sensibility and approach attentive to how *form* makes *worlds*."[15] It is especially relevant that a project aiming to disrupt hegemonic binaries and span disciplinary boundaries would take as its object of attention the political, social, material, and symbolic "lines that cross us" and do so through artistic expression.

The Artwork

Border Disruptions, the art installation exhibited at the conference, visualizes our complex inquiries around borders, including ideas of fugitivity and confinement, seduction and entrapment. Over six feet high and stretching twenty-eight feet long, it evokes a border wall in its extended rectangularity. It is composed of narrow vertical translucent strips of disrupted (cut) images, with each strip suspended from the top, contiguous with or overlapping but unattached to its neighbour. As part of an unstable ensemble, individual pieces never coexist in identical relative relationships from one installation to the next. While extensive in length, the embodied experience of the work is that of verticality; at close proximity, it nearly engulfs the viewer's field of vision. The imagery, blurred as if in motion and punctured by light and darkness, plays just on the cusp of discernibility. A shape emerging on one slice is picked up a few strips later: Is that a fence? A cage? A forest? The colours range from fleshy soft hues of sand, pink, and gold to strikes of charcoal gray and splashes of hot red, orange, and yellow. A searchlight or a dawning sun? There is no internal point of spatial reference, no horizon line. Itself perhaps is a horizon, a border wall, or both.

Dispersed throughout this chapter are horizontal strips cut from images of the exhibited work. These strips enact an entangled expression of our practice, disrupting a binaristic performance of collaboration: artwork = contribution of artist plus (and separate from) written work = contribution of social scientist. Instead, each iteration of our work together asks us (and our respective modalities) to transgress and transform our/their prescriptive forms. They perform the entangled work of our respective disciplines, creating an interstitial manifestation, a third thing. As an exhibited work of art reconstituted and interjected into the body of a text, reoriented from the previous iteration, it extends an opportunity for an expanded set of questions. For example, what can a shift from verticality to horizontality do for our perspective? Make a move away from hierarchy? Infuse a barrier with motion? Turn sedimentation on its side? Appearing throughout the text, the strips are intended to open/ cut space for pause, for a different (nonverbal) language, a gentle stutter to the flow of words. Can these image-borders do the both/and work of disrupting and connecting? Can such imagery, interrupting a text, also interweave (or diffract) multiple ways of knowing? Herein lies an invitation. Or perhaps a provocation.

We weave this work (text and image) across, under, and through the theoretical threads that serve as a connective fiber for our evolving collaboration: Gloria Anzaldúa's *borderlands* theory; Karen Barad's "agential cuts" (cutting together-apart) in the context of diffraction, the "queer" phenomena of light's simultaneous behavior as particle and wave; Donna Haraway's "staying with the trouble"; and Jacques Rancière's political dissensus.[16] All the while we attend to interdisciplinarity's "transgressive charge—to always be pushing at, and defamiliarizing, the limits of disciplinary boundaries."[17]

In the sections that follow, we reflect on the development of our collaborative practice, sharing our insights as potential signposts for future/ fellow border workers. Framed by feminist and decolonial scholarship, we chronicle our learning to work across disciplinary borders, through which three iterative (nonlinear) practices emerged. Negotiating inevitable areas of tension and divergence, border work exposed our need for a *common language*. For us, finding a common language was not a precondition for collaborative work but a central part of collaboration itself. Next is *exploration*, which we understand not as rendering things discrete and knowable at a distance but rather as an intersubjective experience immersed in the realities of limited time and resources and in sometimes contradictory experiences and modes of expression. We discover that this exploration is necessarily slow and that slowness also enacts a substantive quality to working the border through resisting capitalistic imperatives of productivity and centring relationality and care. The third emergent element of our practice is invitation. The desired fruition of our work is not a "product" in the neoliberal sense. Rather, this collaboration opens into *invitation*. It cultivates an ongoing openness to one another and invites others into the continuing creative process, disrupting the boundary between maker and consumer, between science and aesthetics, and importantly, between academic inquiry and political practice.

Finding Common Language

As we dug into our shared practice, our divergent orientations to the topic of borders came into clearer focus—a site of productive exchange versus a tool of exclusion and violence. It became important to find a common language that would enable us to move back and forth between art and geography and between sign and form. We identified two feminist scholars whose work gave us what we needed to make sense of the resonances and tensions emerging between us and to develop our common language with which to speak of them. Anzaldúa was a feminist theorist and poet who wrote extensively about language, identity, and belonging as a *mestiza* growing up in the Texas-Mexico borderlands. Anzaldúa queers border thinking by emphasizing the dual rather than binarist nature of borders—how they can be violent and life-giving, dividing and conjoining. Barad is a physicist and feminist theorist who uses insights from quantum mechanics to trouble received wisdom about the nature of the world and of scientific knowledge production. Barad puts her work in conversation with Anzaldúa's in order to demonstrate how feminist and queer epistemologies better reflect the infinitely more complex and multiple worlds that quantum physicists have just begun to understand.[18]

Anzaldúa's borderland theory captures the dual nature of borders. For her, a border is a sharp thing cutting scars on the earth, dividing "safe" from "unsafe," "us" from "them." A *borderland*, however, is "vague and undetermined"; it is a geography of liminality—a state of neither-nor/both-and "created by the unnatural emotional residue of an unnatural boundary." Both painful and full of possibility, "in a constant state of transition," borderlands are rich with the potential of connection.[19] Political borders inscribe divisions within the social landscape and, often, within the subject herself. For Anzaldúa, we are all bordered subjects. Divisions and lines can be read as attempts to contain the multiple worlds that inhabit the same space. This insight helped us move forward beyond our tension around borders as violent and divisive as well as sites of contact and possibility. They are both—not multiple components added up to a single whole but overlapping, inseparable wholes.

In envisioning the artwork, we began to pull out images from Heather's 35 mm film archive, taken in Morocco and South Carolina, that captured various dualities we recognized as being at play in our dialogue: mobility and immobility, light and dark, freedom and captivity, division and unity, opaqueness and porosity. We began to experiment with translucent materials that could be layered and overlapped. Emphasizing the dual (or multiple) rather than the binary displaced the notion of discrete space, loosening the fixity of borders. Describing the relation of light to darkness in the optical phenomenon of diffraction, Barad demonstrates how light refuses absolute separation from darkness.[20] Passing through two slits in a piece of paper, light overlaps, which we might expect to create more light but in fact produces darkness: (more ≠ more). In other experiments, light appears mingled within the boundaries of a shadow, troubling a politics (and ontology) of separation, of location: Where is here? Where is there? Which side is dark? Which side is light? Diffraction displays the liveliness of light that "troubles the very notion of *dicho-tomy* (cutting into two)" disrupting "some of the most sedimented and stabilized/stabilizing binaries."[21] Reflecting on the creative ways that people engage local border walls, Luis Alberto Urrea tells a story of kids in Nogales who play volleyball together across the US-Mexico border wall—one team on one side, the other team on the other, the game reworking the border as an arena of play. Urrea recalled that the US side of Nogales reminded him of the East German side of the Berlin Wall (stark, heavily patrolled, clear-cut of brush and trees for more visibility), while the Mexican side resembled the West German side (full of people, life, murals, street vendors, and musicians). To Urrea, this begs the question, On which side does freedom reside? Where is the "better life"?[22] In this enacted relationality across a border wall, we see a diffractive troubling of some of America's most sedimented national and political narratives. In the self-acclaimed "Land of Freedom," we ask again, Where is here? Where is there?

As our project continued to take physical shape, Barad's work provided further language and metaphor to encapsulate our emerging collective imagination of borders as dynamic entities. Barad writes about how performances of differentiation, what she calls "agential cuts," are not absolute separations but merely *reorganizations* of always-entangled materials and socialities. Returning to diffraction, in one experiment, when light passes through two slits of paper at the same time, it behaves simultaneously as particle and wave. Barad calls this phenomenon "together-apart." In other experiments, a single particle of light can pass through each of the slits in its entirety at the same time, a result that challenges the Newtonian theory that light must, in such conditions, take the form of a wave. This shows, Barad argues, that differentiation does not require division. Barad's insight was helpful at two levels of our collaboration: We composed materials and images through cutting, sticking, moving, and removing with the understanding that each arrangement revealed something new and yet was bound up in all the other arrangements before and after. It also removed the sense of separateness between process and product. Each installation is a "cut" or snapshot of something always in motion—iterative and iterating recompositions.

"Together-apart" also helped us reconcile how our individual, uniquely held relationship to the theme remained discernible even as a collectively held relationship took shape. As Barad affirms, "Entanglements are not unities. They do not erase differences; on the contrary, entanglings entail differentiatings, differentiatings entail entanglings. One move—cutting together-apart."[23] Rather than seeking integration or consensus, this "together-apart" practice aimed for dissensus.

For political theorist Rancière, dissensus is a site from which the political—as an undisciplined range of possible relations, subjects, and practices—can emerge.[24] While dissensus produces an unruly space of politics by blurring lines of commonly held interrelationalities and hierarchies, consensus represents the evacuation of the political from a social world predicated upon order (police) and membership (citizenship), a reinforcement of hierarchical divisions. In rejecting the depoliticization of social space, dissensus rejects partisanship (each group rigorously delimiting and policing their side). Feminist and queer theorists, such as Haraway and Barad, articulate dissensual practice as one of "staying with the trouble" in order to disrupt or dislodge boundaries perceived as fixed.[25] As we bring art and political geography together-apart, we "displace the borders of art, just as doing politics means displacing the border of what is recognized as the sphere of the political." It is no coincidence, claims Rancière, "that some of the most interesting artworks today engage with matters of territory and borders."[26]

Dissensual practice is a practice of thinking and creating *otherwise*, of unadhering to common conceptions of becoming "disciplined" in multiple senses of the term. In other words, it is a practice to become undisciplined. In academic life, this means disrupting or even undoing the labor of honing our research skills or creative practices. In the context of border work, this paradigm challenges us to examine possible unintended consensual performances that reinforce problematic hierarchies. Is advocating for the protection of "innocent" migrant children reinforcing the militarization of border enforcement against "bad *hombres*"?[27] In creating artwork, is resistance to representational imagery in order to prevent objectification making the artwork less legible and therefore less accessible? Through our process, revisiting debates we thought we had resolved could feel like moving backward, wasting time, or failing. But it is also the case that "failing, losing, forgetting, unmaking, undoing, unbecoming, not knowing may in fact offer more creative, more cooperative, more surprising ways of being in the world."[28]

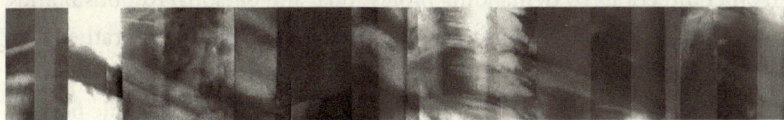

Exploration and Slowness

Recognizing that exploration is often bound up in a colonial relation between (knowing) subject and (perceived) object, our explorations strove for a deeper encounter between subjects and an ethical commitment to each other and our subject matter that exceeded the demands of "getting work done."[29] We felt our way forward carefully in the subject-space of borders and migration. How do we portray our inquiry without reproducing images of the "suffering migrant" that circulates so frequently in media and humanitarian discourse? How do we avoid propagating one-dimensional perceptions and preserve the multiplicity held both in border regions and in the varied experiences of people who navigate them?

As we explored, we had to trust that something was happening even though very little "creation" had taken place. Marilyn Strathern argues that we need to shift our thinking about creative knowledge production, especially within interdisciplinary teams, as only taking place once the time-consuming preliminaries—drumming up interest or resources, getting people on the same page, working out logistics—are complete.[30] These activities are not the run-up to interdisciplinary work but the work itself. This was especially true of our project: each time we sought to reach across the boundaries of time, space, finite resources, understanding, or enthusiasm, we were "working the border."

Collaborations are process oriented and take time. Choosing such collaborations is an act of resistance to the coloniality of time against which productivity is measured and through which it is assigned value. In our case, the "rightness" of our collaboration stemming from our long friendship and ongoing fascination with each other's work motivated our willingness to commit to such a time-intensive endeavor, especially as we constantly felt pulled in other directions by demanding professional and personal responsibilities. We sought to find a rhythm that supported each other's work rather than burdening it. Necessarily, the project unfolded slowly, which ultimately provided the space for a more meaningful and deeper practice.[31] While perhaps seemingly insignificant, it is in these micropolitical shifts, the "bit-by-bitness,"[32] that otherwise worlds are made.[33] We were cultivating "a willingness to take on the space of the unknown in a transformative way." Speaking of fugitive navigation on the way to freedom, Manu Vimalassery observes, "To reach the goal, you don't move in straight lines, on predictable paths, or along foreordained, agreed-upon courses . . . the uncertainty of a journey to an unknown destination. This uncertainty has a name, which is the name of the journey itself, and of the destination: liberation."[34] In our own "bit-by-bit," nonlinear, uncertain ways, we were/are working toward a liberatory practice.

Invitation

The composition and recomposition of the art piece and the project as a whole are not confined to the bounds of our own work. A collaboration between art and social science offers the capacity for invitation and encounter—into a shared physical presence with the artwork and intellectual space with each other—to think inclusively (and in an embodied way) through the issues that drive our inquiry, to (re)compose together. At "The Line Crossed Us" border studies conference, we were able to share this work with scholars, activists, and artists interested in how borders have shaped landscapes, made or unmade nations, and reinforced colonial geographies and how they continue to be resisted, undermined, and reworked. As we talked together, walking along the piece, we described our exploration and shared some of the vocabulary that enabled our collaboration. We invited those present to share the relational space and conceptual territory of our project rather than regard the *results* of the project. The scale and the expressionistic tenor of the work required slowness, time to absorb and process. The imagery is difficult to discern, flickering on a tenuous edge of recognition and suggestion. In the arhythmic arrangement of narrow vertical strips, image fragments of almost-discernible places, objects, and textures are hard to pin down. Associations emerge and recede. Engaging in our common language, people began to move forward and add language of their own. Words like "fugitivity" emerged; some expressed feeling "overwhelmed" by a sense of the enormity of boundaries; others saw "fragility" in the construction as an indication of the inherent "instability" of boundary making. Someone questioned its political work: Does the beauty of the piece erase the violence that borders often engender? In our intention to disrupt rather than reenact conventional border conceptions, beauty can do the work of invitation, drawing people into the space of relationality. Beauty can create an affective (emotional and psychological) opening, softening the metaphorical ground toward receptivity. It can afford comfortable ground to grapple with uncomfortable realities, a hospitable space to "stay with the trouble." The cut that manifested in our initial installation began to change before our eyes as others made their own cuts together-apart.

Invitation into the interdisciplinary process even at the moment of creation returns us to expanding entanglements of relationship and interresponse-ability. The Great Lakes Feminist Geography Collective[35] argues that slow, collective scholarship reflects a feminist ethic of care for oneself and for others and is bound up in "the struggle for . . . the decolonization of knowledge, in which experimentation, creativity, different epistemologies, and dissidence are all valued and encouraged."[36] Loveless points out that the values of deliberate, creative collaboration (curiosity, curation, carefulness) share the same root word: to care, which also "brings warning (caution), desire (to know), and considered choice (the care at stake in curation)."[37] In other words, an invitation to join in our endeavor is also an invitation into relationships that exceed our most comfortable or cherished boundaries—of the university, of the nation, of the self as a solitary and self-contained agent. Haraway insists that this is what is required if we are to survive these "disturbing times, mixed-up times, troubling and turbid times. The task is to make kin in lines of inventive connection as a practice of learning to live and die well with each other in the thick present."[38]

Issuing an expansive, unbounded, excessive invitation into relationship might be the *how* for addressing the most troubling problems of our troubled times. The *who* of these relationships is multiple, other, more-than—in Anzaldúa's words, *nepantla* (neither here nor there). Haraway calls it (us) *oddkin*: "Staying with the trouble requires making oddkin; that is, we require each other in unexpected collaborations and combinations, in hot compost piles. We become-with each other, or not at all."[39] We can imagine a better world only if we get serious about our entanglements with all the other (Indigenous, colonial, ecologically dynamic, more-than-human) worlds out there (in here).[40]

Migratory Futures

This chapter describes our ongoing art–social science collaboration to intervene in struggles over borders and boundaries that loom large in social and political life today. We discover that true interdisciplinary collaboration has the potential to enliven knowledge creation through developing new languages in common, through exploration of other terrains of knowing, and through inviting others into the process. Such work is processual—that is, the line between process and product is necessarily blurry and, as such, is not readily legible to neoliberal metrics of productivity and does not always produce recognizable "results." Instead, such a practice makes space for multiple worlds, for care-full collectives of singular knowledges, individuals, creative processes, methodologies. Such a practice is imbued with decolonial possibility.

But interdisciplinarity, as a collaboration within the university across various academic disciplines, has its limits. All the disciplines within the university were germinated and nurtured in the colonial project; in the extraction of objects and people for study or (forced) labour; in the privileging of scientific practices of describing, measuring, categorizing, and so on; in the division of vocation (of artist, scientist, theorist) from the laity.[41] Furthermore, the production of colonial knowledge has often begun with exploration in order for knowledge to be "treated, enunciated, and represented in new contexts."[42] Thus, a project whose aim is to disrupt colonizing forms of knowledge and imagine emancipatory futures must migrate beyond the confines of the academy altogether. We contend that debordering knowledge production through interdisciplinary collaboration preserves space for the varied, conflicting experiences of living with borders in the settler-colonial nation-state and conditions the possibilities for meaningful political and social change.

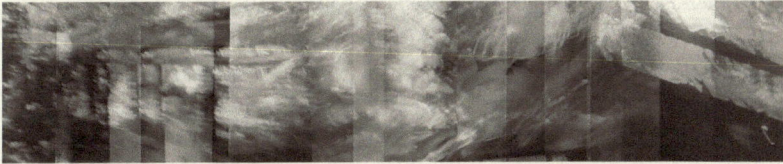

"Working the border" continues to be an invitation to all of us to traverse boundaries and consider how exploration might be more affirmatively understood or reworked as a position of receptivity, listening, and relinquishing ownership or other proprietary claims. Disrupting borders unmoors colonial markers of "here" and "there," enacting an unruly spatiality. Our hope in our continuing collaboration is that valuing unruliness, staying with the trouble, and making oddkin might countermap a strange and lively territory of possibility.

Notes

1. A. Barbosa et al., *The Intercontinental Biosphere of the Mediterranean: D9.2 Case Study Report*.
2. The images appearing throughout the text are recomposed grayscale cuts from a previously installed artwork entitled *Border Disruptions*. Rather than discrete representations of work that exist outside the text, these images are an integral aspect of this chapter, reiterated from their previous variation into a new

form, doing new work within this specific context. They are reprinted with permission of the artists-authors.

3. Gloria Anzaldúa, *Borderlands / La Frontera: The New Mestiza*.

4. Karen Barad, "Quantum Entanglements and Hauntological Relations of Inheritance," 265–66.

5. Sheila McManus, Paul McKenzie-Jones, and Julie Young, eds., *Challenging Borders: Contingencies and Consequences*.

6. McManus, McKenzie-Jones, and Young, *Challenging Borders*.

7. Corey Johnson et al., "Interventions on Rethinking 'the Border' in Border Studies."

8. Jacques Rancière, "Contemporary Art and the Politics of Aesthetics."

9. Renée Marlin-Bennett, "Art-Power and Border Art."

10. Derek Briton, "From Integrated to Interstitial Studies," 373–74.

11. Manu Vimalassery, "Fugitive Decolonization."

12. Gavin Little, "Connecting Environmental Humanities: Developing Interdisciplinary Collaborative Method," 3–4.

13. Donna Haraway, *Staying with the Trouble: Making Kin in the Chthulucene*.

14. Raphael Foshay, "Introduction: Interdisciplinarity for What?" xxix.

15. Natalie Loveless, *How to Make Art at the End of the World: A Manifesto for Research-Creation*, 102.

16. Anzaldúa, *Borderlands / La Frontera*; Karen Barad, *Meeting the Universe Halfway: Quantum Physics and the Entanglement of Matter and Meaning*; Barad, "Diffracting Diffraction"; Haraway, *Staying with the Trouble*; Rancière, "Contemporary Art."

17. Loveless, *How to Make Art*, 60.

18. Barad, *Meeting the Universe Halfway*; Barad, "Diffracting Diffraction."

19. Anzaldúa, *Borderlands / La Frontera*, 3.

20. Barad, "Diffracting Diffraction," 171.

21. Barad, "Diffracting Diffraction," 168.

22. Luis Alberto Urrea and Krista Tippett, "What Borders Are Really about and What We Do with Them."

23. Barad, "Diffracting Diffraction," 176.

24. Jacques Rancière, *Dissensus: On Politics and Aesthetics*.

25. Haraway, *Staying with the Trouble*.

26. Rancière, "Contemporary Art," 47.

27. "To Some, Trump's 'Bad Hombres' Is Much More Than a Botched Spanish Word."

28. Jack Halberstam, *The Queer Art of Failure*, 2.

29. Linda Tuhiwai Smith, "On Tricky Ground: Researching the Native in the Age of Uncertainty."

30. Marilyn Strathern, "Experiments in Interdisciplinarity," 87–88.
31. A. Mountz et al., "For Slow Scholarship: A Feminist Politics of Resistance through Collective Action in the Neoliberal University."
32. Haraway, *Staying with the Trouble*, 40.
33. Loveless, *How to Make Art*, 102.
34. Vimalassery, "Fugitive Decolonization."
35. The Feminist Geographies Specialty Group (FGSG) of the American Association of Geographers (AAG) promotes explorations of how gender, women, and other axes of social power are actualized through space. https://www.aag.org/groups/feminist-geographies/.
36. Mountz et al., "For Slow Scholarship," 1254.
37. Loveless, *How to Make Art*, 47.
38. Haraway, *Staying with the Trouble*, 1.
39. Haraway, *Staying with the Trouble*, 4.
40. Anzaldúa, *Borderlands / La Frontera*.
41. Linda Tuhiwai Smith, *Decolonizing Methodologies*, 70.
42. Smith, *Decolonizing Methodologies*, 70.

Bibliography

Anzaldúa, Gloria. *Borderlands / La Frontera: The New Mestiza*. San Francisco, CA: Aunt Lute Books, 1987.

Barad, Karen. "Diffracting Diffraction: Cutting Together-Apart." *Parallax* 20, no. 3 (2014): 168–87. http://doi.org/10.1080/13534645.2014.927623.

Barad, Karen. *Meeting the Universe Halfway: Quantum Physics and the Entanglement of Matter and Meaning*. Durham, NC: Duke University Press, 2007.

Barad, Karen. "Quantum Entanglements and Hauntological Relations of Inheritance: Dis/Continuities, SpaceTime Enfoldings, and Justice-to-Come." *Derrida Today* 3, no. 2 (2010): 240–68. https://www.jstor.org/stable/48616359.

Barbosa, Ana, Beatriz Martín, Alejandro Iglesias-Campos, Juan Arévalo Torres, Julian Barbière, Virgilio Hermoso, Sami Domisch, et al. *The Intercontinental Biosphere of the Mediterranean: D9.2 Case Study Report*. Berlin: Ecologic Institute, 2018.

Briton, Derek. "From Integrated to Interstitial Studies." In *Valences of Interdisciplinarity: Theory, Practice, Pedagogy*, edited by Raphael Foshay, 367–90. Edmonton, AB: AU Press, 2012.

Foshay, Raphael. "Introduction: Interdisciplinarity for What?" In *Valences of Interdisciplinarity: Theory, Practice, Pedagogy*, edited by Raphael Foshay, 1–30. Edmonton, AB: AU Press, 2012.

Halberstam, Jack. *The Queer Art of Failure*. Durham, NC: Duke University Press, 2011.

Haraway, Donna. *Staying with the Trouble: Making Kin in the Chthulucene*. Durham, NC: Duke University Press, 2016.

Johnson, Corey, Reece Jones, Anssi Paasi, Louise Admoore, Alison Mountz, Mark Salter, Chris Rumford. "Interventions on Rethinking 'the Border' in Border Studies." *Political Geography* 30, no. 2 (February 1, 2011): 61–69. https://doi.org/10.1016/j.polgeo.2011.01.002.

Little, Gavin. "Connecting Environmental Humanities: Developing Interdisciplinary Collaborative Method." *Humanities* 6, no. 91 (2017): 1–22.

Loveless, Natalie. *How to Make Art at the End of the World: A Manifesto for Research-Creation*. Durham, NC: Duke University Press, 2019.

Marlin-Bennett, Renée. "Art-Power and Border Art." *Arts & International Affairs*, October 27, 2019. https://theartsjournal.net/2019/10/27/marlin-bennett-2/.

McKenzie-Jones, Paul, Sheila McManus, and Julie Young, eds. *Challenging Borders: Contingencies and Consequences*. Athabasca, AB: AU Press, 2024.

Mountz, Alison, Anne Bonds, Becky Mansfield, Jenna Loyd, Jennifer Hyndman, Margaret Walton-Robers, Ranu Basu, et al. "For Slow Scholarship: A Feminist Politics of Resistance through Collective Action in the Neoliberal University." *ACME: An International Journal for Critical Geographies* 14, no. 4 (2015): 1235–59. https://acme-journal.org/index.php/acme/article/view/1058.

Paasi, Anssi. *Territories, Boundaries and Consciousness: The Changing Geographies of the Finnish-Russian Border*. Chichester: John Wiley, 1996.

Rancière, Jacques. "Contemporary Art and the Politics of Aesthetics." In *Communities of Sense: Rethinking Politics and Aesthetics*, edited by Beth Hinderliter, Vered Maimon, Jaleh Mansoor, and Seth McCormick, 31–50. Durham, NC: Duke University Press, 2009.

Rancière, Jacques. *Dissensus: On Politics and Aesthetics*. New York: Continuum, 2010.

Smith, Linda Tuhiwai. *Decolonizing Methodologies*. London: Zed Books, 2012.

Smith, Linda Tuhiwai. "On Tricky Ground: Researching the Native in the Age of Uncertainty." In *The Sage Handbook of Qualitative Research*, edited by N. K. Denzin and Y. S. Lincoln, 85–107. Thousand Oaks, CA: SAGE, 2005.

Strathern, Marilyn. "Experiments in Interdisciplinarity." *Social Anthropology* 13, no. 1 (2005): 75–90.

Strathern, Marilyn. "Social Property: An Interdisciplinary Experiment." *PoLAR* 27, no. 1 (May 2004): 23–50.

"To Some, Trump's 'Bad Hombres' Is Much More Than a Botched Spanish Word." PBS NewsHour, October 20, 2016. https://www.pbs.org/newshour/politics/trumps-bad-hombres-draws-jeers-spanish-lessons.

Urrea, Luis Alberto, and Krista Tippett. "What Borders Are Really about and What We Do with Them." OnBeing.org, July 12, 2018. https://onbeing.org/programs/luis-alberto-urrea-borders-are-liminal-spaces/.

Vimalassery, Manu. "Fugitive Decolonization." *Theory & Event* 19, no. 4 (2016). https://muse.jhu.edu/article/633284.

3 The Line Crossed Us?

Remapping the Geo-body of a Nation: How Young People in Finland Understand Shifting Borders

Chloe Wells*

Like a chasm runs the border
In front, Asia, the East
Behind, Europe, the West
Like a sentry, I stand guard.

—Uuno Kailas, "On the Border" (1931)

Nation-state borders are at once geographic borderlines and borderings: social, cultural, and mental constructions. Far more than merely lines on maps and markers in physical space, borders are also abstract concepts constantly reproduced and invested with emotional significance by individual actors.[1] Borderlines delineate what Thongchai Winichakul termed the "geo-body" of a nation-state—not merely the territory it occupies but ideas and associations that produce real-world effects, including emotional responses, such as pride, loyalty, and bias and even love and hate.[2] These national bodies are made visible as maps, copies of which can be endlessly reproduced. In this

* This chapter is dedicated to my Grandad, John "Jack" Wells (1919–2017), who trained at the British Commonwealth Air Training Plan School in Lethbridge during World War II.

way, maps become emblematic icons, or "logo-maps," capable of reifying an abstract entity as a physical object, a "thing."[3]

As Franck Billé observes, as visual symbols, logo-maps play "a crucial role in the inculcation of national identity" and in defining the boundary between "us" and "them."[4] Changes to the shape of a nation-state's geo-body and hence to its logo-map may therefore be traumatic. Billé argues that a nation's citizens frequently perceive a loss of territory "as akin to a violent assault on the physical body," which can produce "territorial phantom pains"—persistent and deep-seated feelings of emotional connection to a place no longer there, not unlike pains felt in a lost limb.[5] Such phantom pains occur when territories imagined as integral to national identity are severed from the nation-state's body via an act of cartographic violence: the forced redrawing of national borders. Physically, such territories are gone, yet "on an emotional level, they remain 'attached' to the national body."[6] Over time, however, attachments to territories that are now outside a nation-state's borders may fade away, and an earlier logo-map may be forgotten. The old one is then replaced by a new one, the "continual re-imprinting" of which eventually leads to "a cognitive remapping of the national contours."[7]

In this chapter, I investigate the long-term impact of changes to a nation's geo-body through the eyes of Finnish youth. Researchers Spyros Spyrou and Miranda Christou have stressed the importance of studies that focus "on children's engagement with place and territory and their meaning-making activities as they go about their daily lives," as the perspectives of children and youth can enrich our overall understanding of borderlines and of bordering processes.[8] As such studies indicate, young people are not simply passive consumers of representations of their nation-state but actively negotiate and construct these representations.[9] Along the same lines, I seek to shed light on processes of bordering by examining how young people in Finland perceive their country's territorial shape, how they represent its borders via mental mapping, and how they frame these changes discursively. More specifically, I explore the ways in which young people understand the changes to Finland's eastern border that occurred during World War II, with special attention to the influence of spatial socialization on their perceptions and interpretations. I also raise the question of how far (if at all) young people still feel an affective attachment to these lost territories—that is, how far emotions travel across generational borders.

The concepts of a geo-body and territorial phantom pains fit the Finnish context well. At the close of World War II, Finland was forced to cede roughly

10 percent of its territory to the Soviet Union (see figure 3.1). Among the ceded areas were sections of the transborder region of Karelia, positioned in narratives of Finnish nation building as key not only to the defence of Finland against what was often termed the "eastern threat" but also to the country's sense of cultural identity. Karelia was thus important not only territorially but symbolically and spiritually as well.[10] Also ceded were territories in Lapland—the Petsamo region in the far northeast and portions of the municipality of Salla, farther south along the eastern border—as well as several islands in the Gulf of Finland. Finally, although the area was not permanently ceded, Finland was obliged to lease territory on the Porkkala peninsula, only about thirty kilometres west of Helsinki, to the Soviet Union for temporary use as a naval base.

Maps depicting Finland's borders played an important role in establishing a distinctly Finnish national identity prior to the country's independence, in 1917, and then in Finland's assertion of its nationhood in the decades following.[11] By the end of the nineteenth century, Finland had come to be anthropomorphized as the Finnish Maiden, traditionally depicted as a young blond-haired woman, her arms outstretched in a gesture of welcome, wearing a traditional Finnish blouse and a billowing skirt.[12] On maps, the slender northwestern extension of Finnish territory sandwiched between Sweden and Norway is her right arm, while the Petsamo region—which first became part of Finland in 1920, only to be reclaimed by Soviet Russia in 1944—formed her left arm. The territorial losses that Finland suffered during World War II may thus be understood, visualized, and remembered as physical assaults on the Finnish Maiden's body.

Although Karelia did not form a visually distinctive part of the Finnish Maiden's body, Finnish geographer Anssi Paasi notes that the ceded Karelian territory "became highly important for national narratives, heritage and collective memories" and was hence "a sore object of emotional 'territorial phantom pains'" for those Finns who were displaced from the area.[13] Expressions of territorial phantom pain—a lingering emotional attachment to "lost Karelia"—can also be found in Finnish media discourses and in popular culture, including Finnish pop songs about getting Karelia back. Unlike the Petsamo area, Karelia had long been bound up with national and cultural identity, particularly since the late nineteenth century, when it became the focus of a romantic form of ethnic nationalism popular among artists and writers who saw in Karelia the essence of "Finnishness."

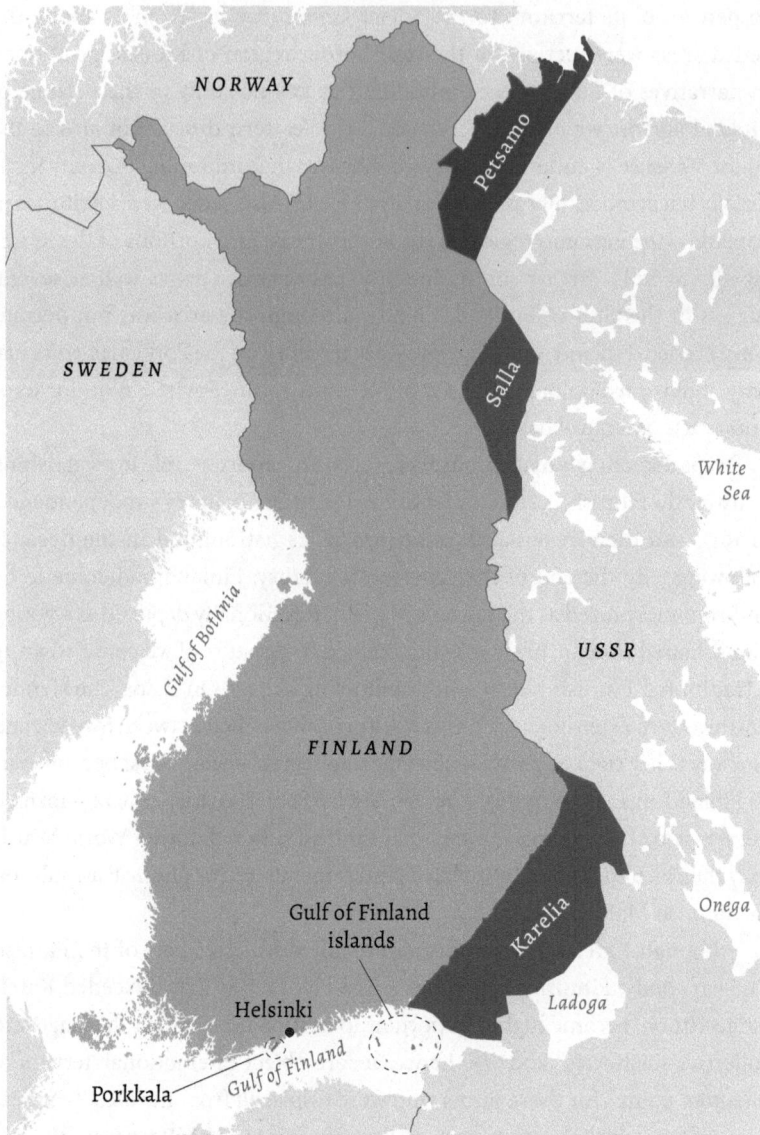

Figure 3.1 The territories that Finland ceded to the Soviet Union during World War II. Much of Finnish Karelia, portions of the municipality of Salla, and five islands in the Gulf of Finland were ceded in 1940, while Petsamo was ceded in 1944, at which time territory on the Porkkala peninsula was also temporarily leased to the Soviet Union. All these territories were emptied of their Finnish populations, who resettled inside Finland.

Finland's Shifting Borders in Historical Perspective

Historically Swedish territory, Finland came under Russian control following Russia's 1808–9 war with Sweden, and in 1812 Russia created the autonomous Grand Duchy of Finland.[14] The Karelian border drawn in 1812 was still in place in December 1917, when Finland declared its independence from Russia on the heels of the Bolshevik Revolution. The next two years were marked by turmoil, as the so-called Whites—supporters of the provisional Finnish government set up in 1917—fought the revolutionary forces of the Finnish Socialist Workers' Republic (the Reds). After a bloody civil war in the spring of 1918, the Whites prevailed, and in 1920 the newly constituted Republic of Finland and the Russian Soviet Federative Socialist Republic signed the Treaty of Tartu, which established the border between the two. Although Finland's Karelian border was unaltered, its northeastern border changed quite dramatically in 1920 as a result of the addition of the Petsamo area, which the Russians ceded to Finland in exchange for two districts of East Karelia that the Finnish Army had occupied during this tumultuous period.

As these initial struggles might suggest, the looming presence of the Soviet Union, just across the border, was a central factor in Finland's post-independence process of nation building. As Paasi points out, "The Finnish state as a national 'We' has typically been constructed in exclusive terms in relation to Russia/the Soviet Union ('The Other')," with the physical border-line making concrete this conceptual division.[15] Uuno Kailas's well-known poem "Rajalla" (On the border), the opening stanza of which is quoted in the epigraph, expresses this nationalist perspective. The poem refers to the borderline between the newly independent Republic of Finland and the Soviet Union, which Kailas likens to an unbridgeable gulf, a chasm. Saija Kaskinen points to the antagonism toward the Soviet Union visible in the poem, which portrays Finland "as the guardian of Western culture against an invasion from the East."[16]

No such invasion materialized, however, until the outbreak of World War II. During the war, Finland experienced two periods of warfare against the Soviet Union, the second in alliance with Nazi Germany. These are known as the Winter War (November 1939–March 1940) and the Continuation War (June 1941–September 1944). The Winter War began when the Soviet Union invaded Finland and lasted for only three and a half months. It ended with the signing of the Moscow Peace Treaty, according to which, as mentioned earlier, Finland was obliged to cede a significant portion of its territory: the Karelian Isthmus (the area between the Gulf of Finland and Lake Ladoga) and Ladoga Karelia (adjacent territory to the north of Lake Ladoga extending roughly halfway down its northeastern shore), part of the northern municipality of Salla, and five islands near the eastern end of the Gulf of Finland (see figure 3.1). A new Finnish-Soviet border was drawn across Karelia, to the west of the 1920 borderline, thus substantially shrinking Finland's share of the Karelian region.

The Continuation War began in June 1941, just a few days after Nazi Germany launched a major offensive against the Soviet Union. Although not formally allied with the Axis powers, Finland saw in the German attack on its long-standing enemy an opportunity to recover the part of Karelia it had ceded in 1940 and perhaps gain even more. Supplied by Nazi Germany and supported by German troops, the Finnish Army succeeded in recapturing the lost Karelian territory in little more than two months, thereby restoring the 1920 borderline. The army then advanced into Soviet Karelia to occupy territory extending along the entire northeastern shore of Lake Ladoga and all the way northeast to the western shore of Lake Onega while also slightly expanding its share of the Karelian Isthmus (see figure 3.2). This advance was fuelled in part by the expansionist and ultra-nationalist vision of "Greater Finland," which would include essentially all of Soviet Karelia.[17]

Finland retained control of the territory it had captured for the better part of three years. In June 1944, however, Soviet forces embarked on a major, multi-pronged offensive and by September had recaptured most of the territory that Finland had occupied. This led to the signing of the Moscow Armistice, which restored the 1940 border. In addition, Finland was forced to cede the Petsamo area (such that Norway now bordered the Soviet Union) and to lease territory on the Porkkala peninsula to the Soviets for a period of fifty years for the construction of a naval base.[18] Finland's border was ratified in the 1947 Paris Peace Treaties and has remained unaltered since then.

World War II caused a traumatic, permanent loss of property, community, and way of life for those who lived in and were forced to leave the areas that Finland ceded to the Soviet Union. In total, somewhere around 420,000 people, over 11 percent of Finland's wartime population, were evacuated from their homes and subsequently resettled elsewhere in postwar Finland.[19] Karelia was the largest of the ceded areas, and it also contained the city of Vyborg, a cultural hub situated in the Karelian Isthmus on the Gulf of Finland.

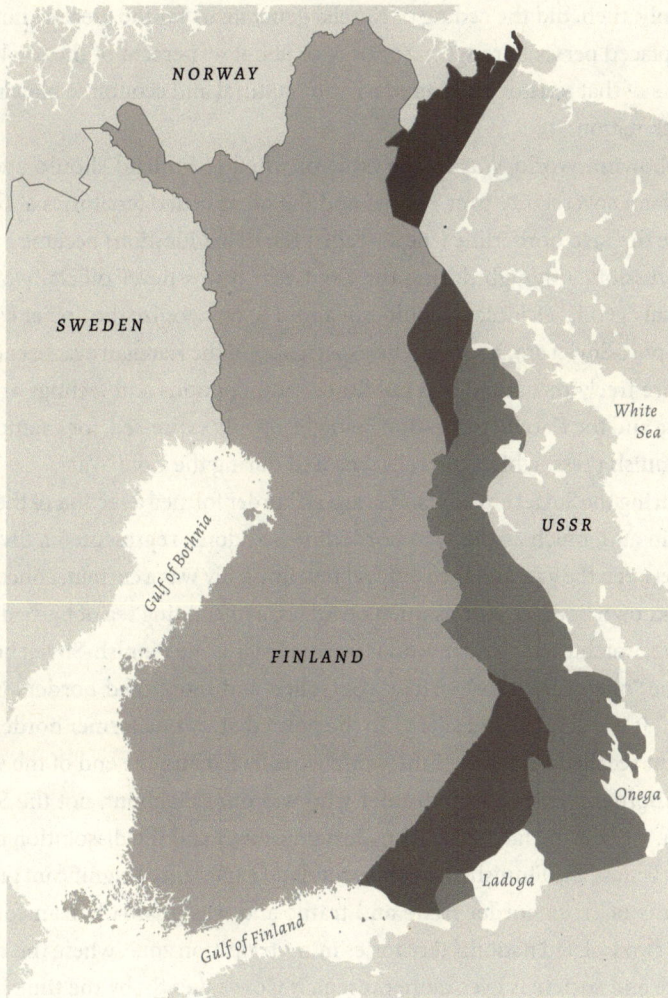

Figure 3.2 The maximum extent of the advance of the Nazi Germany–backed Finnish Army during the Continuation War. At the start of the war, in June 1941, Finland set out to reclaim the portions of Salla and Karelia that it had lost to the Soviet Union in March 1940, at the conclusion of the Winter War. That it had accomplished by September 1941, at which point the army pushed on for another three months, deeper into the Soviet Union, capturing regions of Karelia that had never previously been Finnish territory. The Petsamo region, in the far northeast, was part of Finland in 1941 but was ceded to the Soviet Union in 1944, at the end of the Continuation War.

Not only, then, did the ceding of Karelia generate by far the greatest number of displaced persons (roughly 407,000, or about 97 percent of the total), but the loss of that territory delivered a major cultural and economic blow to the Finnish nation.[20]

Following World War II, the issue of whether Finland should attempt to reclaim sovereignty over Karelia and the other ceded territories and thus restore the 1920 borderline (the so-called Karelian Question) became a topic of discussion, although during the Cold War it was never officially on the political agenda, as Finland could not afford to antagonize the Soviet Union. In the post-Soviet era, however, the experiences of the Karelian evacuees could be more freely recounted and published, and opinions and feelings around Karelia and the Karelian Question could be openly expressed, for example, in the Finnish press, which had self-censored during the Cold War.[21]

During the Soviet era, Finland's eastern border formed a section of the Iron Curtain and, much as the 1920 borderline had done, represented a dividing line between the east and the west. Yet that line truly was a curtain, concealing an unknown beyond. As Kaskinen observes, a forbidding sea of barbed-wire fencing, watchtowers, and ominous warning signs, the Finnish-Soviet border became "one of the most strictly controlled and monitored borders in the world." It was "closed and silent," to the point that, as one former borderland resident recalled, "It felt as if the world is really flat and the end of the world is the Border. . . . It was the Border who was our neighbour, not the Soviet Union."[22] After the fall of the Iron Curtain in 1991 and the dissolution of the Soviet Union, the Finnish-Russian borderland experienced significant growth in terms of cross-border trade and traffic and was gradually transformed "from two isolated national territories into a transition zone, where the 'other' culture and society is ever more present."[23] Consequently, by the time I conducted my research, attitudes toward the border had begun to shift, and it was not necessarily seen as the barrier it once was.

Spatial Socialization and Mental Maps

For many people in Finland, the loss of Karelia and the other territories ceded during World War II has come to seem quite distant, yet some may still experience territorial phantom pains. Why an individual or group of people might feel territorial phantom pains in relation to former national territory can be explained in part by the concept of spatial socialization.

In Paasi's definition, spatial socialization is "the process through which individual actors and collectivities are socialized as members of specific territorially bounded spatial entities and through which they more or less actively internalize collective territorial identities and shared traditions."[24] In other words, it is through spatial socialization that people come to feel that they belong to a particular expanse of territory (be it a nation or a local neighbourhood) and also learn what membership in that territory implies—what it means, for example, to be Finnish. At the same time, they develop a sense of ownership of that territory, the feeling that the territory belongs to them, just as they belong to it. At the national level, spatial socialization occurs not only through formal education (especially classes in history and geography) but also through everyday encounters with maps—on TV weather forecasts, for example, or in newspapers and magazines. Not too long ago, for example, an outline map of Finland even began to appear on milk cartons.[25]

At the time I conducted my research, the high school students with whom I worked were constantly being exposed to the processes of spatial socialization that operate via formal education in Finland as well as to informal processes at work in the society at large (although the milk cartons had yet to come along). For example, during a group discussion in the city of Oulu, on Finland's west coast, students were asked how they had learned about Karelia. They reported that, although they did learn about it in school, it was also "general knowledge," as one put it. Another called it "internal knowledge," while a third commented that "it would be weird if you're a Finn and you haven't heard of Karelia." A student in the northern city of Rovaniemi further noted that there are "a lot of . . . stories in magazines" about Karelia. Their comments well illustrate the effects of spatial socialization. Regardless of their geographic location, students viewed knowledge of Karelia as part of their identity as Finns.

Rovaniemi and Oulu were two of the eleven cities in Finland that I visited in 2017 in the course of my study (see figure 3.3). In what follows, I draw on data collected during thirty-eight mixed-methods focus groups, comprising a total of 325 high school students (aged 16 to 19).[26] These data consist of transcripts of discussions that took place during the groups, 315 pairs of maps of Finland drawn by participants, and 958 pieces of written material.[27] The transcripts and the written materials were analyzed qualitatively, according to a method known as thematic content analysis.[28] The maps were analyzed mainly via quantitative grouping, although the analysis also included qualitative interpretations.

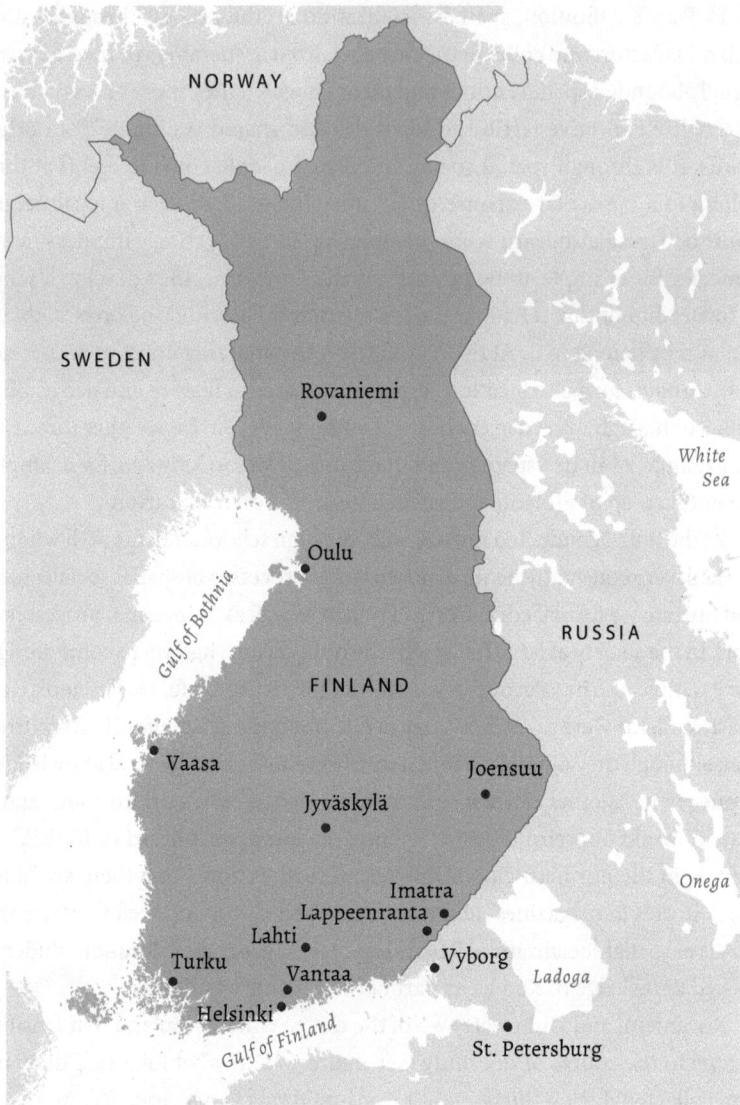

Figure 3.3 The location of the eleven focus groups, as well as of Vyborg and the Russian city of St. Petersburg, known during the Soviet era as Leningrad. Prior to World War II, Vyborg was the main city in Finnish Karelia, but it lay in territory ceded to the Soviet Union in 1940. The following year, during the Continuation War, Finnish-German forces temporarily recovered that territory and then, in the Karelian Isthmus, advanced to a point only a few dozen kilometres north of Leningrad, where they remained until 1944.

During the groups, students were asked about the events of World War II and about their knowledge and perceptions of Karelia, in particular. In order to stimulate discussion, I also asked them to draw mental maps of the outline of Finland before and after the war. In brief, in a mental mapping exercise, a participant draws a map based on an image they have formed in their mind. As subjective impressions, mental maps provide insight into spatial perceptions—how participants conceive of or imagine a certain place.[29] The maps were not entirely individual efforts, however. Participants were encouraged to talk to each other about their maps as they were drawing them, and the talk during the mapping task added another layer to the analysis.

Locating the Past in the Present: Perceptions and Interpretations

As was clear from the maps they drew, students were aware that Finland's eastern border changed as a result of World War II. The loss of the Petsamo area was shown in 89 percent of the map pairs, and 66 percent marked the ceded Karelian territory. In contrast, the other ceded territories—Salla and the islands in the Gulf of Finland—and the leased area of Porkkala were indicated on only a very few maps: Salla on 8 percent, with the gulf islands and Porkkala each marked on only 2 percent. As a general rule, the maps were simple outlines that included few other details. All but twenty-five of the 315 map pairs (92%) showed Finland as if it were a free-floating island, without any indication of what lies beyond its borders: Russia to the east, Sweden to the west, Norway to the north, and Estonia to the south, across the Gulf of Finland.

About 5 percent of the map pairs were anthropomorphic, depicting Finland as a human figure, sometimes complete with human face. Participants also anthropomorphized Finland in comments made during the mental mapping task. For example, in an apparent allusion to the Finnish Maiden, a student in Imatra described Finland as "a skirt-wearing woman who has her hands up."[30] In some cases, participants gave Finland's body a voice to call attention to a key feature on a map. Several indicated that Petsamo was understood as Finland's lost arm: "I lost me hand!" "I have been amputated," "Where's the other hand [mis toinen käsi]?" (see figures 3.4, 3.5, and 3.6), while a fourth map announced that "Karelia has been lost [Karjala menetetty]" (see figure 3.7). In discussions during the mapping task, Petsamo was also sometimes imagined as having been violently severed from the national body.

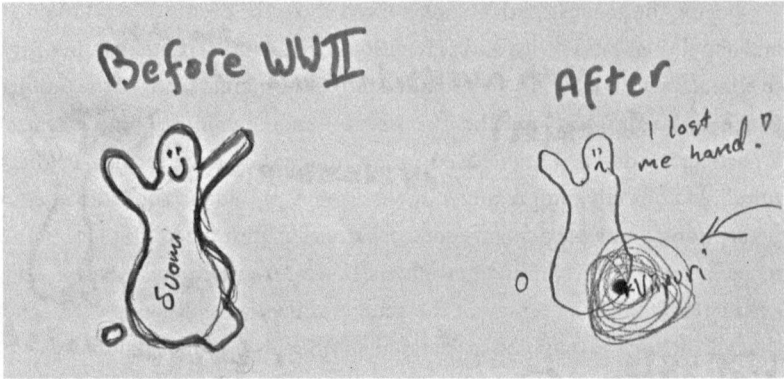

Figure 3.4 Finland (Suomi) before and after World War II as depicted by a high school student in Oulu, a city on Finland's west coast, roughly at the country's "waist." With respect to Karelia, the student emphasizes the loss of Vyborg (Viipuri)—Finland's second-largest city at the time—to the Soviet Union. Used with permission.

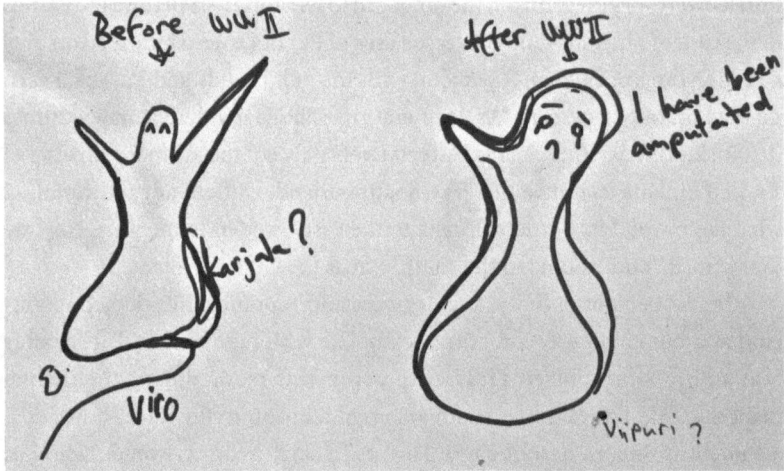

Figure 3.5 Another pair of mental maps showing Finland before and after World War II, also drawn by a student in Oulu. This student explicitly interprets the loss of Finland's Petsamo arm as an act of dismemberment but seems hesitant about the location of Karelia (Karjala) and the city of Viipuri. The "before" map is unusual in marking one of the countries adjacent to Finland: Estonia, known to Finns as Viro, on the southern side of the Gulf of Finland. Used with permission.

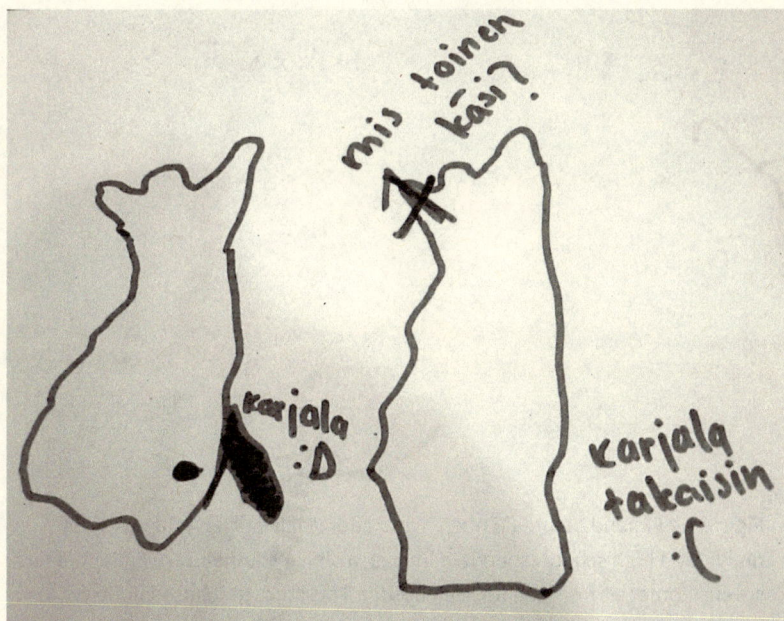

Figure 3.6 Finland before and after World War II, as drawn by a high school student in the city of Turku, in southwestern Finland. Although clearly aware that territory was sacrificed in the far north, the student seems uncertain of its location and has crossed out the wrong "arm." Nor does the black peninsula-like protrusion labeled "Karjala" correspond very well to the shape of the Karelian territory ceded to the Soviet Union. All the same, the call to the Russians to return Karelia ("Karjala takaisin"), with the sad face beside it, acknowledges the pain of its loss. Used with permission.

As a student in Lappeenranta commented, "After the Second World War, the arm was pulled off."[31]

Prior to the war, the Petsamo region—the Finnish Maiden's second arm—was a striking visual feature on a logo-map, jutting out at a sharp angle to the northeast. Its subsequent loss, which does resemble an amputation (a war wound, so to speak), is very noticeable and therefore more likely to be recalled and represented on a mental map.[32] As noted earlier, Karelia was not an especially distinctive feature on a map, however, and for those accustomed to the postwar logo-map, its prewar shape is harder to envisage, as is evident in these maps. While the loss of Karelia is remembered for other reasons,

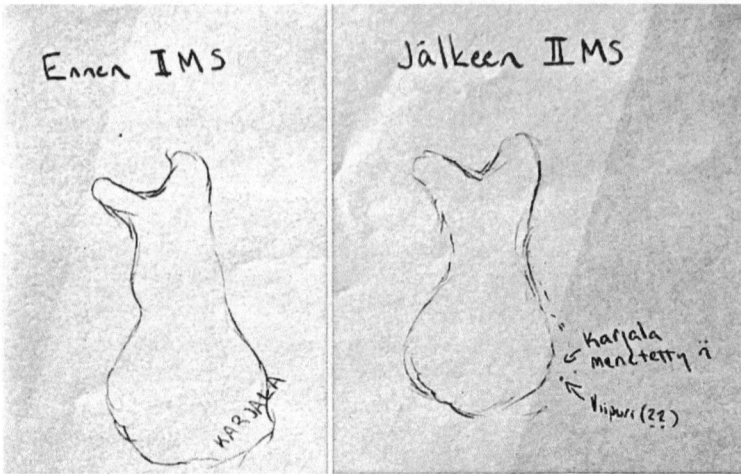

Figure 3.7 Finland before ("Ennen") and after ("Jälkeen") World War II, as drawn by a high school student in Imatra, a city in southeastern Finland only seven kilometres from the Russian border. This student focused entirely on Karelia, ignoring changes to Finland's northeastern border with the Soviet Union, notably the loss of Petsamo. In contrast, "Karjala menetetty" ("Karelia has been lost") explicitly acknowledges the sacrifice of Karelian territory. Used with permission.

students seemed somewhat uncertain of its shape, variously depicting the territory as a protruding rectangle, a crescent, and an inland panhandle.

Immediately after the map-drawing task, I asked participants, "What happened in Finland during World War II?" In their responses, students generally remembered the loss of Karelia, Petsamo, and Salla and also mentioned the leasing of Porkkala to the Soviet Union, even though the location of Porkkala was marked on only 2 percent of the maps they drew. Sometimes participants left out one or another of the ceded areas. For example, a participant in the city of Turku, in the southwestern corner of Finland, neglected to mention Petsamo, in the far northeast, commenting that, after the Continuation War, "we lost Salla, Ladoga Karelia, and the Karelian Isthmus, then Finland's outer islands, and then Porkkala was rented out for fifty years."[33] In several groups, participants collaborated in order to create a list of the ceded areas and when they were lost. A student in one of the Helsinki focus groups noted that at the end of the Winter War, "peace came and Finland lost Karelia," and then went on to say, "Finland also lost Porkkala cape. After the war. Then all the train windows had to always be covered, when the train went by there"—an eerie reminder of the Soviet presence beyond the curtains.[34] Another participant added, "Petsamo was lost in the peace of Moscow '44" (a reference to the Moscow Armistice).[35]

Some of the focus groups discussed Finland's expansionist aims at the beginning of the Continuation War (1941–44). As a group participant in Vaasa commented, after the territorial losses of the Winter War (1939–40), "peace was not considered to be final, it was only temporary"—referring to the Continuation War, in which Finland set out to recover the territory it had lost.[36] A student in Oulu explained to me that, before the Continuation War, "everyone just thought that, okay, Finland just want[s] their old areas back, but then hunger grows when you eat . . . so we went a bit over." Note that the student uses the national "we" to include herself in an anthropomorphized Finland, which hungrily "eats" the additional territory.

During a focus group session in Helsinki, I asked participants to define "Greater Finland," an idea that had become popular around the time that Finland declared its independence. While definitions differ, Greater Finland is commonly understood to encompass the entire Karelian region, from the western shore of the White Sea, in the north, down to the southern tip of Lake Onega and then west along the Svir River to the southern shore of Lake Lagoda and finally to St. Petersburg. One student, however, acknowledged the existence of a far more aspirational vision of Greater Finland, noting that "some think it was only a bit more, than, like, the border that was there before the wars, but some think it should be until the Urals."[37] In this ambitiously expansive definition—the Urals are a mountain range some 1,500 kilometres east of St. Petersburg, generally regarded as the dividing line between eastern and western Russia—Finland would include a vast tract of territory covering much of the northern half of eastern Russia.[38]

Although the ceded territory of Petsamo was mentioned in focus groups everywhere, I specifically asked about it only in focus groups in Rovaniemi—of all the cities I visited the one closest to the territory itself (although still several hundred kilometres away). The fact that 94 percent of the students in Rovaniemi represented the loss of the Petsamo region on their "after" maps, whereas only 16 percent indicated the Karelian territory that had been ceded, suggests the influence of proximity on spatial perception.[39] Despite its remote location, well inside the Arctic Circle, the Petsamo region had provided Finland with access to the Barents Sea, in the Arctic Ocean, via the ice-free harbour at Liinahamari, and was also an important source of nickel. One participant commented that, in comparison to Vyborg, Karelia's largest city, "Petsamo was a greater loss, in my opinion."[40] When I asked the group about this comment, one replied that Petsamo is "an economically more important area . . . economically the bigger loss is Petsamo."[41]

Later, I asked whether the group thought Petsamo should be part of Finland. "Definitely," answered one participant, while another noted that "it could bring lots of jobs here to Lapland."[42] The same participant also said that it would be "lovely" if both Vyborg and Petsamo were to "belong to Finland again, but it's not worth starting a war over them," and then added that "if there's a situation where it's possible to get them back, like in a sensible way, then, certainly."[43] Members of other Rovaniemi focus groups voiced similar views. One expressed indifference regarding the fate of Vyborg ("It's all the same to me where it is") but declared that "of course" Petsamo should be part of Finland: "It gives access to the Arctic Ocean."[44] "Finland would be rich," said another, "if we still had Petsamo,"[45] while a third felt that "there's literally zero chance it'll ever be part of Finland, but it would be nice." Overall, these participants clearly regretted the loss of Petsamo, yet the reasons they gave were economic and pragmatic. There was little evidence of cultural or emotional ties to Finland's northeastern arm, and its amputation did not seem to be associated with any territorial phantom pains.

The ceded area of Salla was mentioned in passing in a number of groups but discussed at length in only one, replicating mainstream Finnish discourse more broadly, in which this ceded area has been largely ignored.[46] A participant in Oulu brought up Salla because of family ties: "My mother's father used to talk about the town called Salla where he used to live," she recalled, "and I'll remember probably forever how he said that his mother was baking bread when the announcement came that they have to leave and she couldn't stay and wait for the bread to be ready—they had to go right away. [. . .] It makes me feel that we have things so good in these times."[47]

During the focus groups, participants also discussed their perceptions of Karelia.[48] Two recurring and related themes were the idea that Karelia rightly belonged to Finland (on which opinions varied) and the significance of the region to Finnish national identity. "Karelia had been a really important area for Finland for the whole of Finnish or Swedish history," said a student in Oulu, "and there's a lot of our ancient history there,"[49] while a member of a focus group in Turku commented: "It was originally a part of Finland but then we sort of had to give it away to the Russians." When participants were asked, "What do you know about Karelia?" the slogan "Return Karelia" ("Karjala takaisin") was often their instant response (and one student even included it on an "after" map: see figure 3.6). When a student in Lahti was asked where he had heard the slogan, he replied, "Well, it's kinda a nationalistic thing—it belongs to Finns' culture."[50]

Echoing the theme of Karelia as inherently Finnish, a student in Oulu explained to me that "many Finns think it should belong to Finland." It is an area, she said, that "we would like to have back, but we probably never will." Participants also reflected on the desire to see Finland's territorial integrity restored in the summaries they wrote at the end of the group sessions. Linking this desire to national identity, a student in Rovaniemi wrote, "It's part of Finnishness to yearn to get back those areas lost in the war."[51] In contrast, another student in Oulu rejected any sense of national loss: "Can Karelia ever be returned? No. Finns don't miss it anymore." All the same, the student said, "It was important that Karelia was discussed."[52]

As the happy "before" faces and the unhappy "after" faces that appeared on their maps suggest, the students in my sample had learned, through processes of spatial socialization, that Karelia is integral to Finnish identity and that its loss should be mourned, although not necessarily put to rest. At the same time, as their comments illustrate, they had not always fully internalized that message and reacted to it in various ways—one pointing to the probable futility of hopes for restoration, and another challenging the very message itself.

The comments that students made during focus group discussions also illustrate the role of spatial socialization in the replacement of an existing logo-map with a new one. For example, a student in Vaasa clearly regarded the post–World War II border as correct, commenting that "Finland would be an awkward shape" if the border were adjusted back to its pre–World War II position. Arguing against the idea that the city of Vyborg should be part of Finland, another student in Vaasa noted its disappearance from the map and remarked that Finland "would be an ugly shape" if Vyborg were included.[53] Like the first, this student had internalized the post–World War II logo-map, on which Finland's southeastern border appears as a smooth curve from which no sections of territory protrude.

The lost part of Karelia did not appear to prompt much by way of territorial phantom pains in my participants, suggesting that, as Jussi Laine and Martin van der Velde observe, "the rough edges of the Karelian scar are slowly healing and fading in people's memory."[54] With the exception of a few anthropomorphic maps and comments (see, for example, figure 3.5), students did not associate the loss of Petsamo with the idea of a violent assault on Finland's geo-body, and they seldom mentioned Salla and the other lost territories, let alone with any sense of longing. My research participants may have recognized that "to yearn to get back those areas lost in the war" is part of being Finnish, but they felt little of that yearning themselves.

Conclusion

The redrawing of Finland's border at the end of World War II created a new logo-map. The loss of territory integral to the Finnish geo-body provoked intense emotional pain among those upon whom the previous logo-map had been thoroughly imprinted. For them, remapping was difficult, and emotions associated with that loss have been slow to recede. Through processes of spatial socialization, however, young people today have internalized the new logo-map and have thus come to regard the redrawn border as correctly delimiting "their" space. At the same time, they know the history and have also learned via spatial socialization to view Finland's forced sacrifice of territory as an unfair blow to the Finnish nation. This leaves them with the task of integrating various understandings of Finnish territory into their personal sense of national identity and of negotiating historical emotions that they have not themselves experienced.

The fading of memories and the emotions they once evoked is a natural process, one that occurs under any circumstances. Yet with respect to Finland's changed borders, the lack of strong emotions among the students with whom I worked reflects an additional circumstance. Not only had these young people no personal experience of Finland's eastern border being anywhere other than in its current location, but they were born roughly a decade after the fall of the Iron Curtain, at a time when Finland's border with Russia was relatively open. They had no personal recollection of the Soviet Union's existence or of the geopolitical climate in which the people of Finland once lived. All the same time, these young people had been exposed to a parallel narrative that also influenced their sense of national identity. They grew up surrounded by ideas and imaginaries concerning Finland's the eastern border that derived from the memories of those who *did* recall the events of World

War II and their aftermath—the ongoing threat posed by the Soviet "Other" and a "closed and silent" border that felt like the "end of the world."

As one might predict, the tension between the past and present was especially visible in relation to Karelia, not the least because that territory had been home to the vast majority of those people evacuated from the ceded areas. Collectively, those evacuees represented a powerful storehouse of memories, permeated by feelings of sorrow, nostalgia, and a lingering sense of outrage—all bound up today in the slogan so often heard in my focus groups: "Karjala takaisin." It is difficult to overestimate the enduring emotional significance of Karelia to Finnish national consciousness. Although the students in my sample were too far distant from that original moment of rupture to experience the same pain, their awareness of the past complicated their feelings around the border.

Since 2017, when my focus groups took place, the situation surrounding the Finnish-Russian border has, of course, altered dramatically. In 2020, the onset of the COVID-19 pandemic led to the closure of all Finland's borders. This would have been the first time in their lives that my participants ever encountered a closed border. Russia's subsequent invasion of Ukraine, in February 2022, not only sent shockwaves throughout Finland, as it did through most of the world, but also raised fears about further Russian aggression. In response, Finland temporarily closed its eastern border while at the same time welcoming refugees from Ukraine.[55] A little over a year later, in April 2023, Finland ended its long-standing policy of neutrality by joining NATO, much to the displeasure of Russia. Finland temporarily closed its border again in November 2023, after Russia began putting pressure on the country by channelling undocumented migrants to border regions. Then, in the face of Russian threats to mobilize troops, the Finnish government announced in April 2024 that the border would remain closed indefinitely.

Once again, then, the border is closed and silent, shrouded in an atmosphere of threat, and the sense of cautious optimism felt in 2017 now seems sadly premature. Even though the Finnish geo-body remains intact, the students who participated in my study will, like other Finns, have been obliged to reconsider their feelings around the country's eastern border. As I hope this chapter has illustrated, borders are in large measure states of mind, ever subject to bordering. Once drawn, a borderline need not change in order to provoke new perceptions and new emotions, which in turn reshape the spatial socialization that young people subsequently internalize. It remains to be seen whether this generation will be taught that to regard Finland's border with Russia as a danger zone is an inherent part of what it means to be Finnish.

Notes

1. For a discussion of bordering, see James W. Scott, "Bordering, Border Politics and Cross-Border Cooperation in Europe." On the social construction of borders, see Vladimir Kolosov, "Theoretical Approaches in the Study of Borders," 50–51; as well as Vladimir Kolossov (an alternative spelling) and James Scott, "Selected Conceptual Issues in Border Studies."

2. See Thongchai Winichakul, *Siam Mapped: A History of the Geo-body of a Nation*, 17.

3. Franck Billé, "Territorial Phantom Pains (and Other Cartographic Anxieties)," 10. Note that page numbers refer to the copy of Billé's article available at https://api.repository.cam.ac.uk/server/api/core/bitstreams/2ede3afc-3d6a-4a12 -8e66-8b1318cace86/content.

4. Billé, "Territorial Phantom Pains," 10. As Billé notes, the concept of a "logo-map" derives from Benedict Anderson's classic study *Imagined Communities: Reflections on the Origin and Spread of Nationalism* (first published in 1983), in which Anderson traces the origin of the map as logo to the production of imperial maps on which each state is represented in a different colour (13).

5. Billé, "Territorial Phantom Pains," 5.

6. Billé, "Territorial Phantom Pains," 18. See also Małgorzata Łukianow and Chloe Wells, "Territorial Phantom Pains: Third-Generation Postmemories of Territorial Changes."

7. Billé, "Territorial Phantom Pains," 18.

8. Spyros Spyrou and Miranda Christou, "Introduction," 5.

9. On youth and the construction of nationhood, see, for example, Pirjo Jukarainen, "Definitely Not Yet the End of Nations: Northern Borderlands Youth in Defence of National Identities"; and Janette Habashi, "Palestinian Children: Authors of Collective Memory." On young people and bordering, see Martina McKnight and Madeleine Leonard, "Bordering in Transition: Young People's Experiences in 'Post-Conflict' Belfast"; as well as the other essays in Spyros Spyrou and Miranda Christou, eds., *Children and Borders*.

10. On Karelia and its significance to the Finnish people, see Christopher S. Browning and Pertti Joenniemi, "Karelia as a Finnish-Russian Issue: Re-negotiating the Relationship Between National Identity, Territory and Sovereignty"; Jussi Laine and Martin van der Velde, "Spiritually Ours, Factually Yours: Karelia and Russia in Finnish Public Consciousness"; and

Kimmo Katajala and Ilkka Liikanen, "The Politics of History of the Lost Land: Shifting European, National and Regional Approaches to the History of Karelia."

11. On the role of maps in this process, see Katariina Kosonen, "Making Maps and Mental Images: Finnish Press Cartography in Nation-Building, 1899–1942."

12. For a history and analysis of the Finnish Maiden, see Johanna Valenius, *Undressing the Maid: Gender, Sexuality and the Body in the Construction of the Finnish Nation.*

13. Anssi Paasi, "Dancing on the Graves: Independence, Hot/Banal Nationalism and the Mobilization of Memory," 25. See also Saija Kaskinen, "If the Borders Could Tell: The Hybrid Identity of the Border in the Karelian Borderland," 1190. Finland was not alone in this experience. At the end of World War II, Poland was, like Finland, forced to cede to the Soviet Union territory central to Polish national identity, which again entailed a massive displacement of people. For a comparison of the transgenerational persistence of territorial phantom pains, see Małgorzata Łukianow and Chloe Wells, "Territorial Phantom Pains: Third-Generation Postmemories of Territorial Changes."

14. On the earlier evolution of the Swedish border with Russia, see Ilkka Liikanen, "Territoriality, State, and Nationality in the Making of Borders of Finland: The Evolving Concept of Border in the Peace Treaties Between Russia and Sweden, 1323–1809"; and Kimmo Katajala, "Line, Zone or Sieve? Conceptualising the 1617 Russo-Swedish Border."

15. Paasi, "Dancing on the Graves," 25. On the historical construction of the Finnish-Russian border more broadly, including its role in nation building and its ideological and socio-spatial significance to the Finnish people, see Paasi, *Territories, Boundaries and Consciousness: The Changing Geographies of the Finnish-Russian Border.*

16. Kaskinen, "If the Borders Could Tell," 1192, which is also the source of the translation quoted in the epigraph. "Rajalla" was first published in 1931, in *Uni ja kuolema* (Sleep and death), and reprinted the following year in the anthology *Runoja* (Poems). See also "Uuno Kailas—Finnish Nationalist Poet, Author, and Translator," Alternative Finland, June 9, 2013, http://www .alternativefinland.com/uuno-kailas/.

17. On the nationalist aspirations surrounding the Continuation War, see Browning and Joenniemi, "Karelia as a Finnish-Russian Issue," 14–15.

18. The newly leased territory on the Porkkala peninsula replaced territory on the Hanko peninsula—located at the southwestern tip of the country by the entrance to the Gulf of Finland—that Finland had been forced to lease to the Soviet Union at the end of the Winter War (although the Soviets

occupied the area only until December 1941). Although the Porkkala lease was for fifty years, by the mid-1950s the Soviets had, for a combination of military, political, and economic reasons, come to regard the Porkkala naval base as unnecessary. The base was therefore closed early in 1956, and the Soviet Union returned the territory to Finland. Even though the area had not been permanently ceded, while the base was operational Porkkala was in fact Soviet territory, completely sealed off from Finland itself. Over seven thousand Finnish residents were evacuated from the area, and although Finns could still travel by train from Helsinki to Turku, they had to cover the windows and were strictly forbidden to take photographs.

19. For the figure of 420,000, see Olli Vehviläinen, *Finland in the Second World War: Between Germany and Russia*, 75.

20. For the number of Karelian evacuees, see Ulla Savolainen, "The Return: Intertextuality of the Reminiscing of Karelian Evacuees in Finland," 171.

21. On the expression of public opinion regarding the Karelian Question as it emerged in the pages of Finland's national newspaper, see Laine and van der Velde, "Spiritually Ours." For reminiscences of Karelian evacuees, see Evgenia Golant, "Sharing the Stories of Those Migrated from Karelia"; and Savolainen, "The Return."

22. Kaskinen, "If the Borders Could Tell," 1192.

23. Virpi Kaisto and Olga Brednikova, "Lakes, Presidents and Shopping on Mental Maps: Children's Perceptions of the Finnish-Russian Border and the Borderland," 59. See also Pirkkoliisa Ahponen, "Miserable or Golden Karelia? Interpreting a Cross-Border Excursion of Students from Finland to Russia"; and Virpi Kaisto, "The Finnish-Russian Borderland as a Lived Space: Perceptions, Experiences, and Identities in Everyday Life." As Kaisto notes, by the early 2010s "border crossings were at their peak, and visiting neighbouring cities across the border had become customary for many individuals residing in the border cities" (11). This trend toward ease of movement was interrupted in March 2020, when the COVID-19 pandemic set in and all of Finland's borders were temporarily closed. Then, in the wake of Russia's invasion of Ukraine in February 2022, tensions along the border escalated, and any nascent sense of rapprochement swiftly dissolved.

24. Paasi, *Territories, Boundaries and Consciousness*, 8. See also Paasi, "Dancing on the Graves," 25; and Kirsi Pauliiina Kallio, "Rethinking Spatial Socialisation as a Dynamic and Relational Process of Political Becoming."

25. For an image, see "Kotimaista rasvaton maito 1l [Domestic skim milk, 1 litre]," Kaupat, accessed April 8, 2024, https://www.s-kaupat.fi/tuote/kotimaista -rasvaton-maito-1l/6415712506032.

26. I was the sole facilitator during the focus groups, which took place in a combination of English and Finnish. (When I quote a comment that was originally in Finnish, I have provided the Finnish text in a note.) During the discussions, I followed a script with questions but also added my own comments and ad hoc questions, usually for purposes of clarification, as I would not be able to go back to one of the participants later on and ask, "What did you mean by that?" For more on my positionality and role during the groups, see Chloe Wells, *Vyborg Is Y/ours: Meanings and Memories of a Borderland City Amongst Young People in Finland*, 74–75.

27. The written materials consisted of 319 lists of what each of the participants associated with the name "Vyborg" ("Viipuri," in Finnish), Karelia's main city, lost to the Soviet Union during World War II; 318 summaries that participants wrote at the end of the study detailing what their group had discussed and/or what they found interesting to discuss; and 321 feedback forms filled out by participants at the end. As participation was voluntary, not all of the 325 students completed all three tasks, so the totals are slightly under the total number of participants. Similarly, five participants did not draw mental maps, while another five maps had to be discarded because they were single maps, not pairs. For a more detailed description, see Virpi Kaisto and Chloe Wells, "Mental Mapping as a Method for Studying Borders and Bordering in Young People's Territorial Identifications."

28. In contrast to quantitative methods, in thematic content analysis the significance of a theme depends not on how many times it appears in the data but rather on "whether it captures something important in relation to the overall research question." Virginia Braun and Victoria Clarke, "Using Thematic Analysis in Psychology," 82.

29. For more on mental mapping and on using the method with young people, see Elen-Maarja Trell and Bettina van Hoven, "Making Sense of Place: Exploring Creative and (Inter)Active Research Methods with Young People"; Thomas F. Saarinen, "Student Views of the World"; and Efrat Ben-Ze'ev, "Blurring the Geo-body: Mental Maps of Israel/Palestine." See also Kaisto and Wells, "Mental Mapping."

30. "No piirränks mää siihen, hameellisen naisen. Jolla käet pystyssä" (lit., "Well I'll draw it like this, as a skirt-wearing woman. Who has her hands up"). All translations from Finnish are my own.

31. "Toisen maailmansodan jälkeen vedettiin pois käsivarsi."

32. In a study of global sketch maps likewise carried out with students, Thomas Saarinen found that the edges of continents and countries that have a distinctive shape (such as Italy, "the boot") were more often depicted on the

maps of the world drawn by his participants. Saarinen, "Student Views of the World," 155–56.

33. "Me menetettiin siin jatkosodan jälkeen Sallan, Laatokan Karjalan ja Karjalankannaksen, sit Suomen ulkosaaret ja sit Porkkala vuokrattiin viidekskymmeneks vuodeks." Finns refer to the islands in the Gulf of Finland as the "outer islands" ("Suomenlahden ulkosaaret").

34. "Sit tuli rauha ja Suomi menetti Karjalan," followed by "Suomi menetti sit kansa Pokkaanniemen. Sit sen sodan jälkeen. Sit kaikkien junien ikkunat piti peittää aina, ku juna meni siit ohi kohalta."

35. "Menetettiin Petsamo Moskovan rauhassa 44."

36. "Rauhaa ei pidetty lopullisena, vaan se oli väliaikanen."

37. "Et joidenki mielest se oli sellanen vaan vähän enemmän, kun siit niinku ennen sotia olevast rajast, mut jotkut ajattelee et sen pitäis olla Uralilla asti."

38. For a map of this grandiose vision, see Janne Sundqvist, "Suur-Suomi olisi onnistunut [Greater Finland possible only with the help of Nazi Germany]." As Sundqvist notes, this vision appeared "in the wildest dreams" of Finnish nationalists ("Hurjimmissa haaveissa rajat piirrettiin lännessä Norjaan ja idässä Uralin valorisation").

39. For further discussion of location-based differences that emerged in this study, see Kaisto and Wells, "Mental Mapping."

40. "Petsamo oli suurempi menetys mielestäni."

41. In full: "No sinänsä Petsamo saattaa ollaki isompi, koska niinku taloudellisesti tärkeempi alue. No yhteydet ja noi että sinänsä taloudellisesti isompi menetys on Petsamo."

42. "Tottakai"; "se ois voinu tuua paljon työpaikkoja tänne Lappiinki."

43. "Mie koen varmaan sen niin, että ois se ihanaa jos molemmat ois taas Suomen niinku, kuuluis taas Suomeen, mut ei niitten takia kannata alottaa sotaa et ne saatas takasi vaa juuri et jos tulee tilanne, jossa ne on mahollista saada niinku järkevällä tavalla takasi nii ehottomasti."

44. "Ihan sama mulle oikeestaan, että missä se on"; "Tottakai . . . pääsis käymään Jäämerellä."

45. "Suomi olis rikas, jos se [Petsamo] ois."

46. See Eerika Koskinen-Koivisto, "Transnational Heritage Work and Commemorative Rituals across the Finnish-Russian Border in the Old Salla Region," 199–200.

47. See Golant, "Sharing the Stories," for similar accounts of daily life suddenly interrupted by forced evacuation.

48. Specifically, the students were asked, "What do you know about Karelia?" "What comes to mind if you hear the word 'Karelia'?" and "Where is Karelia?"

A more detailed discussion of how students responded to these questions can be found in Łukianow and Wells, "Territorial Phantom Pains"; and in Chloe Wells, "Suomen nykynuorten käsityksiä Karjalasta [Perceptions of modern Finnish youth about Karelia]."

49. "Karjala on ollut Suomelle niinku tosi tärkeä alue koko Suomen tai Ruotsin historian ajan ja siellä on paljon meiän niinkö muinaishistoriaa."

50. "No se on vähä sellanen, nationalistinen juttu se liittyy, suomalaiseen kulttuuriin."

51. "Kuuluu Suomalaisuuteen haikailla sodassa menetettyjä alueita takaisin."

52. "Voiko ikinä saada Karjalan takaisin? Ei enää Suomalaisia kaipaa. Tärkeätä oli se, että puhuttiin karjalasta."

53. In full: "Suomen kartastaki tulis ruman mallinen jos se ois." For a more detailed analysis of the students' perceptions of Vyborg, see Wells, *Vyborg Is Y/ours*.

54. Laine and van der Velde, "Spiritually Ours," 74.

55. Finland was not, of course, alone in welcoming Ukrainian refugees, but their arrival did prompt comparisons to the evacuation of Finnish territories lost to Russia over eighty years earlier. One story in the Finnish news media shared the traumatic memories stirred for one Karelian child evacuee (now nearly ninety) when he saw images of Ukrainians fleeing their own country. See Miki Wallenius, "Kuvat Ukrainan pakolaisista toivat oman pakomatkan 87-vuotiaan Eino Kilpiäisen uniin: 'En tiennyt tulevaisuudesta mitään'" (Images of refugees from Ukraine caused 87-year-old Eino Kilpiäinen's to dream if his own evacuation journey: "I knew nothing of the future"). See also Riina Rastas, "Ukrainan sota on nostanut evakoiden muistot pintaan: 'Moni kokee, että Karjala on menetetty nyt kolmannen kerran'" (The war in Ukraine has brought the memories of the evacuees to the surface: "Many feel that Karelia has now been lost for a third time").

Bibliography

Ahponen, Pirkkoliisa. "Miserable or Golden Karelia? Interpreting a Cross-Border Excursion of Students from Finland to Russia." *Journal of Borderlands Studies* 26, no. 2 (2011): 145–59. https://doi.org/10.1080/08865655.2011.641324.

Ben-Ze'ev, Efrat. "Blurring the Geo-body: Mental Maps of Israel/Palestine." *Middle East Journal* 69, no. 2 (2015): 237–54. https://doi.org/10.3751/69.2.14.

Billé, Franck. "Territorial Phantom Pains (and Other Cartographic Anxieties)." *Environment and Planning D: Society and Space* 32, no. 1 (2014): 163–78. https://journals.sagepub.com/doi/10.1068/d20112.

Braun, Virginia, and Victoria Clarke. "Using Thematic Analysis in Psychology." *Qualitative Research in Psychology* 3, no. 2 (2006): 77–101. https://doi.org/10.1191/1478088706qp063oa.

Browning, Christopher S., and Pertti Joenniemi. "Karelia as a Finnish-Russian Issue: Re-negotiating the Relationship Between National Identity, Territory and Sovereignty." EU-Russia Paper no. 18. Centre for EU-Russia Studies, University of Tartu, 2014.

Golant, Evgenia. "Sharing the Stories of Those Migrated from Karelia." *At the Well* (blog), Kone Foundation, April 10, 2018. https://koneensaatio.fi/en/stories/sharing-the-stories-of-those-migrated-from-karelia/.

Habashi, Janette. "Palestinian Children: Authors of Collective Memory." *Children and Society* 27, no. 6 (2013): 421–33. https://doi.org/10.1111/j.1099-0860.2011.00417.x.

Jukarainen, Pirjo. "Definitely Not Yet the End of Nations: Northern Borderlands Youth in Defence of National Identities." *Young Nordic Journal of Youth Research* 11, no. 3 (2003): 217–34. https://doi.org/10.1177/11033088030113002.

Kaisto, Virpi. "The Finnish-Russian Borderland as a Lived Space: Perceptions, Experiences, and Identities in Everyday Life." Joensuu: University of Eastern Finland, 2024.

Kaisto, Virpi, and Olga Brednikova. "Lakes, Presidents and Shopping on Mental Maps: Children's Perceptions of the Finnish–Russian Border and the Borderland." *Fennia* 197, no. 1 (2019): 58–76. https://doi.org/10.11143/fennia.73208.

Kaisto, Virpi, and Chloe Wells. "Mental Mapping as a Method for Studying Borders and Bordering in Young People's Territorial Identifications." *Journal of Borderlands Studies* 36, no. 2 (2021): 259–79. https://doi.org/10.1080/08865655.2020.1719864.

Kallio, Kirsi Pauliina. "Rethinking Spatial Socialisation as a Dynamic and Relational Process of Political Becoming." *Global Studies of Childhood* 4, no. 3 (2014): 210–23. https://doi.org/10.2304/gsch.2014.4.3.210.

Kaskinen, Saija. "If the Borders Could Tell: The Hybrid Identity of the Border in the Karelian Borderland." *Journal of Current Cultural Research* 6, no. 6 (2014): 1183–1205. https://doi.org/10.3384/cu.2000.1525.14611183.

Katajala, Kimmo. "Line, Zone or Sieve? Conceptualising the 1617 Russo-Swedish Border." *Nordic and Baltic Studies Review* 2 (2017): 177–90. https://doi.org/10.15393/j103.art.2017.755.

Katajala, Kimmo, and Ilkka Liikanen. "The Politics of History of the Lost Land: Shifting European, National and Regional Approaches to the History of Karelia." In *How to Address the Loss? Forced Migrations, Lost Territories and the Politics of History: A Comparative Approach in Europe and at Its Margins in the XXth Century*, edited by Anne Bazin and Catherine Perron, 81–108. Brussels: Peter Lang, 2018.

Kolosov, Vladimir. "Theoretical Approaches in the Study of Borders." In *Introduction to Border Studies*, edited by Sergei V. Sevastianov, Jussi P. Laine, and Anton A. Kireev, 33–59. Vladivostok: Far Eastern Federal University Press, 2015.

Kolossov, Vladimir, and James Scott. "Selected Conceptual Issues in Border Studies." *Belgeo* 2013, no. 1. https://journals.openedition.org/belgeo/10532.

Koskinen-Koivisto, Eerika. "Transnational Heritage Work and Commemorative Rituals across the Finnish-Russian Border in the Old Salla Region." In *Transnational Death*, edited by Samira Saramo, Eerika Koskinen-Koivisto, and Hanna Snellman, 200–213. Helsinki: Suomalaisen Kirjallisuuden Seura, 2019.

Kosonen, Katariina. "Making Maps and Mental Images: Finnish Press Cartography in Nation Building, 1899–1942." *National Identities* 10, no. 1 (2008): 21–47. https://doi.org/10.1080/14608940701819769.

Laine, Jussi, and Martin van der Velde. "Spiritually Ours, Factually Yours: Karelia and Russia in Finnish Public Consciousness." *Europa Regional* 24 (2017): 65–79. https://nbn-resolving.org/urn:nbn:de:0168-ssoar-54451-8.

Liikanen, Ilkka. "Territoriality, State, and Nationality in the Making of Borders of Finland: The Evolving Concept of Border in the Peace Treaties Between Russia and Sweden, 1323–1809." *Russian Sociological Review* 13, no. 4 (2014): 105–15. https://doi.org/10.17323/1728-192X-2014-4-105-115.

Łukianow, Małgorzata, and Chloe Wells. "Territorial Phantom Pains: Third-Generation Postmemories of Territorial Changes." *Memory Studies* 17, no. 2 (2024): 177–92. https://doi.org/10.1177/17506980221126602.

McKnight, Martina, and Madeleine Leonard. "Bordering in Transition: Young People's Experiences in 'Post-Conflict' Belfast." In *Children and Borders*, edited by Spyros Spyrou and Miranda Christou, 164–79. Basingstoke, UK: Palgrave Macmillan, 2014.

Paasi, Anssi. "Dancing on the Graves: Independence, Hot/Banal Nationalism and the Mobilization of Memory." *Political Geography* 54 (2016): 21–31. https://doi.org/10.1016/j.polgeo.2015.07.005.

Paasi, Anssi. *Territories, Boundaries and Consciousness: The Changing Geographies of the Finnish-Russian Border*. Chichester, UK: John Wiley, 1996.

Rastas, Riina. "Ukrainan sota on nostanut evakoiden muistot pintaan: 'Moni kokee, että Karjala on menetetty nyt kolmannen kerran'" (The war in Ukraine has brought the memories of the evacuees to the surface: "Many feel that Karelia has now been lost for a third time"). *Maailman Kuvalehti*, August 29, 2022. https://maailmankuvalehti.fi/2022/3/pitkat/ukrainan-sota-on-nostanut-evakoiden-muistot-pintaan-moni-kokee-etta-karjala-on-menetetty-nyt-kolmannen-kerran/.

Saarinen, Thomas F. "Student Views of the World." In *Image and Environment: Cognitive Mapping and Spatial Behaviour*, edited by Roger M. Downs and David Stea, 148–61. London: Arnold, 1973.

Savolainen, Ulla. "The Return: Intertextuality of the Reminiscing of Karelian Evacuees in Finland." *Journal of American Folklore* 130, no. 516 (2017): 166–92. https://doi.org/10.5406/jamerfolk.130.516.0166.

Scott, James W. "Bordering, Border Politics and Cross-Border Cooperation in Europe." In *Neighbourhood Policy and the Construction of the European External Borders*, edited by Filippo Celata and Raffaella Coletti, 27–44. Cham, Switzerland: Springer, 2015.

Spyrou, Spyros, and Miranda Christou, eds. *Children and Borders*. Basingstoke, UK: Palgrave Macmillan, 2014.

Spyrou, Spyros, and Miranda Christou. "Introduction." In *Children and Borders*, edited by Spyros Spyrou and Miranda Christou, 1–26. Basingstoke, UK: Palgrave Macmillan, 2014.

Sundqvist, Janne. "Suur-Suomi olisi onnistunut vain natsi-Saksan avulla [Greater Finland possible only with the help of Nazi Germany]." *YLE*, May 26, 2014, https://yle.fi/a/3-7263681.

Trell, Elen-Maarja, and Bettina van Hoven. "Making Sense of Place: Exploring Creative and (Inter)Active Research Methods with Young People." *Fennia* 188, no. 1 (2010): 91–104.

Valenius, Johanna. *Undressing the Maid: Gender, Sexuality and the Body in the Construction of the Finnish Nation*. Helsinki: SKS / Finnish Literature Society, 2004.

Vehviläinen, Olli. *Finland in the Second World War: Between Germany and Russia*. New York: Palgrave, 2002.

Wallenius, Miki. "Kuvat Ukrainan pakolaisista toivat oman pakomatkan 87-vuotiaan Eino Kilpiäisen uniin: 'En tiennyt tulevaisuudesta mitään'" (Images of refugees from Ukraine caused 87-year-old Eino Kilpiäinen to dream of his own evacuation journey: "I knew nothing of the future"). *YLE*, April 23, 2022. https://yle.fi/a/3-12409866.

Wells, Chloe. "Suomen nykynuorten käsityksiä Karjalasta [Modern Finnish youths' perceptions of Karelia]." *Idäntutkimus* 26, no. 4 (2019): 61–74. https://doi.org/10.33345/idantutkimus.88848.

Wells, Chloe. *Vyborg Is Y/ours: Meanings and Memories of a Borderland City Amongst Young People in Finland*. Joensuu: University of Eastern Finland, 2020.

Winichakul, Thongchai. *Siam Mapped: A History of the Geo-body of a Nation*. Honolulu: University of Hawai'i Press, 1994.

4 From Lines in the Sand to the Wave/Particle Duality

A Quantum Imaginary for Critical Border Studies

Michael P. A. Murphy

The 2009 "Lines in the Sand" agenda represented an ambitious call to action for researchers in the interdisciplinary space of critical border studies.[1] This agenda was a collective effort of "a range of political theorists, historians, human geographers, anthropologists, and international relations scholars" dissatisfied with the "'line in the sand' metaphor as an unexamined starting point for the study of borders."[2] It proposed three axes for further inquiry in critical border studies: "border epistemology," encompassing questions about the enduring appeal of borders, the search for alternative ways of knowing, alternative topological framings, and experiential/existential characteristics; "border ontology," including questions about how the border acts as a foundation both for current conceptualizations of world order and for new ontological registers; and "the space-time of borders," referencing both the spatial and temporal dimensions of borders, as well as their localization at the margins.[3]

The "Lines in the Sand" agenda, as well as the subsequent special section in *Geopolitics*, sought to move beyond the conventional epistemologies, ontologies, and spatiotemporal conceptualization of borders. One of the central tensions to emerge from the "Lines in the Sand" project was between the microscopic and macroscopic emphasis points—while shifting away from a generic "concept of the border" toward "the notion of bordering practices" and "the lens of performance," it was unclear how microscopic and macroscopic levels of critical analysis were to relate.[4] To be sure, both microscopic and macroscopic analyses have demonstrated the value that they bring to the study of borders; the value or criticality of both perspectives is not at issue. Rather, the disjuncture is that big-picture analyses of security and sovereignty discourses seem a world away from the micropolitical studies of lived experience and materiality.[5] While these novel and nuanced perspectives offer researchers in the critical border studies community a wide range of insights, the reproduction of the conceptual distinction between the border-as-micro and the border-as-macro meant that critical border studies could not escape the structuring principle of its own thought. The "line in the sand" had moved from a core concept of how critical border studies scholars understood borders to instead become an organizing principle that divided macro-focused approaches from micro-focused approaches.

What I explore in this chapter is the possibility that critical studies of borders might benefit from a fourth axis around which questions can circulate: physics. Specifically, in this chapter I state the case for critical border studies to join innovative scholars of critical social theory and critical international relations theory in rejecting the dominant Newtonian assumptions of social science, moving from a Newtonian physical imaginary to one grounded in quantum social theory. As we continue to move beyond the line in the sand, we require new conceptual frameworks that remain open to the complex forms of life that have been marginalized by the dominant Western modes of inquiry that too often seek lawlike regularity, ontological separability, causal linearity, and other Newtonian artefacts. Just as critical social theorists and critical international relations theorists have found that quantum assumptions of complexity, uncertainty, and entanglement fill the sails of critique with a new wind, I argue that critical border studies scholars stand to gain from a quantum leap.

Anzaldúa and Barad

One reason I am hopeful for the possibility of a quantum critical border studies is that—in many ways—this dialogue is already ongoing. Our journey to quantize critical border studies begins not in the laboratory or in the emerging literature of quantum social theory or quantum critical international relations but in the borderlands. Or, more precisely, in *Borderlands / La Frontera*, Gloria

Anzaldúa's masterpiece that in fact inspired the development of key elements of Karen Barad's quantum social theory.[6]

Borderlands is a deeply personal, insightful, and original text and has rightfully been recognized as a substantial contribution from feminist theory and Chicano studies to the understanding of borders, borderlands, and identity. Anzaldúa rejects the assimilatory pressures of code consistency, infusing *Borderlands* with multiple languages, dialects, metres, and styles of writing. She problematizes the idea and stability of the border as a concept, introduces the necessarily indeterminate experience of the borderland, and explores the *mestiza* consciousness that arises there.[7] From the physical border to the understanding of identity, Anzaldúa rejects the binaries and dichotomies that dominant societies impose in favour of a new *mestiza* consciousness of the people who "are forced to live in the interface."[8] While *Borderlands* does, in concrete terms, discuss the Mexico-US border region, it is a wide-ranging work that explores a variety of ideas, genres, identities, languages, and experiences.

It is precisely this work—*Borderlands*—that marks this chapter as a quantum return rather than a quantum turn in (critical) border studies. Through the contribution of Anzaldúa, the queered notion of borders and boundaries came to inform the very structure of quantum social theory through the work of a similarly visionary theorist, Barad. Not a traditional social theorist, Barad was first trained as a physicist before a profound shift in their scholarly journey toward queer and feminist social theory. In the somewhat autobiographical "Diffracting Diffraction: Cutting Together-Apart," Barad outlines the profound impact of Anzaldúa's work at a crucial time in their transition from physics to social theory:

> Santa Cruz and Claremont, CA 1991: I am sitting outdoors with Gloria
> Anzaldúa talking about quantum physics and mestiza consciousness.
> It's the late winter and Anzaldúa has come to Pomona College to talk
> with our faculty seminar group. I am teaching in the Physics Depart-
> ment, sitting in on Deena Gonzalez's *Latina Feminist Traditions* class,
> and co-organizing a multi-disciplinary faculty seminar on the nature
> of theory—we're studying *Borderlands*.[9]

And this is no mere historical anecdote. The conceptualization of diffraction—the concept that lies at the very heart of Barad's *Meeting the*

Universe Halfway—was profoundly influenced by *Borderlands*, as Barad continues to explain in this reflective article.

Traditionally, diffraction has described the patterns of interference between waves; however, in Barad's theory of agential realism, the significance of diffraction goes *all the way down*, with ontological and epistemological significance for the nature of matter and mattering alike. Diffraction produces fuzzy borders and complex interactions that destabilize conventional assumptions around the separability of objects, linearity of causal relations, and fixity of binary divisions. To this end, Barad states that "diffraction owes as much to a thick legacy of feminist theorizing about difference as it does to physics."[10] Anzaldúa's rejection of light/darkness as a binary (the "colonizer's story") is presented as a direct influence on the interpretation of light diffraction: "Darkness is not mere absence, but rather an abundance. Indeed, darkness is not light's expelled other, for it haunts its own interior. Diffraction queers binaries and calls out for a rethinking of the notions of identity and difference."[11] And Anzaldúa's quantum influence is not limited to energy but extends to mass as well; it was in a personal conversation between Barad and Anzaldúa around quantum physics and *mita' y mita'* that Barad would discover a framing of quantum properties of matter: "Elections are queer particles, *mita' y mita*.' They are particles. They are waves. Neither one nor the other. A strange doubling."[12] And to overcome this diffractive confounding of traditional categories, Barad returns to Anzaldúa's *mestiza consciousness*.[13] From the diagnosis of the world to the development of an alternative mode of living within it, Barad admits returning frequently to Anzaldúa.[14]

The radical claims of Baradian quantum social theory—which they call "agential realism"—rely on a reimagination of the world that is grounded in an active diffraction. Barad describes a world where relations precede relata, where differences are made to matter through the interactions that produce them, where the foundational units are entangled phenomena instead of discrete entities and the "action" is internal to the phenomenon rather than external between separate units.[15] This foundational ontological connectivity relies on a rejection of separability between inside and outside, and this conceptual move comes to Barad from Anzaldúa's rejection of bordering. To this end, a critique grounded in Baradian quantum social theory is always and already applicable to a critical theory of borders. By reclaiming the intellectual energy of this theory, we can develop radical critical understandings and reimaginings of borders, life, and identity.

Critical Quantum International Relations Theory

The growing momentum behind quantum approaches to international relations theory through the 2010s demonstrated that the insights that quantum ideas offered to other fields of social inquiry—such as mathematical psychology, queer theory, and economics—were conceptually productive for understanding political dynamics at the international level. Alexander Wendt's *Quantum Mind and Social Science*, which draws on broad and interdisciplinary literature to argue for an ontological reimagination of consciousness and all its implications as quantum phenomena, remains the most highly cited work in this field.[16] James Der Derian's ongoing research, including the quantum-themed Project Q symposia at the University of Sydney, has called for a revolution in international theory.[17] Their work—individual and collaborative[18]—has opened new space for a robust and multiperspectival debate on the value of quantum ideas for reimagining international relations.

Of specific interest to critical border studies is the intersection of quantum social theory with critical theories of international relations. Often drawing on Barad's *Meeting the Universe Halfway*, critical quantum international relations has established itself as a conversation that builds on a shared commitment to complexity, uncertainty, critical epistemologies and methodologies, and non-linear causality.[19] Laura Zanotti's *Ontological Entanglements* provides a sharp critique of "substantialist" assumptions in international relations theories and the ethical failings that follow therefrom while providing a quantum alternative that approaches a radical ethic of responsibility.[20] Her subsequent work has outlined the affinities between quantum social theory, decolonial ethics, and micropolitical resistance.[21] In a series of articles building up to *Snapshots from Home*, Karin Fierke has similarly explored the critical implications of quantum international relations in the context of Daoist ethics, Buddhist thought, and linguistic entanglements.[22] Forums appearing in *Millennium: Journal of International Studies* and *Global Studies Quarterly* have pushed this conversation further, engaging with affect theory, feminist praxis, the ethics of scholarship, refugees' ungrieved grief, and other topics.[23] This burgeoning literature draws attention to the many ways in which Newtonian assumptions of ontological separability, epistemological certainty, causal linearity, and lawlike regularity inform and ultimately serve to uphold dominant paradigms of Western social science. This implies a choice for all critical scholars: remain in a Newtonian worldview and start every inquiry by fighting back against its most foundational assumptions or adopt a quantum ontology where relations are already complex, causality is already multiple, binaries are already queered, and boundaries are already fuzzy.

Perhaps part of the reason that quantum social theory has found such interest in circles of critical international relations is that there is an intuitively critical disposition that accompanies quantum social theory. My modest suggestion in this chapter is that the same may be true for critical border studies, and—in light of Anzaldúa's writings on borderlands influencing Barad's foundational writings in quantum social theory—the affinity may be even more conceptually emancipatory and productive than it has already been for critical scholars in international relations.

The Quantum Border: Three Concepts, Two Theories

Quantum social theory provides a map for overcoming the micro/macro divide precisely because that kind of scalar binary is already queered within quantum social theory, thereby opening new and freer space for critical inquiry. The point here is not that critique in a Newtonian modality cannot object to the conceptual constraints of objectivity, separability, and causal linearity—indeed, there are a panoply of critical projects that begin with a deconstruction or rejection of dominant ideas—but that creative energies can flow more freely in a sympathetic imaginary.[24] Shifting to a quantum model facilitates new projects by starting from a position of entanglement, complexity, and uncertainty rather than first fighting to get there.[25]

What I offer in the remainder of this section is a short introduction to how three connected concepts from quantum social theory—the wave/particle duality, the social wavefunction, and measurement—can help us understand how two theoretical approaches to the study of the border fit together: securitization and new materialism. All five of these conceptual engagements remain necessarily introductory; further reading can be found in the notes. It is my hope that by demonstrating the prima facie case for how the pieces of the puzzle fit together, interested readers may explore how more in-depth treatments of the associated concepts may add new conceptual tools to their toolboxes.

The wave/particle duality is a defining feature of quantum mechanics, both in historical terms of its development and in substantive terms of the theory's distinctiveness from Newtonian physics. While competing paradigms argued variably that light was either a shower of particles or a wave, an early discovery of quantum mechanics was that both sides of the argument were correct—in some contexts, there was evidence of light behaving like particles, and in others, evidence of light behaving like waves. Albert Einstein proposed a "heuristic view" that light was in fact both wave *and* particle.[26] Simply put, light is a particle in its interactions and a wave on its own, producing particle-like interactions at a small scale and wave-like patterns over a larger scale. In quantum social theory, this makes intuitive sense because we are able to recognize the patterns of social phenomena over time (Alexander Wendt offers the example of a country); specific glimpses of the component parts of a state are smaller and do not represent the whole "thing"—for example, a flag, a police officer, national food, and so on.[27]

One of the implications of the wave/particle duality is that the trajectory of light is not a linear, predictable path but an undulating expansion through space-time. If we want to make sure that we have an accurate model of where light is (based on prior measurements), we must incorporate all of its potential spread into the calculation; this mathematical expression is called the wavefunction.[28] In quantum social theory, the term *social wavefunction* is used to describe the blurring together of uncertainties in the social realm that can be recognized through patterns over time but not predicted with absolute certainty—for example, the complex intersections of identity, the potential future decisions an individual may make, and so on.[29] As with humans, so with nonhumans; the social significances, meanings, and futures of nonhuman animals, material objects, and ideas all have uncertain futures and identities that exist in superposition until they collapse into one definitive state.[30] For example, the meaning of particular colours of clothing may shift as new political or social movements adopt a colour, or a discriminatory public policy may produce differential experiences for people depending on their race or gender.

For the scholar, one of the most relevant types of interactions that sees the uncertainty of the wavefunction replaced by the certainty of the particle is found in measurement. There are a number of constituent concepts in quantum mechanics that connect to measurement and change. The observer effect describes the collapse of the wavefunction during observation such that uncertain waves are replaced with certain particles. Heisenberg's uncertainty principle highlights that certain connected concepts cannot be certainly known at once; for example, a measurement device that finds the position of a photon will disturb the movement of the photon and render its momentum unknown (and vice versa). The choices we make about what to measure influence what we find. Finally, Bohr's complete description principle argues that the description of a phenomenon is only complete if the measurement apparatus is described.[31] As quantum social theory has argued, these principles call for a radical recognition of the impact of researchers on their research.[32] Not only instrumentation quality but the choices that inform research design, team formation, and individual experiences and expertise can have a profoundly creative impact on the findings produced. Surely, this will come as little surprise to critical scholars; however, the elegance of the argumentation, proceeding from the subatomic to the social, provides a new and powerful argument for the nonobjectivity of research.

Macrowaves

The border appears as a wave when we seek to analyze the macrostructural dimensions of the border, and the most important structural concept at play at the border is that of sovereignty. When considering sovereignty, the border accrues conventional notions of containment, defence, and frontier. The border is the boundary of sovereign control, and protecting the border is a necessary precondition for security within that state's territory. The border is also a source of insecurity for sovereignty, as external threats conventionally challenge sovereign authority at the border. While these accounts of sovereignty at the border may appear realist, not all sovereign-focused accounts of border politics are. Two ways that critical scholarship has investigated the place of sovereignty at the border are through discussions of securitization and the state of exception.

Securitization theory describes the process by which something becomes a security issue.[33] One of the first and still most-cited approaches within the tradition of critical security studies, securitization theory is a linguistic and constructivist approach that seeks to identify how security is intersubjectively constructed. In general, this occurs by a securitizing actor declaring something to be a threat and demanding extraordinary powers to respond to that threat and a relevant audience either granting or not granting assent to that "securitizing move."[34] A successful case of securitization moves the issue from the realm of normal politics to one in which the securitizing actor—in practice, typically a state executive—has extraordinary powers without democratic constraints. Subsequent developments to this theory have offered a broader range of mechanisms to explain how securitizing moves occur and questioned what counts as assent.

Securitization at the border has been analyzed through a variety of case studies and methodological approaches. Mark Salter and Genevieve Piché explore the securitization of the Canada-US border through a series of policy documents, official statements, and government acts (rather than one single securitization speech act).[35] Salter had earlier examined how the Canadian government's risk management approach to border functions led to the securitization not only of the border as such but also of proximate "spill-over" categories.[36] In the case of America's southern border, Jason Ackleson analyzed differences between pre- and post-9/11 border security resulting from securitization speech acts.[37] The same border plays an important role in Avi Astor's study of the 1954 "Operation Wetback," a US government program that increased border controls and government officials' targeting of Mexican immigrants.[38] Cigdem Benam investigated the dynamics of securitization (particularly of migration) in shoring up border controls in the Schengen zone.[39] In all of these cases of securitization, the border is studied as a social structure, an object of discourse whose identity can be securitized through discourse.

What these examples of securitization demonstrate is the interactivity of the border and the capacity of the border to produce patterns and effects. When we analyze the securitization of border crossing or the exceptionality of the port of entry, we are examining the invisible social dimension of the border. The end-state effects of detention at the border, unreasonable search and seizure of property, discriminatory treatment, and even "proper" routines of document authentication depend on the social connection to broader social forces. These social aspects of the border represent some elements of what I am calling the wave nature of the border.

The border-as-wave interacts with other social wave functions in ways that are directly invisible but nevertheless real. When we discuss sovereignty at the border, we are connecting the social nature of the border to the entangled social wavefunction of that state—that is, the body politic constituted by the entanglement of the citizenry. When we discuss the power of the state being performed at the border, we assume that the particular interaction—for example, our interrogation by a border guard whose authority comes from the state—is legible only in the broader context of the social relation to the state. The representative of the sovereign adjudicates our social claim of identity and status, a process by which the social wavefunction of the state interferes with our social wavefunction of identity. The border is a privileged locus of social wavefunction dynamics, as the concept itself is animated by a variety of social structures and identity claims (and adjudications) and can only be understood fully in this context.

Microparticles

Just as the waves of light dissolve into precise particles upon interaction with measurement apparatuses, investigations into the practices and materiality of the border and security have demonstrated how close attention to these topics similarly reveals discrete constitutive parts. Materiality and technology-focused approaches draw attention to the agency, or ability to produce effects, of nonhuman entities. One important way that this has happened is through the influence of the so-called new materialist turn in critical international relations more generally, but it is worth recognizing that technological, architectural, and other approaches exist beyond the limits of new materialism. Even to speak of "new materialism" as a homogeneous group is misleading—while actor-network theory has played an important role in the development of this community, it is far from the only new materialist approach.

Critical border studies and critical security studies scholars have demonstrated how the border is constituted technologically (whether through high-tech innovation or more low-tech options like walls). Mike Bourne, Heather Johnson, and Debbie Lisle discuss the interaction between the border security policymakers and the laboratories engaged in developing new handheld security devices, arguing that given the interplay between the two entities, any analysis of the border should consider the laboratory's effect just as an analysis of the laboratory would have to consider the impact of requests, guidance, and demands from the security policymakers.[40] This remains true in the case of "low-tech" forms of security technologies such as passports. As Salter argues, the crossing of the border is in part dependent on the function of the passport as a key tool in that regime.[41] Indeed, the increasing demands for security at the border are in themselves bound by the biometric capacity of the passport document: despite all the sovereign power of the state, they are unable to overcome the limitations imposed by the passport materials.

Even in the case of fixed borders, careful attention to their function can highlight the agency of that technological materiality. Polly Pallister-Wilkins argues that the border wall has the ability to interrupt human circulation and to capture data through surveillance technologies.[42] While the decisions may be made through a policy of securitization, the effectiveness of the wall is in the physical barrier it creates. Indeed, as the ferocious architecture project has demonstrated,[43] purpose-built structures function as articulations of sovereignty in powerful ways. To analyze architecture, structures, walls, and so on requires attention to the agency of that particular material entity.

But the clearest case of the border as particle is found in Peter Nyers's 2012 commentary on the political significance of dirt.[44] Examining the case of Smuggler's Gulch between the United States and Mexico as well as topsoil theft in the Israel–Lebanon border zone, Nyers demonstrates how the dirt itself becomes central to the political and social success of the states involved. The impact of material changes in the dirt profile of the border is clarified through Nyers's careful microscopic analysis of the physical constitution of the border. To flatten Smuggler's Gulch and make the region more easily patrollable, US government officials flattened mountains and filled canyons—moving enough dirt to cover the Empire State Building.[45] The governments in both cases recognized the centrality of the dirt in the border zone to the future success of their national interest. Thus, while a reading of total dollar amounts may indicate that the proper level of analysis for these interventions is at the (macroscopic) program management level, it is only because of the political agency of dirt that the policy outcomes were even possible. Nyers offers a powerful call to the microagential, drawing attention to that which is often ignored as the least consequential.

As mentioned, every measurement device created by electrodynamic physicists has demonstrated light to be composed of particles. The tests describe in detail the size and mass of a photon, and these findings have facilitated great insight into how light can be mobilized. In an analogous way, investigations into practices and materialities of the border reveal how the same sort of careful attention to border security reveals specific connections, constitutive parts, and causal mechanisms. The interplay between laboratory and border policy entangles these places fundamentally in the ontogenesis of security technologies. The particular arrangement of dirt at a border plays a larger role in determining political possibilities than could ever be known in macrostructural analysis.

These approaches to the study of border security are particle-like because they, like the measurement apparatuses of light, look for particular details.

By highlighting connections, constitutive parts, and causal mechanisms, they disrupt the grand narratives of sovereignty to focus on particularities. This, too, falls in perfect parallel to what takes place in the measurement of light. In the well-known two-slit experiment used to demonstrate the quantum effect of interference, the actual recording of photons passing through the slits can only ever result in particles. The wave effects appear through the firing of many thousands of photons, but this does not change the fact that each measurement is of a particle. At the border, we find that each element is a distinct particle, with its own distinct causes and relations bearing little resemblance to the grand narratives of sovereignty. But as we turn our attention to not wave or particle but their duality, it is useful to keep the two-slit experiment in mind. We may—as have the new materialists—be adamant that our results are particle measurements, but that tells only part of the story. Similarly, the sovereignty-focused approaches can maintain their fervent defence of grand narratives but must also recognize the influence of dirt and architecture on the carrying out of structural politics.

Conclusion

These quantum insights that I have introduced and explored are far from the final chapter in this conversation. Indeed, if the precedent of critical international relations is to offer any guidance, it is that the central intellectual commitments of critical border studies are likely to find productive synergies with quantum social theory. As discussed, the profound legacy of Gloria Anzaldúa as a precursor to quantum social theory only lends further credence to this claim.

While I have provided intentionally accessible and thin introductions to a small number of concepts and research projects in quantum social theory, there is a great deal more to explore. Can the fundamental connectedness of entanglement inform critical border studies scholarship, perhaps building on the prior work of Patricia Noxolo on (post)diaspora identities?[46] How does the superposition of Indigenous and settler-colonial legal traditions inform the uncertainty of borders and law?[47] How do the differential experiences of intersecting social structures of violence and subjugation interfere with life in and around the borderlands?[48] How do surveillance practices produce affect and resistance?[49] These questions and more remain to be asked (and answered) in a continuing dialogue.

The "Lines in the Sand" agenda rejected a simplistic binary structure of a physical demarcation of inside and outside, introducing provocative and thoughtful axes of debate for critical border studies. The project of this volume retains that bold critique but also explores how earlier critique left some stones unturned. In this chapter, I have approached the question of physics as a potential future path for critique, noting the radical possibility of quantum social theory and its recent success in conversation with critical international relations. Quantum critical border studies presents an opportunity to transcend the binary of macro- and micro-, grounding a new critical conversation that moves from lines in the sand to social wavefunctions that continually cross all of our lives.

Notes

1. Noel Parker et al., "Lines in the Sand? Towards an Agenda for Critical Border Studies," 582–87.
2. Noel Parker and Nick Vaughan-Williams, "Critical Border Studies: Broadening and Deepening the 'Lines in the Sand' Agenda," 727–28.
3. Parker et al., "Lines in the Sand," 584–85.
4. Parker and Vaughan-Williams, "Critical Border Studies," 729.
5. But see Chris Rumford, "Towards a Multiperspectival Study of Borders," 887–902.
6. Melina Pereira Savi, "How Borders Come to Matter? The Physicality of the Border in Gloria Anzaldúa's Borderlands/La Frontera," 181–91.
7. Gloria Anzaldúa, *Borderlands / La Frontera: The New Mestiza*.
8. Anzaldúa, *Borderlands*, 37.
9. Karen Barad, "Diffracting Diffraction: Cutting Together-Apart," 172.
10. Barad, "Diffracting Diffraction," 168.
11. Barad, "Diffracting Diffraction," 171.
12. Barad, "Diffracting Diffraction," 173.
13. Barad, "Diffracting Diffraction," 175.
14. Barad also highlights the importance of Anzaldúa in theorizing response-ability and touch. Karen Barad and Daniela Gandorfer, "Political Desirings: Yearnings for Mattering (,) Differently," 62n14; Karen Barad, "On Touching—the Inhuman That Therefore I Am," 219n2.
15. Karen Barad, *Meeting the Universe Halfway: Quantum Physics and the Entanglement of Matter and Meaning*.
16. Alexander E. Wendt, *Quantum Mind and Social Science: Unifying Physical and Social Ontology*.

17. E.g., James Der Derian, "Quantum Diplomacy, German–US Relations and the Psychogeography of Berlin," 373–92; and James Der Derian, "A Quantum of Insecurity," 13–27.

18. E.g., James Der Derian and Alexander Wendt, eds., *Quantum International Relations: A Human Science for World Politics*; and James Der Derian and Alexander Wendt, "'Quantizing International Relations': The Case for Quantum Approaches to International Theory and Security Practice," 399–413.

19. See the following by Michael P. A. Murphy: "Entangled Observers? A Quantum Perspective on Authority in Critical Security Studies," 1–13; "On Quantum Social Theory and Critical International Relations," 244–61; and *Quantum Social Theory for Critical International Relations Theorists: Quantizing Critique*.

20. Laura Zanotti, *Ontological Entanglements, Agency and Ethics in International Relations: Exploring the Crossroads*.

21. Laura Zanotti. "De-colonizing the Political Ontology of Kantian Ethics: A Quantum Perspective," 448–67; "Exploring Agency and Resistance in the Context of Global Entanglements," 103–20.

22. Karin M. Fierke, "Consciousness at the Interface: Wendt, Eastern Wisdom and the Ethics of Intra-action," 141–69; Karin M. Fierke, "Contraria sunt Complementa: Global Entanglement and the Constitution of Difference," 146–69; Karin M. Fierke, *Snapshots from Home: Mind, Action and Strategy in an Uncertain World*; K. M. Fierke and Francisco Antonio-Alfonso, "Language, Entanglement and the New Silk Roads," 194–206.

23. See, e.g., Nadine Voelkner and Laura Zanotti, "Ethics in a Quantum World," ksaco44; Michael P. A. Murphy, "Forum on Laura Zanotti, Ontological Entanglements, Agency and Ethics in International Relations: Exploring the Crossroads (Routledge, 2019)," 117–25; Şengül Yıldız-Alanbay, "The Matter of Affect in the Quantum Universe," 151–61; Elisabeth Prügl, "The Gender Thing: Apparatuses and Intra-agential Ethos," 140–50; Christopher McIntosh, "From Policy Relevance to Present Relevance: Entanglement, Scholarly Responsibility, and the Ethics of Quantum Social Theory," ksaco52; Liberty Chee, "Being of Use: Diffraction and an Ethics of Truth-Telling in Post-Cartesian IR," ksaco49; K. M. Fierke and Nicola Mackay, "Those Who Left/Are Left Behind: Schrödinger's Refugee and the Ethics of Complementarity," ksaco45. This extends beyond the forums as well—e.g., Italo Brandimarte, "Subjects of Quantum Measurement: Surveillance and Affect in the War on Terror," olaco12; Mark B. Salter, "Quantum Sovereignty + Entanglement," 262–79.

24. Murphy, "On Quantum Social Theory."

25. For an accessible introduction to quantum mechanics, see Richard Feynman, *QED: The Strange Theory of Light and Matter.*

26. Albert Einstein, "On a Heuristic Point of View Concerning the Production and Transformation of Light," 177–98.

27. Wendt, *Quantum Mind and Social Science.*

28. Erwin Schrodinger, "The Present Situation in Quantum Mechanics," 327.

29. I explore the concept further in Michael P. A. Murphy, "Violent Interference: Structural Violence, Quantum International Relations, and the Ethics of Entanglement," ksac040.

30. This is known as the "collapse of the wavefunction," and its specific meaning in physics remains hotly contested, with multiple interpretations finding scientific backing. For an introduction, see John Charlton Polkinghorne, *The Quantum World.*

31. Wendt, *Quantum Mind and Social Science*; Niels Bohr, *Atomic Physics and Human Knowledge.*

32. Barad, *Meeting the Universe Halfway*; Murphy, "Entangled Observers?"

33. Through this section, I refer to the "Copenhagen interpretation" of securitization theory. See Ole Waever, "Securitization and Desecuritization," 46–86; and Barry Buzan, Ole Waever, and Jaap de Wilde, *Security: A New Framework for Analysis.* For a review of the "Paris Interpretation" of securitization in borderlands studies, see the recent special issue of the *Journal of Borderlands Studies*: Martin Deleixhe, Magdalena Dembinska, and Julien Danero Iglesias, "Introduction: Securitized Borderlands," 639–47.

34. See Waever, "Securitization and Desecuritization"; and Buzan et al., *Security.*

35. Mark B. Salter and Genevieve Piché, "The Securitization of the US-Canada Border in American Political Discourse," 929–51.

36. Mark B. Salter, "Canadian Post-9/11 Border Policy and Spillover Securitization: Smart, Safe, Sovereign?" 299–319.

37. Jason Ackleson, "Constructing Security on the US-Mexico Border," 165–84.

38. Avi Astor, "Unauthorized Immigration, Securitization, and the Making of Operation Wetback," 5–29.

39. Cigdem H. Benam, "Emergence of a 'Big Brother' in Europe: Border Control and Securitization of Migration," 191–207.

40. Mike Bourne, Heather Johnson, and Debbie Lisle, "Laboratizing the Border: The Production, Translation, and Anticipation of Security Technologies," 307–25.

41. Mark B. Salter, "Passports, Mobility, and Security: How Smart Can the Border Be?" 71–91; "Global Visa Regime."

42. Polly Pallister-Wilkins, "How Walls Do Work: Security Barriers as Devices of Interruption and Capture," 151–64.

43. Benjamin Muller, Thomas N. Cooke, Miguel de Larrinaga, Philippe M. Frowd, D. Iossifova, D. Johannes, Can E. Mutlu, and Adam Nowek, "Collective Discussion—Ferocious Architecture: Sovereign Spaces/Places by Design," 75–96.

44. Peter Nyers, "Moving Borders: The Politics of Dirt," 2–6.

45. Nyers, "Moving Borders," 4.

46. Patricia Noxolo, "I Am Becoming My Mother: (Post)diaspora, Local Entanglements and Entangled Locals," 134–46.

47. Salter, "Quantum Entanglement + Sovereignty"; Norah Bowman, "Here/There/Everywhere: Quantum Models for Decolonizing Canadian State Onto-epistemology," 171–86.

48. Murphy, "Violent Interference."

49. Brandimarte, "Subjects of Quantum Measurement."

Bibliography

Ackleson, Jason. "Constructing Security on the US-Mexico Border." *Political Geography* 24 (2005): 165–84.

Anzaldúa, Gloria. *Borderlands / La Frontera: The New Mestiza*. San Francisco: Aunt Lute Books, 1987.

Astor, Avi. "Unauthorized Immigration, Securitization, and the Making of Operation Wetback." *Latino Studies* 7 (2009): 5–29.

Barad, Karen. "Diffracting Diffraction: Cutting Together-Apart." *Parallax* 20, no. 3 (2014): 168–87.

Barad, Karen. "On Touching—the Inhuman That Therefore I Am." *differences* 23, no. 3 (2012): 206–23.

Barad, Karen. *Meeting the Universe Halfway: Quantum Physics and the Entanglement of Matter and Meaning*. Durham, NC: Duke University Press, 2007.

Barad, Karen, and Daniela Gandorfer. "Political Desirings: Yearnings for Mattering (,) Differently." *Theory & Event* 24, no. 1 (2021): 14–66.

Benham, Cigdem H. "Emergence of a 'Big Brother' in Europe: Border Control and Securitization of Migration." *Insight Turkey* 13, no. 3 (2011): 191–207.

Bohr, Niels. *Atomic Physics and Human Knowledge*. Mineola, NY: Dover, 2010.

Bourne, Mike, Heather Johnson, and Debbie Lisle. "Laboratizing the Border: The Production, Translation, and Anticipation of Security Technologies." *Security Dialogue* 46, no. 4 (2015): 307–25.

Bowman, Norah. "Here/There/Everywhere: Quantum Models for Decolonizing Canadian State Onto-epistemology." *Foundations of Science* 26, no. 1 (2021): 171–86.

Brandimarte, Italo. "Subjects of Quantum Measurement: Surveillance and Affect in the War on Terror." *International Political Sociology* 16, no. 3 (2022): olac012.

Buzan, Barry, Ole Waever, and Jaap de Wilde. *Security: A New Framework for Analysis.* Boulder, CO: Lynne Rienner, 1998.

Chee, Liberty. "Being of Use: Diffraction and an Ethics of Truth-Telling in Post-Cartesian IR." *Global Studies Quarterly* 2, no. 3 (2022): ksac049.

Deleixhe, Martin, Madgalena Dembinska, and Julien Danero Iglesias. "Introduction: Securitized Borderlands." *Journal of Borderlands Studies* 34, no. 5 (2019): 639–47.

Der Derian, James. "Quantum Diplomacy, German–US Relations and the Psychogeography of Berlin." *Hague Journal of Diplomacy* 6, nos. 3/4 (2011): 373–92.

Der Derian, James. "A Quantum of Insecurity." *New Perspectives* 27, no. 2 (2019): 13–27.

Der Derian, James, and Alexander Wendt. "'Quantizing International Relations': The Case for Quantum Approaches to International Theory and Security Practice." *Security Dialogue* 51, no. 5 (2020): 399–413.

Der Derian, James, and Alexander Wendt, eds. *Quantum International Relations: A Human Science for World Politics.* New York: Oxford University Press, 2022.

Einstein, Albert. "On a Heuristic Point of View Concerning the Production and Transformation of Light." In *Einstein's Miraculous Year: Five Papers That Changed the Face of Physics*, 177–98. Princeton, NJ: Princeton University Press, 2005.

Feynman, Richard. *QED: The Strange Theory of Light and Matter.* Princeton, NJ: Princeton University Press, 2006.

Fierke, Karin M. "Consciousness at the Interface: Wendt, Eastern Wisdom and the Ethics of Intra-action." *Critical Review* 29, no. 2 (2017): 141–69.

Fierke, Karin M. "Contraria sunt Complementa: Global Entanglement and the Constitution of Difference." *International Studies Review* 21, no. 1 (2019): 146–69.

Fierke, Karin M. *Snapshots from Home: Mind, Action and Strategy in an Uncertain World.* Policy Press, 2022.

Fierke, Karin M., and Francisco Antonio-Alfonso. "Language, Entanglement and the New Silk Roads." *Asian Journal of Comparative Politics* 3, no. 3 (2018): 194–206.

Fierke, Karin M., and Nicola Mackay. "Those Who Left/Are Left Behind: Schrödinger's Refugee and the Ethics of Complementarity." *Global Studies Quarterly* 2, no. 3 (2022): ksac045.

McIntosh, Christopher. "From Policy Relevance to Present Relevance: Entanglement, Scholarly Responsibility, and the Ethics of Quantum Social Theory." *Global Studies Quarterly* 2, no. 3 (2022): ksac052.

Muller, Benjamin, Thomas N. Cooke, Miguel de Larrinaga, Philippe M. Frowd, Deliana Iossifova, Daniela Johannes, Can E. Mutlu, and Adam Nowek.

"Collective Discussion—Ferocious Architecture: Sovereign Spaces/Places by Design." *International Political Sociology* 10, no. 1 (2016): 75–96.

Murphy, Michael P. A. "Entangled Observers? A Quantum Perspective on Authority in Critical Security Studies." *Critical Studies on Security* 10, no. 3 (2022): 119–31.

Murphy, Michael P. A. "Forum on Laura Zanotti, Ontological Entanglements, Agency and Ethics in International Relations: Exploring the Crossroads (Routledge, 2019)." *Millennium* 49, no. 1 (2020): 117–25.

Murphy, Michael P. A. "On Quantum Social Theory and Critical International Relations." In *Quantum International Relations: A Human Science for World Politics*, 244–61. New York: Oxford University Press, 2022.

Murphy, Michael P. A. *Quantum Social Theory for Critical International Relations Theorists: Quantizing Critique*. London: Palgrave Macmillan, 2021.

Murphy, Michael P. A. "Violent Interference: Structural Violence, Quantum International Relations, and the Ethics of Entanglement." *Global Studies Quarterly* 2, no. 3 (2022): ksac040.

Noxolo, Patricia. "I Am Becoming My Mother: (Post)diaspora, Local Entanglements and Entangled Locals." *African and Black Diaspora* 13, no. 2 (2020): 134–46.

Nyers, Peter. "Moving Borders: The Politics of Dirt." *Radical Philosophy* 174 (2012): 2–6.

Pallister-Wilkins, Polly. "How Walls Do Work: Security Barriers as Devices of Interruption and Capture." *Security Dialogue* 47, no. 2 (2016): 151–64.

Parker, Noel, and Nick Vaughan-Williams. "Critical Border Studies: Broadening and Deepening the 'Lines in the Sand' Agenda." *Geopolitics* 17, no. 4 (2012): 727–33.

Parker, Noel, Nick Vaughan-Williams, et al. "Lines in the Sand? Towards an Agenda for Critical Border Studies." *Geopolitics* 14, no. 3 (2009): 582–87.

Polkinghorne, John Charlton. *The Quantum World*. Princeton, NJ: Princeton University Press, 1989.

Prügl, Elisabeth. "The Gender Thing: Apparatuses and Intra-agential Ethos." *Millennium* 49, no. 1 (2020): 140–50.

Rumford, Chris. "Towards a Multiperspectival Study of Borders." *Geopolitics* 17, no. 4 (2012): 887–902.

Salter, Mark B. "Canadian Post-9/11 Border Policy and Spillover Securitization: Smart, Safe, Sovereign?" In *Critical Policy Studies*, edited by Miriam Catherine Smith and Michael Orsini, 299–319. Vancouver: UBC Press, 2007.

Salter, Mark B. "Passports, Mobility, and Security: How Smart Can the Border Be?" *International Studies Perspectives* 5 (2004): 71–91.

Salter, Mark B. "Quantum Sovereignty + Entanglement." *Quantum International Relations: A Human Science for World Politics* 315 (2022): 262–79.

Salter, Mark B., and Genevieve Piché. "The Securitization of the US-Canada Border in American Political Discourse." *Canadian Journal of Political Science* 44, no. 4 (2011): 929–51.

Savi, Melina Pereira. "How Borders Come to Matter? The Physicality of the Border in Gloria Anzaldúa's Borderlands/La Frontera." *Anuário de literatura: Publicaçao do Curso de Pós-Graduaçao em Letras, Literatura Brasileira e Teoria Literária* 20, no. 2 (2015): 181–91.

Schrödinger, Erwin. "The Present Situation in Quantum Mechanics." *Proceedings of the American Philosophical Society* 124, no. 5 (1980): 323–38.

Voelkner, Nadine, and Laura Zanotti. "Ethics in a Quantum World." *Global Studies Quarterly* 2, no. 3 (2022): ksac044.

Waever, Ole. "Securitization and Desecuritization." In *On Security*, edited by Ronnie Lipschutz, 46–86. New York: Columbia University Press, 1995.

Wendt, Alexander E. *Quantum Mind and Social Science: Unifying Physical and Social Ontology*. New York: Columbia University Press, 2015.

Yıldız-Alanbay, Şengül. "The Matter of Affect in the Quantum Universe." *Millennium* 49, no. 1 (2020): 151–61.

Zanotti, Laura. "De-colonizing the Political Ontology of Kantian Ethics: A Quantum Perspective." *Journal of International Political Theory* 17, no. 3 (2021): 448–67.

Zanotti, Laura. "Exploring Agency and Resistance in the Context of Global Entanglements." In *The Globality of Governmentality*, 103–20. London: Routledge, 2021.

Zanotti, Laura. *Ontological Entanglements, Agency and Ethics in International Relations: Exploring the Crossroads*. London: Routledge, 2019.

Part 2

Cuttings and Crossings

5 Sinixt Existence in "Extinction"

Identity, Place, and Belonging in the Canada-US Borderlands

Lori Barkley, with Marilyn James and Lou Stone

Sinixt, also known as the Lakes or Arrow Lakes Indians, traditional territory (təmxʷúlaʔxʷ) was divided by the US-Canada border in 1846 (see figure 5.1). Two-thirds of Sinixt təmxʷúlaʔxʷ lies in what became known as British Columbia (BC), with one-third in what is now Washington State. In the United States, Sinixt/Lakes are recognized as one of the twelve Confederated Tribes of the Colville Reservation, established in 1872.[1] In 1956, the Canadian government deemed the Arrow Lakes Band "extinct for purposes of the *Indian Act*."[2] Regardless, Sinixt exist in numerous borderlands: hard borders between states, borders negotiated in the contemporary land claims process in BC, and academic borders that perpetuate problematic truths, like Sinixt "extinction."

This chapter outlines the complicated colonial history and use of borders to perpetuate the myth of Sinixt "extinction" in Canada and challenges academics to deconstruct borderlands of established "truths."[3] The maze of borderlands Sinixt negotiate are threefold. First, the 1876 Indian Act and "being crossed" by the Canada-US border perpetuate the perception of Sinixt "extinction" in Canada. Second, borders created through the British Columbia Contemporary Land Claims Process further contribute to Sinixt "extinction." And finally, Sinixt erasure in multiple legal, academic, and public discourses compounds their "extinction."

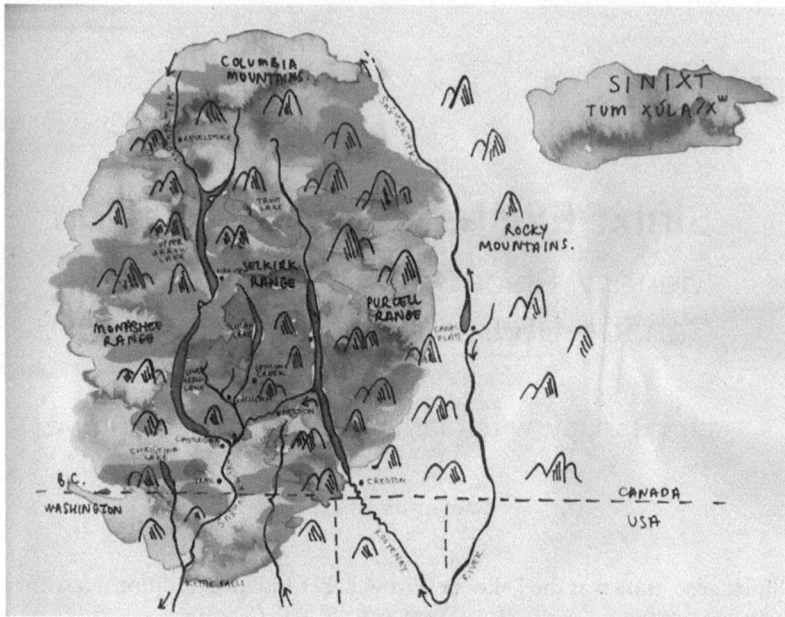

Figure 5.1 Sinixt təmxʷúlaʔxʷ. Marilyn James and Taress Alexis, *Not Extinct: Keeping the Sinixt Way* (2nd ed., New Denver, BC: Maa Press, 2018), 1. With permission. *Note:* As Sinixt dialect revitalization progresses, spellings change. This image contains the older spelling *tum xúlaʔxʷ*.

Historical Context

The Arrow Lakes Band (Sinixt) were assigned a single reserve at Oatscott, British Columbia, Canada in 1902 on land described as inaccessible, "precipitous granite bluffs" "utterly worthless for agriculture, and very inferior for grazing."[4] The reserve was only reachable via steamboat or by travelling "83 miles over a very poor road" that was often blocked in winter.[5] Even the local Indian agent expressed concerns that the reserve was insufficient to meet the band's needs. Officially, the Arrow Lakes Band consisted of twenty-six people in 1903 and was down to three by 1929. By 1937, Annie Joseph was deemed "the last surviving adult member of the Arrow Lakes Reserve."[6]

Around that time, Joseph moved to an Okanagan (Syilx) reserve and lived with an Okanagan Indian Band (OIB) member.[7] Understanding that if she married him, she would lose her Arrow Lakes Band status under the Indian

Act, she chose not to.[8] As the last "recognized" member, she also held the timber rights on the Arrow Lakes Reserve, by far its most valuable resource. In 1952, in an effort to "preserve the Arrow Lakes Reserve with its timber resources, for the Indians," both the province and the OIB requested amalgamation of the Arrow Lakes and Okanagan Indian Bands, passed by the OIB and Joseph (acting as the Arrow Lakes Band) in 1953.[9] This would prevent the Arrow Lakes Reserve from reverting to the province as per the 1916 McKenna-McBride Commission, whereby any lands of a tribe or band who "became extinct" would "revert to the Province."[10] However, it is unlikely that Joseph was informed that capital funds held in trust for the Arrow Lakes Band, along with the land, would also be transferred to the OIB for the benefit of their members alone, and the Arrow Lakes Band members "would gain nothing."[11] Amalgamation was denied by the Canadian government for three reasons: (1) it was a strategy to prevent the land from reverting to the province, (2) only the OIB would benefit, and (3) the distance from the Okanagan reserve would make it impractical.[12]

Joseph, the last registered member of the Arrow Lakes Band, died in 1953. Without federal approval of amalgamation, her death signalled that "there were no longer any persons who qualified for membership in the Arrow Lakes Band under the provisions of the Indian Act. It [did] not, of course, mean that the Sinixt people ceased to exist as a tribal group."[13] Following Canada's "extinction" of the Arrow Lakes Band in 1956, Sinixt təmxʷúlaʔxʷ started to disappear from maps, a problem that persists into the present.[14] Colonial regimes rely on maps, whereby imaginary lines become reality. Brazilian environmental educators Michèle Sato, Regina Silva, and Michelle Jaber argue that "maps were, and still are, considered a language of power and legitimacy over land, supportive of the imperialist domination of spaces." Believed to be "ideologically neutral," they are "key weapons of imperialism" that support colonialism and the "hegemonic power of the ruling classes."[15] The implication is that certain people can exercise rights within borders, while others are excluded. Richard Osburn, an attorney with the Cherokee Nation of Oklahoma, argues, "Long before the arrival of the first European, the Native tribes living along what is now the border of the United States and Canada freely interacted. The idea that an imaginary line could run through their lands and permanently separate them was unthinkable."[16] For Sinixt, the Canada-US border irrevocably divided their nation and təmxʷúlaʔxʷ and became the line between extinction and recognition.

In 1961, shortly after "extinction," the United States and Canada signed the Columbia River Treaty (CRT), a significant cross-border agreement regarding hydroelectric power and flood mitigation. The Columbia River is the heart of Sinixt təmxʷúlaʔxʷ; with the "extinction" of the Arrow Lakes Band, any potential Indigenous hindrances to this agreement were eliminated. Sinixt are excluded from Indigenous consultation in current renegotiations of the CRT, while the Okanagan Nation Alliance (ONA) and Ktunaxa, claiming Sinixt təmxʷúlaʔxʷ, are included. It is somewhat ironic that a significant cross-border agreement excludes Sinixt, as their village sites mark their presence along its banks and tributaries and dictated who was able to fish the river for centuries prior to the establishment of the US-Canada border.[17] Moreover, the Columbia River is now one of the most heavily dammed rivers in North America, preventing returning salmon runs. The loss of salmon, a major food supply, was another significant blow to Sinixt existence in Canada. Decimated by smallpox epidemics and pushed out of their territory by resource extraction and the lack of a viable reserve in Canada, Sinixt survival in their təmxʷúlaʔxʷ became nearly impossible.

This is a common experience of Indigenous peoples across Canada and indeed throughout the world, as several authors argue. Anthropologist Angela Robinson describes the paradox of Aboriginal policy: "Across Canada, colonial and federal policies were guided by the dual fallacies of gradual but progressive assimilation and/or the certain extinction of Aboriginal populations, neither of which occurred."[18] Ojibway legal researcher Dan Shaule, in response to a question about Beothuk "extinction," stated, "All First Nations are in the position of extinction when someone else controls their definition."[19] Sadly, Indigenous peoples in Canada often "found themselves transformed from independent peoples . . . to refugees in their own land, outnumbered by newcomers and no longer able to support themselves as they had always done."[20]

Contemporary Land Claims

The next major border process disrupting Sinixt existence was the creation of the British Columbia Treaty Commission (BCTC) in 1992. BC is somewhat unique in Canada with few historic treaties: Douglas Treaties were signed with eleven First Nations on Vancouver Island (1850–54), and Treaty 8 (1899) lands span the Alberta-BC border. Otherwise, no historic treaties exist in BC, with the vast majority of the province being imposed on unceded Indigenous lands. Through the BCTC, BC entered the contemporary land claims process, as University of British Columbia anthropologist Carole Blackburn argues, to create "investor certainty" for resource extraction on untreated Indigenous territory.[21] This has far-reaching consequences for all Indigenous peoples in BC, but most profoundly for "extinct" Sinixt.

To participate in the BCTC, one must have a government recognized by the Canadian state to enter into negotiations—that is, a recognized band. Sinixt, "extinct for purposes of the *Indian Act*," have no such government and are precluded from participating. The process is designed to create certainty about which Indigenous governments must be consulted for development projects and possible compensation. Autonomous Sinixt filed a claim in 2008, asserting contention, but they are still ignored in the processes.[22] The BCTC signed Completed Treaty Agreements with Ktunaxa in 2013, 2014, and 2018.[23] This problem is not unique in the BCTC but rather compounded by Sinixt extinction. As elsewhere in the province (e.g., Nisga'a and Gitxsan), the designation of territory in land claims has "far exceeded the bounds of actual ownership," which is required in the process.[24]

It appears that in the rush to create border certainty, problematic aspects of the BCTC are ignored, even for recognized bands. Judith Sayers, former chief of the Hupacasath First Nation, assistant law professor at the University of Victoria, and chief negotiator for sixteen years, said boundary issues were to be resolved prior to an agreement in principle, but "these governments want settlements so bad that they don't care about overlap. It is first-come, first serve." This has resulted in First Nations turning to the courts for resolution.[25]

Anthropologist Brian Thom furthers, "Ironically, the judges and negotiators have accepted the simplistic, generalized model of the Nisga'a in favour of the complex and nuanced one of the Gitxsan and Wet'suwet'en. This raises the question of how much information the courts or negotiators are willing to take."[26] Similarly, the ONA argues that Sinixt rights "exist in Syilx Okanagan Territory" and that "we are all related and we remain related to the present day."[27] However, the ONA only represents ONA members, and rights do not extend to non-ONA members. Thus, to clear title, agreements are reached in spite of contention. The BC Assembly of First Nations has raised similar concerns: "While there may be an assumption in BC that the proper aboriginal title holder is being represented in Treaty Negotiations, in the context of true recognition followed by reconciliation, this problem with the BC treaty-making process raises serious questions regarding with whom Canada should be, and may currently be, negotiating."[28]

In an open letter to BC government officials, the ONA outlined challenges they face in the BCTC:

> For far too long, the Okanagan Indian Band has been forced to defend Syilx Okanagan territorial boundaries against encroachment from other First Nation communities attempting to assert and claim interests within Syilx Okanagan territory. The unnecessary burden of defending our territorial integrity simply because [of] the provincial government's inability to sort out its own internal processes is completely unacceptable. Our community finds itself in this position time and time again with no resolution to this long-standing issue simply because the province ignores its own obligations to deal with proper Title and Rights holders in a matter that is consistent with the legal realities in a post-*Tshilhqot'in* era.[29]

Overlapping boundaries claimed by those able to participate in the process are discussed and debated, while Sinixt are ignored. Borders of "extinct" peoples are seen as inconsequential, if they are acknowledged at all. As historian Sheila McManus states, ignoring and erasing all traces of Indigenous peoples, including their territorial borders, is at the very heart of the colonial process.[30]

The overarching political context makes it unlikely that the British Columbia Assembly of First Nations (BCAFN) will support Sinixt claims. BCAFN Grand Chief Stewart Phillip is the former chair of the ONA, currently claiming Sinixt territory and engaged in border disputes with Ktunaxa, who are also claiming Sinixt territory.[31] While the BCAFN and recognized bands acknowledge that there are problems with the process between colonially designated bands, they are silent regarding unrecognized or "extinct" Indigenous peoples.[32] Thus, not only does the BCTC create borders for consultation; it also solidifies the border of existence or extinction for Sinixt in Canada. Lines drawn on maps become reality.[33]

While the situation may seem dire, there are glimmers of Sinixt recognition in Canada. In 2017, in exchange for land for road development in Syilx (ONA) territory in Kelowna, BC, the Westbank (ONA) Band was offered land in Sinixt təmxʷúlaʔxʷ, ironically farther from their territory than the Arrow Lakes (Oatscott) Reserve. The Regional District of the Central Kootenay

(RDCK) directors took the position that they would not support the settlement until Sinixt extinction was addressed.[34] Autonomous Sinixt and the Colville Confederated Tribes (CCT) in Washington State opposed the transfer, and the CCT demanded consultation, launching a court case.[35] The CCT press release stated, "We have filed this court case because our repeated requests for a proper and respectful dialogue with Canada and Westbank have been completely ignored, and we believe that the Sinixt people have a right to be consulted about such an important development in their traditional territory in British Columbia."[36] Thus, when Sinixt are included by the ONA as members depends on political expedience. When in competition over control of resources, the ONA and CCT are no longer one people. Conflicts between Autonomous Sinixt and the CCT are also a complicating factor discussed later in the chapter.

The Courts and Government Borders

Within the context of the land claims process and an international border between extinction and recognition, Sinixt, like most Indigenous peoples worldwide, are forced into the courts for recognition of their Aboriginal rights and title. Autonomous Sinixt (through the Sinixt Nation Society) have challenged their "extinction" numerous times (e.g., *Robert Watt v. E. Liebelt and the Minister of Citizenship and Immigration* [1999], *Vance Robert Campbell et al. on their own behalf and on behalf of the Sinixt Nation and the Sinixt Nation Society v. Minister of Forests and Range of British Columbia and Sunshine Logging* [2004 BCSC 1046]). In the appeal of *Campbell v. British Columbia (Forest and Range)* (2012 BCCA 274), the CCT and ONA intervened against Autonomous Sinixt and argued they are the ones to be consulted, not Sinixt Nation.[37] As a result, the case was dismissed, logging went ahead and destroyed cultural sites that the Sinixt Nation was trying to protect, and the Sinixt Nation Society was ordered to pay court costs for the Crown and the logging company.[38] In this case, the right of recognized nations to claim borders of representation was paramount to the destruction of cultural sites.

    R. v. Desautel [2017 BCSC 2389 and 2019 SCC 38734], a hunting rights case involving the Lakes of the CCT and supported by the ONA is currently under appeal at the Supreme Court of Canada.[39] All three lower court rulings supported the Aboriginal right of Sinixt to hunt in Canada. Remarkably, the Sinixt Nation Society had already secured the right to hunt in British Columbia in

1998 through *smum iem* matriarch Marilyn James.[40] Despite this, an enrolled Lakes member of the CCT was sent to Canada to hunt without a licence and invite charges under BC's Wildlife Act.[41]

The *Desautel* defence revolved around whether Sinixt are recognized as Aboriginal peoples *of* Canada and thus enjoy constitutionally protected rights as such. In final arguments, the Crown's position was that the CCT was attempting to "manufacture a group that has some ties to community" but "that community is still just an idea," and they can't be a rights-bearing group without "some form of community."[42] The Crown repeatedly referred to Sinixt as "non-resident aliens" and "strangers to the *Constitution of Act of Canada*" who "abandoned" their rights when they crossed the border.[43] Furthermore, "the Canadian government . . . would not, and did not, have a law allowing *foreign nationals* to have hunting rights in Canada."[44] The fact that Sinixt were part of the CCT meant that they were "no longer the group that they once were" but "foreign nationals attempting to exercise constitutional rights."[45] As "noncitizens, nonresidents" they "can't hold aboriginal rights" and are "outside the sovereignty of the Crown."[46] At one point in the first trial, Judge Morinzski quipped, "You keep saying foreign nationals to make Mr. Desautel as alien as possible, while talking about a person whose ancestors have lived [in Canada] for thousands of years, who have been absent for less than a century."[47]

As border studies historian Benjamin Hoy argues, Canada and the United States interfered with transnational identities and familial bonds that spanned borders, "using Indian status and reservation lands as a cudgel with which to enforce the national orderings . . . envisioned during the nineteenth century."[48] Indigenous peoples crossing borders "violated the sanctity of national spaces." Although Hoy is discussing early nineteenth-century US-Canada border issues with regard to Indigenous peoples, attitudes of state governments toward transnational Indigenous identity have changed little: "Both countries perceived the transnational movements of Native Americans as a financial liability, a diplomatic risk, a challenge to their sovereignty, and a disruption to their Indian policies."[49] It is noteworthy that both Canada (2016) and British Columbia (2019) adopted the *United Nations Declaration on the Rights of Indigenous Peoples*, which states in article 36.1, "Indigenous peoples, in particular those divided by international borders, have the right to maintain and develop contacts, relations, and cooperation, including activities for spiritual, cultural, political, economic and social purposes, with their own members as well as other peoples across borders."[50] Yet both governments' positions in *Desautel* contradict the declaration.

Thus, the Canadian government's stance on Sinixt in Canada spans from confusion to nonrecognition as a way to eliminate their responsibility. In discussing the conditions for the Lakes diaspora, anthropologist Paula Pryce states,

> In Canada, the government never understood the Lakes to be a distinct Interior Salish people whose ancestral territory spanned the international boundary. Instead, they were considered to be either Colville or a hodgepodge of Shuswaps and Kutenais. Rather than acknowledging them to possess legitimate territorial rights north of the boundary, the governments perceived these "Colville" Lakes to be American opportunists who took economic advantage of British and (after 1871) Canadian soil by illegally crossing the line.[51]

There is a long history of "governmental befuddlement" regarding which side of the border Sinixt belong to, particularly when it comes to excluding them from their təmxʷúlaʔxʷ in Canada.[52] Anthropologist James Teit's unpublished fieldnotes from 1910–13 state,

> About twenty years ago, some slight troubles occurred between Lakes and Shuswap at Revelstoke over hunting rights, and the BC government officials took the position that the Shuswaps alone had rights in the district, the Lakes being American Indians from the Colville Reservation, and interlopers in BC. *This was entirely wrong*, there being no more reason to deny the rights of [Lakes] people in B.C., than Okanogan and Kootenay which . . . also inhabit both sides of the line.[53]

Moreover, as University of Toronto law professor Patrick Macklem argues, "the unquestioned adherence to basic categories of the Anglo-Canadian legal imagination [is] effected by the denial and acceptance of native difference." This "denial of difference . . . operate[s] on behalf of domination."[54] The denial of Sinixt as a distinct people with cultural and linguistic differences from neighbouring Indigenous groups with their own territory is not only an eradication of hindrances to development; it is also an effective means to deny their very existence as Aboriginal Peoples of Canada.

These hard borders based on ambiguous and contested understandings persist. In *Desautel*, Brian Williams (Gitanyow hereditary chief), manager of aboriginal relations for BC Parks, Ministry of Environment, testified that transboundary hunting would "disrupt the apple cart" of Aboriginal hunting rights in BC: "The optics of another group coming in and disrupting that . . . could be upsetting to the First Nations we already talk to. . . . We see it already with a lot of First Nations that have overlapping interests, and placing the Crown in a position to try to determine whose rights take priority over whose, those are difficult conversations."[55] He later testified that the province has no way to effectively monitor how many animals are hunted in BC as an Aboriginal right. Furthermore, because Sinixt are "extinct" under the Indian Act, no strength-of-claim assessment was conducted in the case. If Sinixt are not Aboriginal people of Canada, then apparently, Aboriginal relations are not required to assess their constitutionally protected rights.

Academic Borderlands of Understanding

Concomitant with imposed borders, erasure from maps, land claims, and court cases in perpetuating Sinixt extinction is academic research. As an "extinct" people with no reserve in Canada, Sinixt presence is difficult to establish. There is no band council office in Canada from which to seek research permission in Sinixt territory. Does one go to the CCT in the United States to secure research permissions in Canada? If so, it is unlikely that one would work with Autonomous Sinixt in Canada, given the deep divisions between the two entities.

Moreover, band council representatives can change each election cycle, making long research relationships challenging. I (Barkley) have been living, working, and interacting with Autonomous Sinixt in BC for over twenty years. It took several years after the introduction of the BCTC to see Syilx and Ktunaxa presence in the təmxʷúlaʔxʷ, and a few years after that, the CCT. Over approximately ten years, the CCT has employed three different Arrow Lakes coordinators.[56] None of the coordinators sought the counsel of Marilyn James, smum iem matriarch and elder-appointed spokesperson in the "Canadian" təmxʷúlaʔxʷ for over twenty-five years, nor other Autonomous Sinixt, like former CCT councillor Lou Stone.[57]

Building long-lasting, trusting relationships between settler researchers and Indigenous peoples is challenging at the best of times. When those people live across a border and change every few years, building relationships is particularly difficult. Any attempt at understanding the complexities of Sinixt existence in "extinction" relies on deep research relationships with those deemed extinct and living that reality on a daily basis in Canada. This is also necessary to challenge borderlands of academic truths about the status of Sinixt in Canada.

For academics working with neighbouring bands with status under the Indian Act, it is unlikely that the topic of Sinixt or their extinction will be raised. Rather, maps and borders produced by band councils are taken as fact and may contain territory of unrecognized and recognized peoples. For example, the Ktunaxa's traditional territory map includes not only Sinixt təmxʷúla?xʷ but also those of nations covered under Treaty 7 in southern Alberta.[58] At a 2015 meeting of anthropologists and sociologists representing academic institutions from across the province in Ktunaxa territory, this statement of territory spanning several distinct ecological zones from interior rainforest to prairie was presented but went unchallenged. Thus, all in attendance were complicit in Ktunaxa's problematic construction of borders. What is the role of settler academics in challenging the territorial claims of Indigenous nations? Well intentioned or not, academics contribute to these misunderstandings by not wanting to disagree with their research participants or the band councils who support their work.[59]

As Australian political scientist Alissa Macoun argues, "White settlers who identify as critical thinkers or progressives can be particularly invested in being good people, in doing good things, in engaging with destructive histories or problematic power structures, and thus most invested in our own innocence."[60] These "constructions of innocence," combined with the desire of settler academics to be seen doing "good work" in Indigenous communities, can perpetuate Sinixt extinction.[61] Settler academic innocence may support Indigenous innocence of Sinixt as a distinct people, perpetuating their extinction. When intra-Indigenous violence is supported by academics, it becomes a monolith built through the complicity of Indigenous people, academics, settler governments, and the courts, "simultaneously enabling and erasing ongoing colonial violence." Macoun argues that white innocence—and I suggest Indigenous innocence as well—"both erases the state's implication in existing colonial relationships and morally authorizes their continuation."[62]

Are Macoun's words on settler innocence relevant to Indigenous innocence in claiming Sinixt territory? "Settler [and Indigenous] moves to innocence are those strategies or positionings that attempt to relieve the settler [and other nations] of feelings of guilt or responsibility without giving up land or power or privilege, without having to change much at all."[63] Can the same be said for the BCTC process? Is Indigenous "innocence" of bands claiming Sinixt təmxʷúlaʔxʷ a strategy for relieving their guilt or responsibility for perpetuating Sinixt extinction? Unlike settler innocence, however, as marginalized peoples within both the state and the BCTC process, they do so in an attempt to gain *some* power or privilege to continue to underserve their communities within the context of settler colonialism.

This "innocence" is the foundation of colonialism; "we are all colonized *into* innocence," settler and Indigenous alike. Colonialism is the theft of land and resources from rightful owners.[64] Land claims and the drawing of borders are part of the ongoing process of settler colonialism, explicitly designed to ensure the state's "innocence" in ongoing control over Indigenous peoples and *their* resources.[65]

Resulting from the BCTC, the *United Nations Declaration on the Rights of Indigenous Peoples*, and the *Truth and Reconciliation Commission of Canada*, territorial acknowledgements are a common feature of many settler gatherings, academic and otherwise, fostering the sense of white innocence that Macoun critiques. Thus, any nation that claims the land is acknowledged. In Sinixt təmxʷúlaʔxʷ, this may or may not include Sinixt. Every time a statement is made about shared territory or territory of another nation, it creates boundaries for understanding the complexities of Sinixt extinction. This then becomes the reality for settlers, who "innocently" reproduce acknowledgements without understanding the complicated inferences.[66]

In the rush to reconcile something that can never be reconciled—the theft of land and bureaucratic extinction of Sinixt—the complexity of truths is often ignored to reproduce clear borders for a brief acknowledgement of territory. Every time Sinixt are excluded, there is no truth.[67] Without truth, there is no reconciliation. Without truth in the courts, there is no reconciliation. Without truth in land claims, there is no reconciliation. Without truth in academic work, there is no reconciliation. As academics, our aim must always be to delve into the complexity and to ask hard questions of ourselves and our research. As Macoun argues, "Complicity should be the starting point for critical encounters, I am advocating an awareness of complicity among white settlers and the ways that we are located within whiteness and coloniality."[68] Taking this further, there is also an urgent need for greater awareness of settler innocence and complicity in neocolonial violence between Indigenous nations.

Another problem is the singularity of identity seemingly demanded by governments and reproduced in research. Someone can have Sinixt, Syilx, and/or Ktunaxa ancestors. Over time, one of those identities may become paramount, and rather than having multiple identities, one becomes Syilx, for example. When one identifies as Syilx, there is the potential for Aboriginal rights not available to Sinixt in Canada, including a reserve land base and access to band council resources. While ancestors may have considered themselves Sinixt in the past, their descendants now consider themselves to be Syilx, or that Syilx and Sinixt are the same and there is no difference between them.[69]

As Robinson argues regarding Mi'kmaw in Newfoundland and Labrador, governments lumping Indigenous peoples together and ignoring distinctiveness is an effective strategy in imposing one-size-fits-all policy solutions. "This one-identity-fits-all approach to governance asserted a form of neocolonialism that ensured continued and, arguably, increased repression of Aboriginal peoples in the province."[70] In the case of BC, as previous examples demonstrate, the sheer number of different Indigenous groups are glossed over whenever possible in order to simplify the process for colonially imposed governments. Within the BCTC process, this results in Indigenous governments also minimizing diversity and contention if it strengthens their claim, drawing on academia for evidence. This too contributes to borders between Indigenous peoples and creates barriers to understanding the complex history of settlers.

As Thom, referring to *Mathias v. Canada* (2000), states, even "detailed kinship studies may not always correspond with a First Nation's sense of contemporary political identity, particularly if two competing First Nations are closely related, but have overlapping or conflicting claims, such as the current Musqueam and Squamish claim for valuable alienated land in Vancouver."[71] Similarly, Syilx and Sinixt speak related Interior Salishan dialects. In this homogenizing process that shuns heterogeneity, the Syilx dialect is presented by the ONA and the CCT as one and the same, further contributing to the erasure of a distinct Sinixt identity.

The work of Autonomous Sinixt, in the words of James, is to convey the "real truth about land and people's connections to it. Experts, Sinixt, everyone, must put on their bullshit meters to clear their glasses of the dark shades of the past."[72] While the task of experts is to create truths, if the territory is inaccurate and political representation ignores nuance, then no trust can be created with Indigenous peoples. Every time an "expert" ignores Sinixt in their təmxʷúlaʔxʷ, borders of misunderstanding are perpetuated. In the case of the Indian Act, courts, and the BCTC process, ignoring Sinixt realities contributes to their continued "extinction." The same holds true for territorial acknowledgements. The "colonial fog" must be lifted to understand that Sinixt never ceased to exist in their təmxʷúlaʔxʷ, regardless of how many "borders crossed them."

Sinixt exist in multiple borderlands: between extinction and existence, between lumping and distinctiveness, between Canada and the United States; between and within Syilx and Ktunaxa land claims, between academic borders of existence and erasure. The multiplicity of borders fixes or erases Sinixt in a multitude of ways, each with its own set of challenges to their very existence as a distinct people. The call to academics in this chapter is to not reproduce those borderlands that deny Sinixt peoples' very existence as distinct Indigenous peoples of Canada.

Postscript

Since this chapter was written in 2020, there have been some significant developments. The Supreme Court of Canada upheld the lower court's decisions that Sinixt enrolled as members of the CCT do have the right to hunt in Canada. While the question before the courts was about hunting rights, the CCT repeatedly asserted that the ruling reversed Sinixt extinction in Canada. This is an intentional misrepresentation of the case, as extinction was not before the courts.

The decision affirmed their right to use the land without rights to the land itself. Extinction, the right to be consulted about resource extraction, the ability to participate in the land claims process, and the right to the land itself are all beyond the scope of the Desautel case. The Canadian government's assertion that the Arrow Lakes Band is extinct for purposes of the Indian Act remains unchanged.

The Okanagan Indian Band (member of the ONA) again filed with the specific claims tribunal (SCT-7004-20) for financial compensation for *their* loss of the Arrow Lakes Band / Oatscott reserve. Autonomous Sinixt and Ktunaxa Nation requested intervenor status, and both were denied.

The CCT was successful in appealing to the BC Heritage Branch to have the site operator agreement with James rescinded. As part of this process, the CCT has sent out press releases denying that James is Sinixt, despite her Sinixt ancestry being submitted in the Sunshine logging case for all to see. In response, James has reoccupied the Vallican site, an ancient village site the province wanted to turn into a picnic ground and the catalyst for Sinixt resurgence in Canada. James has been protecting this site for decades and has made the small one-room cabin there her permanent residence despite the lack of electricity, running water, or access to wi-fi or cellular service. That remains largely unchanged, with the exception of a solar panel. Her responsibility to protect her ancestors' graves is a cultural law that she must follow, handed down to her from previous matriarchs. She is not trusting the care of her ancestors to colonial governments, Indigenous or settler. The struggle against colonial forces continues.

Acknowledgements

K. L. Kivi, Craig Proulx, and David Thorsen-Cavers provided valuable feedback. Elizabeth Harwood's research and editorial assistance were invaluable.

Notes

1. Sinixt are also known as Lakes or Arrow Lakes.
2. On January 5, 1956, Order-in-Council PC 1956-5 passed the "control, management and administration" of the Arrow Lakes Reserve to the province of British Columbia (R. B. Bryce, Clerk of the Privy Council, in a letter to the Governor General dated January 5, 1956, in author's possession). On January 20, Indian Commissioner W. S. Arneil stated, "We are satisfied that this Band has become extinct" (Letter from W. S. Arneil, Indian Commissioner for B.C. to Land Branch of BC, dated January 20, 1956, in author's possession). Ronald A. Irwin, Minister of Indian Affairs and Northern Development, in response to a letter written by Jacqueline Heywood, co-founder of the Coalition of Supporters of the Sinixt/Arrow Lakes Nation, circa August 1995, stated, "The Arrow Lakes Band ceased to exist as a band for the purpose of the Indian Act when its last member died on October 1, 1953" (in the author's possession).
3. Sinixt are not truly "extinct" but rather bureaucratically extinct in Canada.
4. Andrea Geiger, "'Crossed by the Border': The U.S.-Canada Border and Canada's 'Extinction' of the Arrow Lakes Band, 1890–1956," 129.
5. The steamboat was no longer in service at the time; "the termination process had been set in motion." Geiger, "Crossed by the Border," 138.

6. Bouchard and Kennedy, *Lakes Indian Ethnography*, 156.
7. Bouchard and Kennedy, *Lakes Indian Ethnography*, 156.
8. The Indian Act was imposed on Indigenous peoples, turning them into wards of the state and controlling most aspects of their lives through the band system. "Indian Status" is a legal identity, largely based on band membership; however, having band membership does not guarantee status. Status is required for rights as an "Indian" of Canada. Not all Indigenous peoples in Canada have status, however: "In Canada, more than twice as many people self-identify as Aboriginal than are registered as 'status Indians.'" Maximilian C. Forte, "Introduction: 'Who Is an Indian?': The Cultural Politics of a Bad Question," 4.

   During Joseph's time, Indigenous women lost their status when they married unless they married someone with status in the same band. For males, the wife (including non-Indigenous women) was granted the status of the husband. Upon divorce or the husband's death, the woman lost status. Thus, by marrying an OIB member, Joseph would lose Lakes status and gain OIB status and lose all status as an Indian under the Indian Act if her husband predeceased her. For a longer discussion of Indian status and Sinixt "extinction," see Lori Barkley and Tonio Sadik, "'At the End of the Dog's Tail': Aboriginal Policy and Sinixt in British Columbia, Canada."
9. R. H. S. Sampson, Superintendent of the Okanagan Indian Agency, 1952, cited in Bouchard and Kennedy, *Lakes Indian Ethnography*, 157–58.
10. Geiger, "Crossed by the Border," 144. This created considerable incentive for governments to bureaucratically erase Indigenous peoples. For a more thorough discussion of bureaucratic genocide, see Dean Neu and Richard Therrien, *Accounting for Genocide: Canada's Bureaucratic Assault on Aboriginal People*.
11. L. L. Brown, Superintendent, Reserves and Trusts, June 1953, in Geiger, "Crossed by the Border," 146.
12. Randy Bouchard and Dorothy Kennedy, *First Nations' Ethnography and Ethnohistory in British Columbia's Lower Kootenay/Columbia Hydropower Region*, 100. Joseph died prior to amalgamation. Bouchard and Kennedy, *Lakes Indian Ethnography*, 158.
13. Ron Irwin, Minister of Indian Affairs and Northern Development, to Jacqueline Heywood, co-founder of the Coalition of Supporters of the Sinixt/Arrow Lakes Nation, Nelson, BC, n.d., ca. August 1995. "Tribal groups" are not recognized under the Indian Act, only bands. The Canadian government does not deny that Sinixt exist as a people (i.e., "a tribal group") but rather

that the Arrow Lakes Band is extinct. It is through bands that rights, land and resources are controlled under the Indian Act.

14. For example, *Pulling Together: A Guide for Indigenization of Post-secondary Institutions* by Kory Wilson and Colleen Hodgson excludes Sinixt from their map of "First Nation Territories across British Columbia": https://opentextbc .ca/indigenizationfoundations/wp-content/uploads/sites/220/2018/01/01-0 -first-nations-1.jpg, accessed June 1, 2020.

15. Michèle Sato, Regina Silva, and Michelle Jaber, "Between the Remnants of Colonialism and the Insurgence of Self-Narrative in Constructing Participatory Social Maps: Towards a Land Education Methodology," 106.

16. Richard Osburn, "Problems and Solutions regarding Indigenous Peoples Split by International Borders," 471–85. However, Indigenous peoples did have clear ideas about their territories. For Sinixt, once another people came down from the mountains to the valley floor, visiting protocols were required. As Pryce states, "Identity, like territory, is temporal. It moves and flows, never static, growing out of the thoughts and practices and interactions of individuals in the community." Paula Pryce, *"Keeping the Lakes' Way": Reburial and the Re-creation of a Moral World among an Invisible People*, 35.

17. Marilyn James and Taress Alexis, *Not Extinct: Keeping the Sinixt Way*, 22.

18. Angela Robinson, "Enduring Pasts and Denied Presence: Mi'kmaw Challenges to Continued Marginalization in Western Newfoundland," 386–87.

19. Dan Shaule, personal communication to Lori Barkley, Mary 14, 2013.

20. Adrian Tanner, "The Aboriginal People of Newfoundland and Labrador, and Confederation," 238–52, quoted in Robinson, "Enduring Pasts," 386.

21. Carole Blackburn, "Searching for Guarantees in the Midst of Uncertainty: Negotiating Aboriginal Rights and Title in British Columbia," 586–96.

22. "Contention" means more than one federally recognized band has claimed a particular piece of land (i.e., overlapping land claims). As Jean-François Bayart argues, "Liminal nations hang about or complain in the antechamber of the world without knowing when, or if, the usher will let them in." Jean-François Bayart, *Global Subjects: A Political Critique of Globalization*, 284.

23. For a complete list, see British Columbia, "Ktunaxa Nation."

24. Brian Thom, "Aboriginal Rights and Title in Canada after *Delgamuukw*: Part Two, Anthropological Perspectives on Rights, Tests, Infringement & Justification," 14. The BCTC necessarily creates contention, as bands are required to claim overlapping territories. As with all bargaining, it is prudent to start high, as final land agreements are far smaller than unceded traditional territories. This creates widespread contention, largely ignored by non-Indigenous governments. By filing a claim, Sinixt were attempting

to prevent their təmxʷúlaʔxʷ from being ceded to other Indigenous groups. Unfortunately, this has not been the case, and their claim is ignored by all in the process.

25. Dene Moore, "It's up to First Nations to Resolve Overlapping Claims: B.C. Treaty Commission Report." This position has not changed; see Justine Hunter, "Overlapping Land Claims in Wet'suwet'en Territory Complicate Talks with Government."

26. Thom, "Aboriginal Rights," 15.

27. The Okanagan Nation Alliance (ONA) is the chosen name for Okanagan/Syilx governance, consisting of seven bands in Canada, each with a reserve. The CCT are also a member of the ONA. Like Sinixt, Syilx territory was crossed by the Canada-US border, and they are also one of the CCT member tribes, which further complicates matters. Okanagan Nation Alliance (ONA), "B.C. Court of Appeal Confirms Rights in Arrow Lakes." Sinixt had only one band and reserve, compared to the ONA with seven, one of numerous political disparities dating back over a century that affect the BCTC process.

28. British Columbia Assembly of First Nations (BCAFN), "Reconsidering Canada's Comprehensive Claims Policy: A New Approach Based on Recognition and Reconciliation," 5.

29. Okanagan Nation Alliance, "Open Letter Re: Opposition to Silver Star Mountain Resort—Splatsin First Nation Memorandum of Understanding," February 23, 2017 (in the author's possession).

30. Sheila McManus, personal communication to Lori Barkley, May 12, 2020.

31. See *Okanagan Nation Alliance v. Her Majesty the Queen in Right of the Province of British Columbia as Represented by the Minister of Aboriginal Rights and Reconciliation VLC-S-S-146110*, 2014.

32. The ONA was "outraged" when an incremental agreement was settled with Ktunaxa, arguing it encroached on Syilx territory. Okanagan Nation Alliance (ONA), "Clark Government Misleads Public for Political Gain." In response, the ONA launched a civil claim in BC Supreme Court questioning the legitimacy of the BCTC process. CBC News Online, "First Nations Alliance Launches Court Challenge of B.C. Treaty Process."

33. Noteworthy of all the land claims in BC, Westbank (ONA) is the only rectangle, unimpeded by landscape features like mountain ranges and waterways. BC Treaty Commission, "Interactive Map."

34. Westbank First Nation—Fauquier Community Meeting, Fauquier Community Hall, Fauquier, BC, October 4, 2017. Gregg Nesteroff, "Updated: RDCK Backs Sinixt over Fauquier Reserve." Unfortunately, their approval is not required to convert the property to reserve status.

35. "Autonomous Sinixt is an evolving reference indicating independence by Sinixt Peoples in their təmxʷúlaʔxʷ. From the time of Canadian Crown designation of 'extinction' in 1956, rejection of such a declaration was immediate by The Peoples, albeit informally. This changed in the late 1980s when a former village and burial site was threatened by road building in Vallican, BC. The site was actively protected by many Sinixt persons who considered themselves Autonomous and acting independently on a matter long over-due. This site has become the longest, peaceful ongoing Indigenous occupation in Canada, under control of Autonomous Sinixt. Autonomy is mandatory in order for Sinixt self-government, separate and apart from an assumption of influence by the Colville Confederated Tribes of the United States. Autonomous Sinixt assert the CCT has no jurisdiction in Canada and therefore has no authority on Sinixt matters or conduct of business in Canada." Lou Stone, personal communication to Lori Barkley, June 2, 2020.

    When the CCT heard that Marilyn James, Autonomous Sinixt, was named operator of the Vallican site, they issued a statement of intention "to meet with the Province at the earliest opportunity," arguing that they are the authorized representatives of Sinixt in Canada in BC. Jan McMurray "Marilyn James Signs on with BC Heritage Branch as Vallican Site Operator."

36. John Boivin, "Consult Before Creating Fauquier Reserve: CCT." This also speaks to the ability of recognized Indigenous groups with access to money, lawyers, and communication teams to bring territorial disputes before the courts. Autonomous Sinixt simply cannot match their resources.

37. In their opposition to the Vallican site operator memorandum of understanding between James and the province, the CCT cited this case as to why they should be the authorized representatives of Sinixt in Canada. McMurray, "Marilyn James Signs On," 3. The courts have been silent on who is the authorized representative, as that would require acknowledging their existence as an organized body in Canada (i.e., recognition of Sinixt governance that would need to be consulted).

38. Peter Scott Vicaire, "Campbell v. British Columbia: Costs Awarded to Crown and Sunshine Logging." Sinixt Nation Society was a registered Society under the BC Societies Act. Those ordered to pay costs were its board members, who were listed as the defendants. This also precludes Sinixt Nation from bringing any cases before the courts until the debt is fully paid.

39. The ONA was very involved in the case, including the selection of witnesses. In commenting on the decision, Grand Chief Stewart Phillip, chair of the Chiefs' Executive Council of the Syilx Okanagan Nation, stated, "We

are pleased that the Court of Appeal has confirmed what we have always known—that the Sinixt (in our language, the *sʔaltíkʷt*) were the original inhabitants of the Arrow Lakes region long before the Europeans arrived. We are not extinct" (ONA, "B.C. Court of Appeal"). The use of "we" here indicates inclusion, but the ONA did not respond to CCT over the creation of an ONA member reserve in Sinixt təmxʷúlaʔxʷ. Syilx are not now, nor ever have been, considered "extinct." The scheduled 2020 date for the Federal Supreme Court Hearing was postponed due to COVID-19. This case has progressed this far largely as a result of the vastly superior resources of the CCT over the Sinixt Nation Society. See postscript for an update on the case.

40. *Smum iem* translates as "belongs to the women." In practice, this means that as a matrilineal, matriarchal culture, the responsibility for the təmxʷúlaʔxʷ and everything in it belongs to the women. An Indigenous hunter, following traditional protocols, sought permission from smum iem and shared the meat with them.

41. The elk was processed in Canada and all the meat taken across the border to CCT members; none was distributed to Autonomous Sinixt in Canada going against Sinixt protocols.

42. Fieldnotes, *R. v. Desautel*, taken by Lori Barkley during court proceedings, Nelson, BC, November 30, 2016, book 1:10. This also speaks to the CCT's assertion that "the Desautel case has established that the Lakes Tribe of the CCT is [the] representative body" of Sinixt in Canada. McMurray, "Marilyn James Signs On," 3.

43. Fieldnotes, November 30, 2016, book 3:22; *R. v. Desautel* file (2016) 23646, Nelson, BC.

44. Fieldnotes, November 29, 2016, book 2:55.

45. Fieldnotes, November 30, 2016, book 3:8; fieldnotes, November 20, 2016, book 3:1.

46. Fieldnotes, November 30, 2016, book 3:14.

47. Fieldnotes, November 30, 2016, book 3:25.a.

48. Benjamin Hoy, "A Border without Guards: First Nations and the Enforcement of National Space," 97.

49. Hoy, "Border without Guards," 93. Remarkably, according to the Indian Act of 1876, "Any Indian who resided for five years continuously in a foreign country would lose their status unless the consent of the band with the approval of the Superintendent-General or his agent was first obtained." Hoy, "Border without Guards," 94.

50. United Nations, *United Nations Declaration on the Rights of Indigenous Peoples*.

51. Pryce, *"Keeping the Lakes' Way,"* 60. The Treaty of Washington (1871), in part, was intended to address border disputes.

52. Pryce, *"Keeping the Lakes' Way,"* 62. Shuswap (*Secwépemc*) also have a contemporary land claim including Sinixt təmxʷúlaʔxʷ. The Treaty of Washington (1871) addressed outstanding border issues between Great Britain (Canada) and the United States.

53. Quoted in Pryce, *"Keeping the Lakes' Way,"* 61 (emphasis added).

54. Patrick Macklem, "First Nations Self-Government and the Borders of the Canadian Legal Imagination," 394.

55. Fieldnotes, October 12, 2016, book 2:20.

56. These are unelected, paid positions hired by the Colville Business Council, which represents twelve tribes, including Okanagan. As of 2024, there is yet another new representative.

57. Lou Stone, personal communication to Lori Barkley, December 1, 2019.

58. E.g., Nupqu, "We Are Nupqu," The ONA argue they are claiming Syilx territory as well. See also Pryce, *"Keeping the Lakes' Way,"* 31.

59. The First Nations of British Columbia Map at the Museum of Anthropology (University of British Columbia), indicates Sinixt təmxʷúlaʔxʷ with a dashed line, but it is not named as Sinixt territory. Similar dashes appear in Wet'suwet'en, Gitxsan, and Nisga'a territories, but they are named. See Museum of Anthropology, *First Nations of British Columbia*.

60. Alissa Macoun, "Colonising White Innocence: Complicity and Critical Encounters," 86.

61. Macoun, "Colonising White Innocence," 88. This may be compounded by requirements of research ethics boards to consult with First Nation governments.

62. Macoun, "Colonising White Innocence," 91.

63. Eve Tuck and K. Wayne Yang, "Decolonization Is Not a Metaphor," quoted in Macoun, "Colonising White Innocence," 88.

64. Elizabeth Ferguson (*Dene Tha*), personal communication to Lori Barkley, November 28, 2019.

65. See also Sharon Venne, "Crown Title: A Legal Lie," 14–17.

66. For example, the city of Nelson's official land acknowledgement (where the Sinixt aboriginal rights case was heard) states, "We would like to acknowledge that the land on which we gather is the traditional territories of the Sinixt, the Syilx, and the Ktunaxa peoples, and is home to many diverse indigenous persons, including the Metis" (https://www.nelson.ca/) According to Gregg Nesteroff, "Outgoing councillor Purcell says her motion was modelled on what Selkirk College does." Nesteroff, "Nelson Amends Aboriginal Acknowledgement."

 When the school district, which includes Nelson, wanted to name nations in their acknowledgement, Lower Kootenay Band Chief Jason Louie "admonished" them, stating, "We're not going to concede to [including other BC and American Bands] because we're currently in at treaty process, we're currently exploring the possibility of rights and title. The moment we acknowledge [those bands], we're giving up our territory. We're conceding there's other First Nations here as well." Tyler Harper, "Lower Kootenay Band Criticizes Proposed Changes to School District 8's Acknowledgement."

67. A significant problem is the multiplicity of "truths" about territory. The argument here is that Sinixt truly *exist*.

68. Macoun, "Colonising White Innocence," 90.

69. All of the authors have had this conversation with several people who are members of the Okanagan Nation yet identify as Sinixt and maintain there is no difference.

70. Robinson, "Enduring Pasts," 385; Thom, "Aboriginal Rights."

71. Thom, "Aboriginal Rights," 18.

72. Marilyn James, personal communication to Lori Barkley, ca. 2014.

Bibliography

Barkley, Lori, and Tonio Sadik. "'At the End of the Dog's Tail': Aboriginal Policy and Sinixt in British Columbia, Canada." Academia.edu. 2014. https://www.academia.edu/29837056/_At_the_End_of_the_Dogs_Tail_Aboriginal_Policy_and_Sinixt_in_British_Columbia_Canada.

Bayart, Jean-François. *Global Subjects: A Political Critique of Globalization*. Cambridge: Polity Press, 2007.

BC Treaty Commission. "Interactive Map." 2023. http://www.bctreaty.ca/map.

Blackburn, Carole. "Searching for Guarantees in the Midst of Uncertainty: Negotiating Aboriginal Rights and Title in British Columbia." *American Anthropologist* 107, no. 4 (2005): 586–96.

Boivin, John. "Consult Before Creating Fauquier Reserve: CCT." *Arrow Lakes News*, March 16, 2018. https://www.arrowlakesnews.com/local-news/consult-before-creating-fauquier-reserve-cct/.

Bouchard, Randy, and Dorothy Kennedy. *First Nations' Ethnography and Ethnohistory in British Columbia's Lower Kootenay/Columbia Hydropower Region*. Castlegar, BC: Columbia Power Corporation, 2005.

Bouchard, Randy, and Dorothy Kennedy. *Lakes Indian Ethnography and History*. Unpublished manuscript prepared for the BC Heritage Conservation Branch, Victoria, August 1985.

British Columbia. "Ktunaxa Nation." Accessed June 5, 2020. https://www2.gov.bc.ca/gov/content/environment/natural-resource-stewardship/consulting-with-first-nations/first-nations-negotiations/first-nations-a-z-listing/ktunaxa-nation.

British Columbia Assembly of First Nations (BCAFN). "Reconsidering Canada's Comprehensive Claims Policy: A New Approach Based on Recognition and Reconciliation." Scribd. Last updated July 16, 2013. http://www.scribd.com/doc/165509244/Chiefs-CCP-Discussion-Guide-Revised-July-16-2013.

CBC News Online. "First Nations Alliance Launches Court Challenge of B.C. Treaty Process." August 12, 2014. https://www.cbc.ca/news/indigenous/first-nations-alliance-launches-court-challenge-of-b-c-treaty-process-1.2734282.

Forte, Maximilian C. "Introduction: 'Who Is an Indian?': The Cultural Politics of a Bad Question." In *Who Is an Indian? Race, Place, and the Politics of Indigeneity in the Americas*, edited by Maximilian C. Forte, 2–51. Toronto: University of Toronto Press, 2013.

Geiger, Andrea. "'Crossed by the Border': The U.S.-Canada Border and Canada's 'Extinction' of the Arrow Lakes Band, 1890–1956." *Western Legal History: The Journal of the Ninth Judicial Circuit Historical Society* 23, no. 2 (2010):121–53.

Harper, Tyler. "Lower Kootenay Band Criticizes Proposed Changes to School District 8's Acknowledgement." *Castlegar News*, June 28, 2019. https://www.castlegarnews.com/news/lower-kootenay-band-criticizes-proposed-changes-to-school-district-8s-acknowledgement/.

Hoy, Benjamin. "A Border without Guards: First Nations and the Enforcement of National Space." *Journal of the Canadian Historical Association* 25, no. 2 (2014): 89–115. https://doi.org/10.7202/1032842ar.

Hunter, Justine. "Overlapping Land Claims in Wet'suwet'en Territory Complicate Talks with Government." *Globe and Mail*, March 4, 2020. https://www.theglobeandmail.com/canada/british-columbia/article-overlapping-land-claims-in-wetsuweten-territory-complicate-talks/.

James, Marilyn, and Taress Alexis. *Not Extinct: Keeping the Sinixt Way*. New Denver, BC: Maa Press, 2018.

Macklem, Patrick. "First Nations Self-Government and the Borders of the Canadian Legal Imagination." *McGill Law Journal* 36 (1991): 383–456.

Macoun, Alissa. "Colonising White Innocence: Complicity and Critical Encounters." In *The Limits of Settler Colonial Reconciliation: Non-Indigenous People and the Responsibility to Engage*, edited by Sarah Maddison, Tom Clark, and Ravi De Costa, 85–102. Gateway East, Singapore: Springer, 2016.

McMurray, Jan. "Marilyn James Signs on with BC Heritage Branch as Vallican Site Operator." *Valley Voice*, June 4, 2020, 3.

Moore, Dene. "It's up to First Nations to Resolve Overlapping Claims: B.C. Treaty Commission Report." *Globe and Mail*, October 7, 2014. https://www.theglobeandmail.com/news/british-columbia/its-up-to-first-nations-to-resolve-overlapping-claims-bc-treaty-commission-report/article20968990/.

Museum of Anthropology. *First Nations of British Columbia*. 1994. https://moa.ubc .ca/wp-content/uploads/2014/08/SchoolProgram-FirstNationsMap.pdf.

Nesteroff, Gregg. "Nelson Amends Aboriginal Acknowledgement." MyNelsonNow, October 23, 2018. https://www.mynelsonnow.com/35585/nelson-amends -aboriginal-acknowledgement/.

Nesteroff, Gregg. "Updated: RDCK Backs Sinixt over Fauquier Reserve." MyKootenayNow, November 17, 2017. https://www.mykootenaynow.com/23527/ rdck-backs-sinixt-fauquier-reserve/.

Neu, Dean, and Richard Therrien. *Accounting for Genocide: Canada's Bureaucratic Assault on Aboriginal People*. Black Point, Nova Scotia: Fernwood Publishing, 2003.

Nupqu. "We Are Nupqu." 2018. http://www.nupqu.com/the-company/.

Okanagan Nation Alliance (ONA). "B.C. Court of Appeal Confirms Rights in Arrow Lakes." May 3, 2019. Accessed November 17, 2019. https://www.syilx.org/ b-c-court-of-appeal-confirms-rights-in-arrow-lakes/.

Okanagan Nation Alliance (ONA). "Clark Government Misleads Public for Political Gain." April 2013. Author's personal collection.

Okanagan Nation Alliance v. Her Majesty the Queen in Right of the Province of British Columbia as Represented by the Minister of Aboriginal Rights and Reconciliation VLC-S-S-146110. 2014 https://www.firstpeopleslaw.com/files/file/ 5f3ecc4e4fdab/2014_08_08_Notice_of_Civil_Claim.pdf.

Osburn, Richard. "Problems and Solutions regarding Indigenous Peoples Split by International Borders." *American Indian Law Review* 24, no. 2 (1999/2000): 471–85. https://doi.org/10.2307/20070641.

Pryce, Paula. *"Keeping the Lakes' Way": Reburial and the Re-creation of a Moral World among an Invisible People*. Toronto, Ontario: University of Toronto Press, 1999.

Robbins, David M. "Aboriginal Peoples, British Columbia & Canada: The Constitutional Division of Land Interests & Legislative Powers." Paper prepared for the Westbank First Nation's conference "Making or Breaking the Treaty Process: The Constitutional Status of Treaty Settlement Land," Kelowna, BC, May 31, 2006. Author's personal collection.

Robinson, Angela. "Enduring Pasts and Denied Presence: Mi'kmaw Challenges to Continued Marginalization in Western Newfoundland." *Anthropologica* 56, no. 2 (2014): 383–97.

Sato, Michèle, Regina Silva, and Michelle Jaber. "Between the Remnants of Colonialism and the Insurgence of Self-Narrative in Constructing Participatory Social Maps: Towards a Land Education Methodology." *Environmental Education Research* 20, no. 1 (2014): 102–14.

Tanner, Adrian. "The Aboriginal People of Newfoundland and Labrador, and Confederation." *Newfoundland Studies*, 14, no. 2 (1998): 238–52.

Thom, Brian. "Aboriginal Rights and Title in Canada after *Delgamuukw*: Part Two, Anthropological Perspectives on Rights, Tests, Infringement & Justification." *Native Studies Review* 14, no. 2 (2001): 1–42. http://iportal.usask.ca/docs/Native _studies_review/v14/issue2/pp1-42.pdf.

Tuck, Eve, and K. Wayne Yang. "Decolonization Is Not a Metaphor," *Decolonization: Indigeneity, Education & Society* 1, no. 1 (2012): 1–40.

Venne, Sharon. "Crown Title: A Legal Lie." In *Whose Land Is It Anyway? A Manual for Decolonization*, edited by Peter McFarlane and Nicole Schabus, 14–17. Vancouver: Federation of Post-Secondary Educators of BC, 2017.

Wilson, Kory, and Colleen Hodgson. *Pulling Together: A Guide for Indigenization of Post-secondary Institutions*. Victoria, BC: BCcampus, 2018. https://opentextbc.ca/ indigenizationfoundations/.

United Nations. *United Nations Declaration on the Rights of Indigenous Peoples*. September 13, 2007. https://www.un.org/development/desa/indigenouspeoples/ wp-content/uploads/sites/19/2018/11/UNDRIP_E_web.pdf.

Vicaire, Peter Scott. "Campbell v. British Columbia: Costs Awarded to Crown and Sunshine Logging." *Turtle Talk* (blog), August 26, 2011.https://turtletalk.blog/ 2011/08/26/campbell-v-british-columbia-costs-awarded-to-crown-and-sunshine -logging/.

6 Seeking Safe Harbour

Indigenous Refugees and the Making of Canada's Numbered Treaties

Ryan Hall

We tend to think of our current historical moment as one marked by radical and growing instability, especially regarding the role of borders. Around the world, issues relating to the movement of peoples, the policing of immigrants and refugees, and the security of international boundaries have moved to the centre of increasingly bitter political divisions. Governments' handling of refugees has become a flashpoint for fractious debates about the security and collective moral conscience of wealthy nations in particular. In this corner of the world, US Americans and Canadians sometimes see their treatment of immigrants and refugees as constitutive of their national differences. For example, in late 2015, when US Republican presidential candidates openly debated the merits of refusing entry to Syrian orphan children based on security concerns, Canadian prime minister Justin Trudeau visited Toronto's Pearson International Airport and publicly greeted Syrian refugees to Canada. In this case, welcoming refugees represented a way for Canadians to present themselves as more enlightened and humane than Americans. Indeed, Canada has become a destination for immigrants and refugees who find the United States increasingly unwelcoming. Issues of refugees and immigration are closely intertwined in Canada and the United States today, but as this chapter will demonstrate, this interconnection is far from new.[1]

Our current era of human movement and political rancor should prompt Canadians and Americans to reflect with fresh eyes on the foundations of their own physical presence in these lands and the role of refugees in that story. In the case of western Canada, where the conference that produced these papers was held and where the press that published them is located, this would mean revisiting the treaties between Indigenous First Nations and Canadian officials that directly precipitated the settlement of western Canada. Canadians ratified eleven treaties between 1871 and 1921—known today as the "Numbered Treaties"—that transferred most of the Canadian interior out of Native hands. The first seven of the eleven Numbered Treaties all transpired in the decade of the 1870s, which was itself a time of heightened political instability and concern about border crossing. In large part, the treaties represented attempts by Canadian officials and Indigenous nations to wrest some measure of stability during an era of perceived disorder.

This chapter will argue that the presence of refugees played a central role in these treaties, especially Treaty 7, and was therefore a crucial factor in establishing settler society in western Canada. During the 1860s and 1870s, western Canada became a destination for thousands of Indigenous people displaced by America's so-called Indian Wars. To Canadian officials, the arrival of these refugees fuelled fears of international Indigenous alliances, cross-border raiding, ruinous resource depletion, and impeded settlement. As more Indigenous people fled north of the border seeking safety, the urgency of treaties grew exponentially. The Canadians who demanded and perpetrated the treaties saw them as both a necessary bulwark against potential refugee-caused disorder and a way to exclude Indigenous refugees from Canadian life. At the same time, displaced Indigenous people themselves made important contributions to treaties. On the northwest plains in particular, Native survivors who fled genocidal warfare in Montana had a crucial part in the negotiation and implementation of Treaty 7. Refugees were essential figures before, during, and after the Numbered Treaties.

Understanding this history requires expanding the frames we usually use to understand the history of treaties and Indigenous people. Typically, treaty making is approached as a distinctly national phenomenon, a key moment in the formation of Canada as a settler nation. Perhaps because of this national emphasis, the historiography of Canadian treaties rarely looks seriously at border politics.[2] Likewise, despite a number of pathbreaking studies that engage with Indigenous and settler histories across international borders, Indigenous people are still generally understood in national terms as residents of particular ancestral territories that mark them as "American Indians" or

"Aboriginal Canadians."[3] The notion of seeing Indigenous people (whose identity is generally defined by their connection to specific homelands) in the same terms as refugees (whose identity is defined by their lack of place) can therefore feel counterintuitive.[4] In order to understand the position of Indigenous refugees in the history of the Numbered Treaties, we need to recognize Indigenous people as transnational actors and the treaties themselves as transnational events.

To label Indigenous people as "refugees" is, of course, reflective of colonial worldviews. The word *refugees* was first coined by Europeans to describe religious exiles during the Reformation and today generally refers to any people who, out of fear for their safety, have left their home country to seek refuge elsewhere.[5] By definition, Indigenous claims far predate the imposition of nation-states and international borders, and Indigenous homelands continue to overlap and transcend these constructions. At the same time, Indigenous border crossing reflected an increasingly inescapable political reality for Indigenous people in the nineteenth century: international borders existed, and many Indigenous people deliberately sought to use them for their benefit. By the 1860s and 1870s, US and Canadian officials regularly labeled Indigenous people who crossed the forty-ninth parallel as "refugees."[6] Nevertheless, the scholarship of nineteenth-century Indigenous refugee studies remains fragmentary.[7] By seeking out new connections between Indigenous history, refugee history, and treaty history, we can unlock surprising and important new stories that reframe the origins of western Canada itself.

The Refugee "Threat" and Canadian Expansion

Prior to Confederation, the British North American colonies that would later become Canada established a long history of welcoming Indigenous refugees from south of the border. For example, following the American War of Independence, the colony of Upper Canada welcomed several thousand Haudenosaunee (Iroquois) refugees led by the Mohawk chief Thayendanegea, or Joseph Brant, who fled north after his British allies surrendered to American separatists in 1783. Haudenosaunee people established thriving homelands north of the border, and many fought as British allies when the United States and Great Britain again went to war in 1812.[8] A similar process unfolded in 1862, when between one thousand and two thousand Dakota people escaped persecution in Minnesota by fleeing north into what later became Manitoba.

These Dakota refugees, who asserted traditional territorial claims north of the border and called on previous generations' military alliances with the British, established peaceful communities and built working relationships with settlers partly by incorporating themselves into the region's agricultural wage labour economy. Although the Dakota refugees were never afforded treaty relationships, they successfully lobbied British officials for several small reserves that exist to this day.[9]

Beginning with Confederation, Canadians adopted a more aggressive approach to dominating Indigenous lands and peoples, which would soon lead them to see the issue of refugees differently. In 1867, the distinct British colonies of Upper and Lower Canada (which became Ontario and Quebec), New Brunswick, and Nova Scotia united as the Dominion of Canada. They quickly added to their territorial claims by incorporating Manitoba in 1870, British Columbia in 1871, and Prince Edward Island in 1873. In 1870, the dominion acquired the charter to Rupert's Land—the drainage of Hudson Bay that encompassed most of what is now Alberta, Saskatchewan, and Manitoba—from the Hudson's Bay Company. Canada remained a small and uncertain country despite these vast territorial claims, with a settler population of just 3.2 million, less than a tenth of that south of the border. Yet Canadian leaders imagined a similar future to the Americans'. To fortify their claims, they conceived of a widespread program of Indigenous dispossession through treaties and the establishment of "reserve" lands. With reserves would come political subjugation and forced assimilation partially modelled on that of the United States.[10]

Canada's nascent political leadership, including many of those today known as the "Fathers of Confederation," worried openly about their lack of control over their expansive western territories. When Canadian officials added British Columbia to the dominion in 1871, they included an explicit promise that they would begin building a transcontinental railway linking British Columbia to the eastern provinces within two years and would complete it within ten. The proposed railway would need to pass through the territories of Indigenous nations that had yet to sign treaties with the government, and officials therefore needed to remove them or secure their permission to operate in their territories. Once they could confine and control Native people, officials imagined that the railway would bring farmers and other settlers onto the prairies, thus expanding the dominion and securing Canada's claim to the region against potential American interference. The process seemed orderly in theory, and boosters explicitly touted the relative peacefulness of settlement in the Canadian West compared with that of the United States in order to attract settlers. From the perspective of Canadian expansionists, dispossessing and controlling Native people through treaties formed the essential first step toward building railroads, facilitating settlement, and strengthening the nation.[11]

As Canadians embarked on their project of continental expansion, events in the United States threatened to undermine it. Between the 1840s and the 1870s, the United States expanded rapidly into the lands west of the Mississippi River, where officials sought to systematically extinguish Native titles and restrict Indigenous people to reservations. This invasion led to a series of bitter and catastrophic conflicts throughout the West known as the "Indian Wars," which only grew in intensity once Americans settled their own Civil War in 1865.[12] The most long-lasting and iconic of these conflicts pitted the US Army against the Dakota people's plains kin, the Lakota Sioux. The largest and most powerful Indigenous nation on the North American plains, the Lakota had established an expansive homeland across what is now Nebraska, South Dakota, Wyoming, and Montana after migrating from midwestern woodlands a century earlier. The Lakota had weathered multiple conflicts with US soldiers and settlers beginning in the 1850s, and in 1868 they forced US officials to grant them an enormous reservation comprising much of what is now South Dakota. When Americans abrogated this agreement by invading the Black Hills in 1874, the Lakota were again pulled into war, this time under the leadership of a holy man named Sitting Bull, who notched an astonishing victory by annihilating the US Army's Seventh Cavalry at the Battle of Little Bighorn on June 25, 1876. Aware that the victory would lead to a greater mobilization of US troops and that the Lakota were already losing access to bison herds and trade goods, Sitting Bull chose to lead his people north. In the late summer and fall of 1876, Sitting Bull and his followers escaped across the border, and within months, around three thousand Lakota refugees streamed into lands claimed by Canada.[13]

The following year, the Nez Perce people of what is now Idaho likewise looked to Canada to escape US soldiers. The Nez Perces' conflict with the United States began in 1860, when the discovery of gold led to a mass invasion of prospectors and settlers into their homelands. Over time, the Nez Perce people became divided between those who chose to settle on government-imposed reservation lands and others who rejected confinement. After the

Lakota victory at Little Bighorn in 1876, US Army officials and Indian agents placed greater pressure on the Nez Perces to restrict themselves to the reservations. By June 1877, these tensions exploded into a war between US soldiers and warriors from the nontreaty faction led by a Nez Perce chief named Joseph. During the summer of 1877, Chief Joseph and his eight hundred followers led US soldiers on an epic chase through Idaho, Wyoming, and Montana. In September 1877, after realizing that they would not receive protection from the Crows of southern Montana as they had hoped, the Nez Perces set their sights northward in hopes that they could find refuge in Canada alongside Sitting Bull's Lakota.[14]

The arrival of thousands of Indigenous refugees into Canada in 1876 and 1877 unnerved Canadian expansionists. Although officials allowed Native refugees to remain in Canada, settlers and government officials alike looked at them with enormous concern.[15] First and foremost, Canadians worried about the possibility of military alliances between Indigenous nations already present in Canada and the refugees from the United States. Government officials had imagined this scenario as early as 1857, when the Canadian geographer Henry Youle Hind used his seminal report on the western prairies to warn that disaffected Native people from the United States could join with Indigenous groups north of the border to oppose future settlement on the prairies.[16] In 1876, Alexander Morris, the governor of Canada's Northwest Territories, worried that Indigenous people already in Canada would inevitably feel sympathy for the Lakota, and he urged his superiors to send larger military forces west.[17] These concerns became widespread among the broader public in 1876 and 1877. For example, when the Nez Perces neared the Canadian border in September 1877, the Toronto *Globe* breathlessly speculated that the "northern tribes [were] ready for revolt" and that they would surely join together in an antiwhite alliance if possible.[18] The *Manitoba Free Press* likewise circulated reports that Sitting Bull would soon rally the Nez Perces and northern Indigenous peoples like the Blackfoot to his cause, warning darkly that "the consequences" would be "fearful to contemplate."[19]

Canadians also fretted about the possibility of refugees using Canada as a base for launching raids into the United States. In the spring of 1876, editors at the *Globe* warned that if the Lakota were to cross into Canada, it would be "used by them as a place of secure retreat, from which, at convenient seasons, to harass United States troops or settlers."[20] These worries persisted well after the Lakota arrived in Canada that summer. For example, as news of the Nez

Perce conflict circulated in Canada during the summer of 1877, editors at the *Manitoba Herald* predicted that Sitting Bull would see the news and feel inspired to "go again upon the war-path" south of the border.[21] Again, public anxieties paralleled those that Canadian government officials expressed in their own correspondence. Federal officials instructed North West Mounted Police (NWMP) officers to impress upon Sitting Bull and his Lakota followers "the necessity of keeping the peace towards the people of the United States." Allowing Canada to become a launching point for raids into the United States, they worried, would damage relations with their more powerful neighbour beyond repair. It could even give US soldiers an excuse to cross the border and violate Canadian sovereignty.[22]

Canadians likewise worried that an influx of refugees would lead to dangerous overcompetition among Native people for scarce resources. During the 1860s and 1870s, populations of bison had declined disastrously across the Great Plains. The advent of more effective guns, the destruction of winter forage in river valleys, and the growing demand for leather bison hides for use in manufacturing rapidly accelerated the long downward trend in bison populations during the 1870s.[23] The Canadian prairies still hosted resilient herds—among the last of their kind on the continent—but the arrival of thousands of refugee hunters could put new pressure on the bison and instigate clashes between Native nations. The Blackfoot people of what is now southern Alberta stood to lose the most by the arrival of competing hunters. By 1875, Blackfoot leaders were already lamenting to visitors that white, Métis, and First Nations bison hunters had begun to invade their lands from other parts of Canada. Indigenous refugees from the south could push this crisis to its breaking point. The *Globe* noted that the greatest danger from a potential Lakota migration into Canada would not be from their attacking settlers but from killing bison and thus instigating a catastrophic intertribal war.[24] Government officials like Morris worried that a rapid collapse of bison populations would force Canadians to act quickly to prevent a famine, for which the fledgling government had little preparation.[25] Although Canadians planned eventually to replace bison ranges with cattle ranches and farms, they feared a crisis in the short term.

Lastly, the presence of refugees raised fears about Canadians' ability to guard the region against US incursions. Though largely forgotten today, US invasion and even annexation were persistent topics of conversation in both countries throughout the nineteenth century. Those concerns ratcheted up after the US Civil War ended and there was no longer a political need for Americans to balance the power of slave and free states. US politicians' open (though ultimately toothless) musings about annexation helped motivate Canadian leaders like Sir John A. MacDonald, Canada's first prime minister, to push for Confederation and the purchase of Rupert's Land.[26] By the 1870s, annexationist conversations centred on the sparsely settled Canadian West, where, during the Métis Resistance of 1870, a cadre of US Senators openly advocated for adding parts of Manitoba to the United States. US commentators blamed outdated British institutions like the Hudson's Bay Company for the Canadians' perceived failure to control and colonize the prairies.[27] Indeed, the United States had a history of using weak colonialization as an excuse for aggression toward their neighbours: in its conquest of northern Mexico between 1846 and 1848, the United States claimed that widespread Comanche and Apache raids had rendered Mexico a failed state with no real claim to its northern frontiers. Could the Americans use the same justification to pursue refugees or even lay claim to western Canada? Even if formal annexation was unlikely, US officials could conceivably use perceived Canadian weakness as an excuse to send soldiers north across the border. Canadians' approach to refugees and treaties should therefore be seen as part of an ongoing strategy to project strength and guard against the existential threat of US interference.[28]

Canadians had many worries about refugees, and beginning in the summer of 1876, they saw reason to believe that some of their fears had already come to fruition. In May, at least a month prior to the Battle of Little Bighorn, Canadian officials learned that Sitting Bull himself sent tobacco to a powerful Blackfoot chief named Crowfoot, who reported to a visiting police official that the gift came with an invitation to form an alliance. According to Crowfoot, the Lakota messenger told him that if the Blackfoot would join the Lakota in their war against enemy nations like the Crows and the United States, the Lakota would provide horses, mules, and human captives to the Blackfoot, and after the war was won, the Lakota would join the Blackfoot in a war against white Canadians north of the border. Crowfoot rejected the invitation, which he said infuriated the Lakota leader.[29] Canadian officials believed in Blackfoot people's good faith desire for a treaty, but the news planted seeds of doubt in some minds. Editors of the Toronto *Globe* intoned that Canada owed Crowfoot and the Blackfoot people its "appreciation" as well as its help in defending against Lakota reprisals. By enveloping the Blackfoot with "protection" and goodwill, Canadians believed they could stifle the refugees' ability to build lasting relationships in the north, thus securing Canadian preeminence.[30]

While Canadian officials and settlers took some comfort in Crowfoot's initial refusal of Sitting Bull's entreaties in 1876, they saw more reason to worry by the following summer. When the snows melted and spring bison hunts began in 1877, the Blackfoot and the Lakota reopened communication. Sitting Bull and his followers had encamped around the Cypress Hills, near what is now the Alberta-Saskatchewan border, just as Crowfoot led his own people near the hills to hunt. When Sitting Bull learned of his Blackfoot counterpart's approach, he once again dispatched an emissary with tobacco before taking it upon himself to lead a peace delegation to Crowfoot's camp. Unburdening themselves of the previous year's acrimony, the two chiefs shook hands and smoked together, and the combined camp held a friendship dance before the Lakota left the next day. (In a testament to their mutual esteem, Sitting Bull later named one of his own children after Crowfoot.)[31] Their newfound friendship included no agreement regarding a military alliance, but it alarmed whites nonetheless. Canadian newspapers reprinted a report from a Montana newspaper that Sitting Bull had successfully rallied the Native people of western Canada to his cause. Meanwhile, Canadians continued to follow closely the news of Nez Perce refugees fighting their way through Montana on their way to join Sitting Bull north of the border.[32] From the Canadian perspective, forces had begun to align against their carefully laid plans.

Apprehensions about Lakota and Nez Perce refugees and their potential inroads among Indigenous peoples north of the border provide crucial context for understanding treaty making. Canadian officials felt great urgency to make a treaty with the nations that might come into frequent contact with the refugees, especially the Blackfoot, Stoney Nakoda, and Tsuut'ina nations of what is now southern Alberta. Forming treaty relationships would prevent cross-border alliances and would send a clear message to the refugees that they would not receive support from other Indigenous nations, nor would they be granted reserves or assistance themselves. When the Lakota migration into Canada began in the summer of 1876, Canadian officials immediately began discussing the urgent need for treaties that would bind "Canadian" Indigenous nations to the federal government. Historian Sheila Robert has revealed extensive communication between concerned leaders. For instance, on July 11, 1876, Governor Alexander Morris lamented to the Canadian secretary of state that the Lakota entreaties to the Blackfoot had made a timely treaty council essential and urged that a treaty council date be set for the following year. Morris noted ominously that the Battle of Little Bighorn had taken place only 180 miles from the Canadian border (a mild exaggeration) and that violence could easily spread northward without preventive action. Another letter, by an unnamed Department of Interior official later that month, made the case more bluntly. "The Blackfeet and the Indians on the Boundary should be treated with as early as possible so as to secure their friendship," it stated, in "the event of the American Sioux and other Indians being driven into or taking refuge in our territory." The spectre of refugees and the many complications that came with them lent urgency to treaty making.[33]

Indigenous people likewise used the presence of refugees to speed the clock toward a treaty. Blackfoot leaders in particular had already been formally lobbying Canadian officials for a treaty prior to the Lakota arrival, having concluded that a formal agreement represented their only option for preventing incursions into their hunting territories. In 1875, a council of chiefs led by Crowfoot dictated a petition formally requesting a treaty council, but by the summer of 1876, their Canadian counterparts had yet to make firm arrangements. Sitting Bull's gift of tobacco therefore represented an opportunity for the Blackfoot to pressure the Canadians for a treaty, and they wasted little time reporting it to NWMP officials. Blackfoot leaders may have also deliberately emphasized or exaggerated the salacious details of the invitation—which Canadians said included the promise of "white women"—to curry favour and build goodwill with the Canadians. In response, officials told Crowfoot that Queen Victoria herself was pleased with his rejection of the Lakota. At the same time, Crowfoot's conversations with Canadian visitors may have carried an implied threat: if a treaty were *not* to happen, the Blackfoot would need to act in their own interests, either by going to war with other nations or even by taking the Lakota up on their offer of an alliance.[34]

Hastened by the perceived threat of refugees, the Treaty 7 council began on September 19, 1877. More than six thousand Blackfoot, Tsuut'ina, and Stoney Nakoda people (along with some Cree representatives who came to sign an adhesion to Treaty 6) gathered at the Bow River to meet with Canadian officials and mounted policemen. No refugee nations were included in the treaty negotiations. The treaty council proceeded swiftly despite Indigenous complaints about the lack of qualified translators (which justifiably persist to the present day). By September 22, just three days after the council commenced, representatives from all the assembled nations signed a treaty that reduced

Indigenous territories to several reserves and thus opened southern Alberta to widespread settlement. As Treaty 7 elders, Sarah Carter, Walter Hildebrandt, and Dorothy First Rider have argued, commissioners' fears about the potential threat of refugee nations may have led them to ignore urgent concerns about the poor translation and fast pace of negotiations. Indeed, the treaty concluded just as the Nez Perces were racing toward the Canadian border, though most would fall tragically short of their goal when US soldiers caught up to them at the Battle of Bear Paw eight days later. The commissioners' anxiety about these refugees, coupled with their zeal for rapid settlement by the new Canadian nation, pushed them to complete a treaty at all costs, with consequences that echo into the present.[35]

Border Crossers in the Treaty Process

Concerns about the impact of Indigenous refugees motivated the treaty process, but to what extent did refugees themselves participate in the negotiation of the treaties? The Canadian government explicitly excluded Dakota, Lakota, and Nez Perce people from treaty negotiations and denied treaty relationships to refugee nations. Nonetheless, framing the treaties simply as excluding American Indigenous refugees and including Indigenous people already present in Canada might obscure important histories of Indigenous exiles, especially with reference to Treaty 7. In fact, many of the Blackfoot people who signed Treaty 7 could themselves be understood as exiles, or even refugees in part, who had fled violence in their American homelands for safety in Canada.

Blackfoot people, like the Lakota and Nez Perces, faced brutal violence south of the US-Canada border during the Indian Wars era. Historically, three nations have together known themselves as Blackfoot: the Kainai, Siksika, and Piikani. Blackfoot territory traditionally spanned from the North Saskatchewan River in the north, south to the Missouri River, and from the base of the Rocky Mountains several hundred miles onto the prairies, which meant that about a third of their homelands lay within the United States. Few if any Blackfoot people lived entirely in the United States, and many Blackfoot people travelled frequently back and forth across the forty-ninth parallel as they had for countless generations before. However, many Blackfoot people spent most of their time south of the border, particularly among the Piikanis, and Montana was the site of ancient winter camps and many essential religious sites.[36] These southern Blackfoot homelands became the site of vicious conflicts with Montana settlers who poured into the region following prospectors' discovery of gold on the Missouri River headwaters in 1862. Small-scale conflicts proliferated throughout Montana territory during the late 1860s as settlers accosted and sometimes murdered Blackfoot people and Blackfoot people raided settlements in turn. These conflicts culminated in January 1870, when US soldiers massacred nearly an entire band of Piikani people on the Marias River (known to the Blackfoot as the Bear River) about forty miles south of the international border.[37]

The conflicts in Montana led many Blackfoot people to seek permanent refuge on the Canadian side of the border. During the 1860s, British fur traders at Edmonton and Rocky Mountain House happily noted that many Blackfoot people began to avoid Montana entirely due to the violence. This flow increased after the 1870 Marias Massacre, when the Piikani people grew desperate to avoid further violence from the Americans. According to witnesses, many survivors of the massacre immediately fled north and trekked up to a hundred miles in subzero temperatures to escape the United States, even though the soldiers stole all their horses. More Piikanis from other bands followed, fearful of attacks on their own communities. They spent the winter following the massacre in the Belly River valley (in and near present-day Lethbridge) and then moved to the Cypress Hills for the summer bison hunts. These Blackfoot survivors were not "refugees" insofar as they were never entirely dislodged from ancestral territories, but they were nonetheless exiled from much of their core homeland and forced to seek safety in the north. They therefore had much in common with the Dakota, Lakota, and Nez Perce people who so preoccupied Canadian officials during the same era. (Dakota and Lakota people likewise claim ancestral lands in Canada, but their communities generally resided in the United States.) Many Blackfoot people never returned south of the border, choosing instead to take their chances with the Canadians.[38]

Displaced Blackfoot people played a significant role in the leadup to Treaty 7 as well as in the treaty negotiations themselves. Although firsthand sources are scarce, we can assume that some Blackfoot people's unique knowledge and experience from south of the border was valued in conversations within the Blackfoot community prior to the 1877 treaty council. The Blackfoot people who had spent significant time in Montana had far more firsthand experience in dealing with settlers and government representatives than those in Canada. In contrast to south of the border, the settler invasion of Alberta had just begun. Fur trade companies had established isolated outposts in the region as early as 1792, but government officials and law enforcement agents had only established a permanent presence north of the border in 1874.[39] As transnational people, the Blackfoot had already experienced a mass invasion of settlers south of the international border, which could provide invaluable perspectives in the north. Those experiences undoubtedly carried warnings about how voracious the settlers' desire for land and resources could be.

Blackfoot people who had fled Montana provided warnings about the potential flimsiness of government treaties. Representatives of all three Blackfoot nations signed a treaty with the United States in 1855 that the government had violated repeatedly by neglecting to deliver promised annuity goods. Moreover, their subsequent attempts to update the treaty in 1865 and 1868 had been rejected by the US Senate even after both the Blackfoot and US treaty commissioners had signed. The voices of the Blackfoot people who left Montana are often obscured in archival sources, but documents yield some occasional glimpses. In 1871, the year after the Marias Massacre, a close associate of the Piikanis named Jean L'Heaureux noted that the Piikanis in Canada "dread[ed] troops and any conference business, since the treachery of the American government officials towards them." Several chiefs who had signed the 1855 treaty with the United States attended the 1877 council with the Canadians, including the Kainai war chief Medicine Calf, who openly challenged the Canadian commissioners by sharing his memory that the Americans were generous with annuity goods at first but became more parsimonious over time. In a carefully crafted speech early in the council, he urged his fellow chiefs to insist that the Canadians pay for the timber that mounted police had already used and that the treaty include permanent yearly compensation for all Blackfoot people. Although Medicine Calf's demands were only partially realized, he provided a hard-earned perspective from south of the border.[40]

As Medicine Calf knew, history and experience carried hard lessons that spanned international borders. The perspectives of these treaty signers are difficult to access in the archival record, but historians should not ignore the lived linkages between American and Canadian treaties. These Indigenous border crossers surely played an important but little-understood role in negotiating Treaty 7.

Conclusion

Indigenous refugees had a crucial part in the conception and negotiation of the Numbered Treaties in Canada. The presence of refugees from America's Indian Wars—and the possibility of more to come—was one of the major motivations for Canadian officials to organize treaties and to finish them quickly. In the case of Treaty 7, Indigenous people likewise used anxieties about Indigenous border crossing to advocate for a treaty themselves. Although most refugees were excluded from treaties, in some cases Indigenous border crossers contributed to the negotiation of treaties by bringing their experience from the United States to their dealings in Canada. In each case, Indigenous people used the border in savvy and creative ways to advance their own interests. While US and Canadian officials saw the border as a dangerous and inconvenient impediment to their ambitions, Indigenous people recognized that they could use the border to their advantage by escaping persecution, sharing crucial knowledge, or gaining political leverage. The border and the Indigenous people who crossed it were central to the era of the Numbered Treaties.

In a broader sense, the history of Indigenous refugees in Canada should be a reminder of the importance of transnational perspectives in North American history. Like so many other historical events, treaties do not happen in isolation and cannot be understood in purely national terms. They are events with a wide array of causes and effects that span international borders. The history of Canadian treaties therefore cannot be understood fully in isolation from events in the United States and vice versa. The histories of these settler nations were deeply intertwined then, and they remain so today.

Notes

1. Gregory Krieg, "Christie on Refugees: Not Even 5-Year-Old Orphans"; Agence France-Presse, "Justin Trudeau Shows Up at Airport to Welcome Canada's First Syrian Refugees"; Jake Halpern, "The Underground Railroad for Refugees."
2. While there are many excellent studies of the Numbered Treaties, few engage extensively with the role of border politics. See, for example, J. R. Miller, *Compact, Contract, Covenant: Aboriginal Treaty-Making in Canada*; and D. J. Hall, *From Treaties to Reserves: The Federal Government and Native Peoples in*

Territorial Alberta, 1870–1905. Jill St. Germain's works utilize a comparative rather than a connective framework for US and Canadian treaties. Jill St. Germain, *Indian Treaty-Making Policy in the United States and Canada, 1867–1877*; Jill St. Germain, *Broken Treaties: United States and Canadian Relations with the Lakotas and the Plains Cree, 1868–1885*.

3. Key regional cross-border studies include Sheila McManus, *The Line Which Separates: Race, Gender, and the Making of the Alberta-Montana Borderlands*; Ryan Hall, *Beneath the Backbone of the World: Blackfoot People and the North American Borderlands, 1720–1877*; Michel Hogue, *Metis and the Medicine Line: Creating a Border and Dividing a People*; David G. McCrady, *Living with Strangers: The Nineteenth-Century Sioux and the Canadian-American Borderlands*; Beth LaDow, *The Medicine Line: Life and Death on a North American Borderland*; and Benjamin Hoy, *A Line of Blood and Dirt: Creating the Canada-United States Border Across Indigenous Lands*.

4. For contested definitions of indigeneity, see United Nations Department of Economic and Social Affairs, *State of the World's Indigenous Peoples*, 4–7. For a current working definition of *refugee*, see Bruce Burson and David James Cantor, "Introduction: Interpreting the Refugee Definition via Human Rights Standards," 1–24.

5. For the origin of the word *refugee*, see Maximilian Miguel Scholz, "Religious Refugees and the Search for Public Worship in Frankfurt am Main, 1554–1608," 765.

6. For examples, see George Wright to Thomas Meagher, April 16, 1867, Records of the Montana Superintendency of Indian Affairs, RG 75, Records of the Bureau of Indian Affairs, M833, National Archives Microfilm Publications, roll 1, p. 2; and J. Norquay to Alexander Morris, January 8, 1873, in Dominion of Canada, *Sessional Papers of the Dominion of Canada: Volume 5, First Session of the Second Parliament, Session 1873*, 14.

7. For works that frame Indigenous histories as refugee studies, see Brenden Rensink, *Native but Foreign: Indigenous Immigrants and Refugees in the North American Borderlands*; Jerome Green, *Beyond Bear's Paw: The Nez Perce Indians in Canada*; Jeff Guinn, *Our Land Before We Die: The Proud Story of the Seminole Negro*; Evan Taparata, "'Refugees as You Call Them': The Politics of Refugee Recognition in the Nineteenth-Century United States," 9–35; and Paul Conrad, *The Apache Diaspora: Four Centuries of Displacement and Survival*.

8. Bothwell, *Your Country, My Country*, 51–56; Alan Taylor, *The Divided Ground: Indians, Settlers, and the Northern Borderland of the American Revolution*, 77–407.

9. McCrady, *Living with Strangers*, 17–30; Benjamin Hoy, "A Border without Guards: First Nations and the Enforcement of National Space," 92–93; David

Mills, Report of Minister of Interior, December 31, 1877, in *Annual Report of the Department of the Interior for the Year Ended 30th June, 1877*, xvii–xviii; Alexander Morris, *The Treaties of Canada with the Indians of Manitoba and the North-West Territories; Including the Negotiations on Which They Were Based, and Other Information*, 12, 276–84. Dakota people maintain that their ancestral homelands extended into what became Canada. Leo J. Omani, "A Written Response from Canada," 283–84.

10. Robert Bothwell, *Your Country, My Country: A Unified History of the United States and Canada*, 117–18; St. Germain, *Broken Treaties*, 14–26. For a summary of Canadian settler colonialism and assimilationism, see Truth and Reconciliation Commission of Canada, *Honouring the Truth, Reconciling for the Future: Summary of the Final Report of the Truth and Reconciliation Commission of Canada*, 37–134.

11. Miller, *Compact, Contract, Covenant*, 148–49, 156; Sheila Robert, "The Negotiation and Implementation of Treaty 7," 47–48; McManus, *Line Which Separates*, 60–76; "Notes on the North-West."

12. For the Indian Wars, see Roxanne Dunbar-Ortiz, *An Indigenous Peoples' History of the United States*, 133–61; Robert V. Hine, John Mack Faragher, and Jon T. Coleman, *The American West: A New Interpretive History*, 2nd ed., 177–222; and Robert Utley, *The Indian Frontier of the American West, 1846–1890*, 65–196.

13. McCrady, *Living with Strangers*, 61–85; Pekka Hämäläinen. *Lakota America: A New History of Indigenous Power*, 337–79; Robert Utley, *The Lance and the Shield: The Life and Times of Sitting Bull*, 106–210. In accordance with Lakota language, this chapter uses Lakota in both the singular and plural forms.

14. Elliott West, *The Last Indian War: The Nez Perce Story*, 123–314; Treaty 7 Elders and Tribal Council with Sarah Carter, Walter Hildebrandt, and Dorothy First Rider, *The True Spirit and Original Intent of Treaty 7*, 226–28.

15. Canadian officials chose to grant refugees sanctuary but did not provide treaties or support for fear of inflaming Indigenous or US resentments. See Joseph Manzione, *"I Am Looking to the North for My Life": Sitting Bull, 1876–1881*, 51–52; and Hoy, "Border without Guards," 93–94.

16. Arthur Ray, J. R. Miller, and Frank Tough, *Bounty and Benevolence: A History of Saskatchewan Treaties*, 96–104.

17. Robert, "Negotiation and Implementation of Treaty 7," 44–45.

18. "The U.S. Indians."

19. "Storm in the North-West," *Manitoba Free Press*.

20. "The Sioux Question."

21. "Indian and Mexican Troubles."

22. Quote from Canada Department of the Interior, *Annual Report of the Department of the Interior for the Year Ended 30th June, 1877*, xviii; St. Germain, *Indian Treaty-Making Policy*, 45.

23. Andrew Isenberg, *The Destruction of the Bison: An Environmental History, 1750–1920*, 93–122; Elliott West, *The Way to the West: Essays on the Central Plains*, 51–79; William Dobak, "Killing the Canadian Buffalo," 33–52.

24. Treaty 7 Elders et al., *True Spirit*, 276–77; "The Indians of the North-West"; "The Land of the Blackfeet"; "Sitting Bull"; John Taylor, "Two Views on the Meaning of Treaties Six and Seven," 26; Utley, *Lance and the Shield*, 191.

25. Morris, *Treaties of Canada*, 283–84.

26. For an overview of annexation debates, which have been underexamined by historians in recent years, see Donald F. Warner, *The Idea of Continental Union: Agitation for the Annexation of Canada to the United States, 1849–1893*; and Bothwell, *Your Country, My Country*, 116–21. The cross-border raids of the pro-Irish Fenian Brotherhood between 1866 and 1871 added to these concerns.

27. Warner, *Idea of Continental Union*, 107–25; James G. Snell, "The Frontier Sweeps Northwest: American Perceptions of the British American Prairie West at the Point of Canadian Expansion (circa 1870)," 381–400; Paul Sharp, *Whoop-Up Country: The Canadian-American West, 1865–1885*, 292–312.

28. Brian DeLay, *War of a Thousand Deserts: Indian Raids and the U.S.-Mexican War*, 226–96; St. Germain, *Indian Treaty-Making Policy*, 45; Hall, *From Treaties to Reserves*, 41.

29. Frederick White to R. W. Scott, December 30, 1876, in Dominion of Canada, *Sessional Papers of the Dominion of Canada: Volume 7, Fourth Session of the Third Parliament, Session 1877*, 21–24.

30. "The Noble Savage."

31. Hugh Dempsey, *Crowfoot: Chief of the Blackfeet*, 91–92; Utley, *Lance and the Shield*, 201–2.

32. "The Storm in the North-West," *Manitoba Free Press* (Winnipeg), September 15, 1877; "The Storm in the North-West," *Globe* (Toronto), September 4, 1877.

33. Robert, "Negotiation and Implementation of Treaty 7," 44–47. See also St. Germain, *Indian Treaty-Making Policy*, 44–45.

34. Treaty 7 Elders et al., *True Spirit*, 276–77; White to Scott, December 30, 1876, in *Sessional Papers 1877*, 21–24.

35. Treaty 7 Elders et al., *True Spirit*, 228–29. For more on translation problems, see Frank Oliver, "The Blackfeet Indian Treaty," 28; Ben Calf Robe, *Siksiká: A Blackfoot Legacy*, 21; White Headed Chief (Spumiapi) interview by Jane Richardson, September 2, 1938, series 1, p. 114, Jane and Lucien Hanks Fonds, M-8458-6, Glenbow Museum Archives, Calgary, Alberta, Canada; Treaty 7

Elders et al., *True Spirit*, 69–77, 143–44; Jack Crow interview by Albert Yellowhorn, January 1, 1973, Indian History Film Project, Canadian Plains Research Center, University of Regina (IHFP), http://hdl.handle.net/10294/508; Useless Good Runner interview by Dila Provost and Albert Yellowhorn, ca. 1973, IHFP, http://hdl.handle.net/10294/546; and Mrs. Buffalo interview by Johnny Smith, March 12, 1975, IHFP, http://hdl.handle.net/10294/504.

36. Hall, *Beneath the Backbone*, 13–36, 144–71; Rosalyn LaPier, *Invisible Reality: Storytellers, Storytakers, and the Supernatural World of the Blackfeet*, 91–145; McManus, *Line Which Separates*, 57–82.

37. Andrew Graybill, *The Red and the White: A Family Saga of the American West*, 54–104; Blanca Tovías, "Diplomacy and Contestation Before and After the 1870 Massacre of Amskapi Pikuni," 269–93. I use the term "Marias Massacre" to differentiate from the US Army's 1863 Bear River Massacre of Shoshone people.

38. Hugh Dempsey, *The Great Blackfoot Treaties*, 66; C. Imoda to Alfred Sully, April 11, 1870, Records of the Montana Superintendency of Indian Affairs, RG 75, Records of the Bureau of Indian Affairs, M833, National Archives Microfilm Publications, roll 2, p. 1; Alexander Culbertson, "Regarding the Alleged Massacre of Piegan Indians by Col. Baker," June 20, 1870, Records of the Montana Superintendency of Indian Affairs, RG 75, Records of the Bureau of Indian Affairs, M833, National Archives Microfilm Publications, roll 2, pp. 4–5; Culbertson, "Journey from the Marias River to the Bow River, Canada, July–August, 1870," Alexander Culbertson Papers, SC 586, Montana Historical Society, Helena, Montana, pp. 8–10; Johnny Healy, *Life and Death on the Upper Missouri: The Frontier Sketches of Johnny Healy*, 227; "Personal."

39. For state expansion in Alberta, see McManus, *Line Which Separates*, 57–82; Hogue, *Metis and the Medicine Line*, 73–99; and Hall, *Beneath the Backbone*, 47, 172–80.

40. Dempsey, *Crowfoot*, 99–100; Jean L'Heureux to J. W. Christie, 1871, Richard C. Hardisty Fonds, M-5902, Glenbow Museum Archives, Calgary, Alberta, Canada, p. 3; Hall, *Beneath the Backbone*, 119–43; McCrady, *Living with Strangers*, 107–8; Morris, *Treaties of Canada*, 270.

Bibliography

Primary Sources

Agence France-Presse. "Justin Trudeau Shows Up at Airport to Welcome Canada's First Syrian Refugees." Public Radio International, December 11, 2015. https://theworld.org/stories/2016/07/30/justin-trudeau-shows-airport-welcome-canadas-first-syrian-refugees.

Canada Department of the Interior. *Annual Report of the Department of the Interior for the Year Ended 30th June, 1877*. Ottawa: Maclean, Roger & Company, 1878.

Dominion of Canada. *Sessional Papers of the Dominion of Canada: Volume 5, First Session of the Second Parliament, Session 1873*. Ottawa: I. B. Taylor, 1873.

Dominion of Canada. *Sessional Papers of the Dominion of Canada: Volume 7, Fourth Session of the Third Parliament, Session 1877*. Ottawa: Maclean, Roger & Company, 1877.

Halpern, Jake. "The Underground Railroad for Refugees." *New Yorker*, March 5, 2017. https://www.newyorker.com/magazine/2017/03/13/the-underground -railroad-for-refugees.

Healy, Johnny. *Life and Death on the Upper Missouri: The Frontier Sketches of Johnny Healy*. Edited by Ken Robison. Self-published, CreateSpace, 2013.

"Indian and Mexican Troubles." *Manitoba Herald* (Winnipeg), July 23, 1877.

Indian History Film Project. Canadian Plains Research Center, University of Regina, Saskatchewan, Canada.

"The Indians of the North-West." *Globe* (Toronto), April 1, 1875.

Krieg, Gregory. "Christie on Refugees: Not Even 5-Year-Old Orphans." CNN, November 17, 2015. https://www.cnn.com/2015/11/17/politics/chris-christie-paris -attacks-refugee-orphans/index.html.

"The Land of the Blackfeet." *Globe* (Toronto), May 24, 1877.

Morris, Alexander. *The Treaties of Canada with the Indians of Manitoba and the North-West Territories; Including the Negotiations on Which They Were Based, and Other Information*. Toronto: Belfords, Clarke & Company, 1880.

"The Noble Savage." *Globe* (Toronto), September 25, 1876.

"Notes on the North-West." *Manitoba Free Press* (Winnipeg), November 4, 1876.

Oliver, Frank. "The Blackfeet Indian Treaty." *Maclean's Magazine*, March 15, 1931.

"Personal." *New Nation* (Winnipeg), May 17, 1870.

"The Sioux Question." *Globe* (Toronto), April 22, 1876.

"Sitting Bull." *Globe* (Toronto), August 5, 1877.

"The Storm in the North-West." *Globe* (Toronto), September 4, 1877.

"The Storm in the North-West." *Manitoba Free Press* (Winnipeg), September 15, 1877.

United Nations Department of Economic and Social Affairs. *State of the World's Indigenous Peoples*. New York: United Nations, 2009.

"The U.S. Indians." *Globe* (Toronto), September 25, 1877.

Secondary Sources

Bothwell, Robert. *Your Country, My Country: A Unified History of the United States and Canada*. New York: Oxford University Press, 2015.

Burson, Bruce, and David James Cantor. "Introduction: Interpreting the
Refugee Definition via Human Rights Standards." In *Human Rights and
the Refugee Definition: Comparative Legal Practice and Theory*, edited by Bruce
Burson and David James Cantor, 1–24. Boston: Brill Nijhoff, 2016.

Calf Robe, Ben. *Siksiká: A Blackfoot Legacy*. Invermere, BC: Good Medicine Books,
1979.

Conrad, Paul. *The Apache Diaspora: Four Centuries of Displacement and Survival*.
Philadelphia: University of Pennsylvania Press, 2021.

DeLay, Brian. *War of a Thousand Deserts: Indian Raids and the U.S.-Mexican War*.
New Haven, CT: Yale University Press, 2008.

Dempsey, Hugh. *Crowfoot: Chief of the Blackfeet*. Norman: University of Oklahoma
Press, 1972.

Dempsey, Hugh. *The Great Blackfoot Treaties*. Victoria, BC: Heritage House, 2015.

Dobak, William. "Killing the Canadian Buffalo." *Western Historical Quarterly* 27,
no. 1 (April 1, 1996): 33–52.

Dunbar-Ortiz, Roxanne. *An Indigenous Peoples' History of the United States*. Boston:
Beacon Press, 2014.

Graybill, Andrew. *The Red and the White: A Family Saga of the American West*.
New York: W. W. Norton, 2013.

Green, Jerome. *Beyond Bear's Paw: The Nez Perce Indians in Canada*. Norman:
University of Oklahoma Press, 2010.

Guinn, Jeff. *Our Land Before We Die: The Proud Story of the Seminole Negro*. New
York: Penguin, 2005.

Hall, D. J. *From Treaties to Reserves: The Federal Government and Native Peoples in
Territorial Alberta, 1870–1905*. Montréal: McGill-Queen's University Press, 2015.

Hall, Ryan. *Beneath the Backbone of the World: Blackfoot People and the North
American Borderlands, 1720–1877*. Chapel Hill: University of North Carolina
Press, 2020.

Hämäläinen, Pekka. *Lakota America: A New History of Indigenous Power*. New
Haven, CT: Yale University Press, 2019.

Hine, Robert V., John Mack Faragher, and Jon T. Coleman. *The American West:
A New Interpretive History*. 2nd ed. New Haven, CT: Yale University Press, 2017.

Hogue, Michel. *Metis and the Medicine Line: Creating a Border and Dividing a
People*. Chapel Hill: University of North Carolina Press, 2015.

Hoy, Benjamin. "A Border without Guards: First Nations and the Enforcement of
National Space." *Journal of the Canadian Historical Association* 25, no. 2 (2014):
89–115.

Hoy, Benjamin. *A Line of Blood and Dirt: Creating the Canada-United States Border
Across Indigenous Lands*. New York: Oxford University Press, 2021.

Isenberg, Andrew. *The Destruction of the Bison: An Environmental History, 1750–1920.* New York: Cambridge University Press, 2000.

LaDow, Beth. *The Medicine Line: Life and Death on a North American Borderland.* New York: Routledge, 2001.

LaPier, Rosalyn. *Invisible Reality: Storytellers, Storytakers, and the Supernatural World of the Blackfeet.* Lincoln: University of Nebraska Press, 2017.

Manzione, Joseph. *"I Am Looking to the North for My Life": Sitting Bull, 1876–1881.* Salt Lake City: University of Utah Press, 1991.

McCrady, David G. *Living with Strangers: The Nineteenth-Century Sioux and the Canadian-American Borderlands.* Lincoln: University of Nebraska Press, 2006.

McManus, Sheila. *The Line Which Separates: Race, Gender, and the Making of the Alberta-Montana Borderlands.* Lincoln: University of Nebraska Press, 2005.

Miller, J. R. *Compact, Contract, Covenant: Aboriginal Treaty-Making in Canada.* Toronto: University of Toronto Press, 2009.

Omani, Leo J. "A Written Response from Canada." *American Indian Quarterly* 28, no. 1/2 (Winter–Spring 2004): 283–88.

Ray, Arthur, J. R. Miller, and Frank Tough. *Bounty and Benevolence: A History of Saskatchewan Treaties.* Montréal: McGill-Queen's University Press, 2000.

Rensink, Brenden. *Native but Foreign: Indigenous Immigrants and Refugees in the North American Borderlands.* College Station: Texas A&M University Press, 2018.

Robert, Sheila. "The Negotiation and Implementation of Treaty 7, through 1880." Master's thesis, University of Lethbridge, 2007.

Scholz, Maximilian Miguel. "Religious Refugees and the Search for Public Worship in Frankfurt am Main, 1554–1608." *Sixteenth Century Journal* 50, no. 3 (Fall 2019): 765–82.

Sharp, Paul. *Whoop-Up Country: The Canadian-American West, 1865–1885.* Minneapolis: University of Minnesota Press, 1955.

Snell, James G. "The Frontier Sweeps Northwest: American Perceptions of the British American Prairie West at the Point of Canadian Expansion (circa 1870)." *Western Historical Quarterly* 11, no. 4 (October 1980): 381–400.

St. Germain, Jill. *Broken Treaties: United States and Canadian Relations with the Lakotas and the Plains Cree, 1868–1885.* Lincoln: University of Nebraska Press, 2009.

St. Germain, Jill. *Indian Treaty-Making Policy in the United States and Canada, 1867–1877.* Lincoln: University of Nebraska Press, 2001.

Taparata, Evan. "'Refugees as You Call Them': The Politics of Refugee Recognition in the Nineteenth-Century United States." *Journal of American Ethnic History* 38, no. 2 (Winter 2019): 9–35.

Taylor, Alan. *The Divided Ground: Indians, Settlers, and the Northern Borderland of the American Revolution.* New York: Alfred A. Knopf, 2006.

Taylor, John. "Two Views on the Meaning of Treaties Six and Seven." In *The Spirit of Alberta Indian Treaties*, edited by Richard Price, 3rd ed., 9–46. Edmonton: University of Alberta Press, 1999.

Tovías, Blanca. "Diplomacy and Contestation before and after the 1870 Massacre of Amskapi Pikuni." *Ethnohistory* 60, no. 2 (March 2013): 269–93.

Treaty 7 Elders and Tribal Council with Sarah Carter, Walter Hildebrandt, and Dorothy First Rider. *The True Spirit and Original Intent of Treaty 7*. Montréal: McGill-Queen's University Press, 1996.

Truth and Reconciliation Commission of Canada. *Honouring the Truth, Reconciling for the Future: Summary of the Final Report of the Truth and Reconciliation Commission of Canada*. Winnipeg: Truth and Reconciliation Commission of Canada, 2015.

Utley, Robert. *The Indian Frontier, 1846–1890*. Rev. ed. Albuquerque: University of New Mexico Press, 2003.

Utley, Robert. *The Lance and the Shield: The Life and Times of Sitting Bull*. New York: Ballantine Books, 1994.

Warner, Donald F. *The Idea of Continental Union: Agitation for the Annexation of Canada to the United States, 1849–1893*. Lexington: University of Kentucky Press, 1960.

West, Elliott. *The Last Indian War: The Nez Perce Story*. New York: Oxford University Press, 2009.

West, Elliott. *The Way to the West: Essays on the Central Plains*. Albuquerque: University of New Mexico Press, 1995.

7 Keeping Them Vulnerable

Female Applicants and the Biopolitics of Asylum in Texas

Claudia Donoso

In this chapter, I focus on the deterrence of female asylum seekers by the US government as a form of control of their mobility and exclusion from the asylum process. I argue that what contributes to the deterrence of female asylum seekers from Central America is the result of biopower manifested in the form of a biopolitics of asylum. This case demonstrates how biopower emphasizes the control of populations in a given territory. The exercise of this form of power within the asylum framework seeks the regularization of those who cannot enter and those who can remain permanently in US territory as long as applicants contribute to the productivity of the state. Intersectional feminism enhances even further our understanding of the rationale behind the deployment of biopower to regularize female asylum seekers from Central America.

In the context under study, biopower seeks to diminish a perceived risk to society through security *dispositifs* that surveil and exclude applicants. In what follows, I aim to address the question of to what extent border enforcement, detention, and denial of asylum claims respond to the biopolitics of asylum. To this end, I begin with a brief explanation of the reasons why women from Central America are fleeing to the United States requesting asylum. I then go on to discuss the concept of biopower developed by Michel Foucault as well as the concept of *dispositif of security* explored by Michael Dillon. Finally, in an intersectional feminist analysis, I examine how the biopolitics of asylum is understood in the case study and translates into the treatment of female asylum seekers through three *dispositifs of security*: border enforcement, detention, and the denial of asylum claims to regularize and control a population considered less productive and a burden to the US economy. Based on qualitative research, the study relies on fifteen semistructured interviews with directors of shelters for asylum seekers, migrant rights advocates, an immigration judge, and immigration attorneys who have represented female asylum seekers at detention centres in Dilley and Karnes, Texas.[1]

Background: Gang Violence Against Central American Women

Gender-based violence by gangs and intimate partners, particularly against girls and women, has become routine in Central America. Two gangs, *Mara Salvatrucha* (MS-13) and *Calle 18*, have terrorized Central American women. Gang members show their masculinity by raping, kidnapping, torturing, and carving tattoos on the bodies of women, girls, and members of the LGBTQ+ community.[2] In a state of impunity, social violence against women expresses itself through the violent murder of women or femicide. The term *femicide* has been defined by feminist sociologist Diana Russell as "the killing of females by males because they are female."[3] Because of patriarchy and misogyny, this culturally permitted practice bolsters male dominance and relies on the presence of systemic impunity and historically rooted gender inequality.[4] Many feminist scholars have studied cases of femicide in Ciudad Juárez on the Mexico-US border.[5] However, this type of hate crime against women also has reached alarming proportions across Central America. In El Salvador, a high rate of gender-based violence continues to make it one of the most dangerous countries to be a woman.[6] In fact, El Salvador has the highest rate of femicide in the world, Guatemala is third, and Honduras is close behind at seventh.[7] Women suffering domestic violence or trying to leave their violent partners are at significant risk. Although partners of the victims carry out these crimes, in a high proportion of cases, the murderers are connected to gang violence.[8] In Guatemala, for example, femicide exists because the state does not guarantee the protection of the rights of women.[9] In Honduras, women's naked and tortured bodies were found with their legs open as a demonstration of male power to spread terror among women.[10] In Honduras, in 90 percent of cases, femicides continue to go unpunished.[11]

In El Salvador, violent deaths of women show signs of severe cruelty, such as stoning, asphyxiation, or hanging. From January through October 2017, 395 women were killed in the country.[12] Thus, many Central American women have been left unprotected by states and have become victims of femicides. The exacerbated levels of crime against women and the weak intervention of Central American states to decrease the levels of impunity have pushed women to flee their home countries and seek safety in the United States, where they face several challenges. Unlike race, nationality, or religion, gang violence is not an obvious ground to grant asylum. Therefore, the main difficulty for those fleeing gang violence is to prove fear of persecution. Traditionally, asylum seekers can only support their claim based on group membership or political opinion.

In what follows, I discuss how, despite the complex insecurity scenario in El Salvador, Honduras, and Guatemala, US security authorities have turned away Central American female asylum seekers fleeing from gang-related violence at the border, separated them from their families, detained them in US detention facilities, and denied their asylum claims. These deterrence mechanisms have become part of a broader system of exclusion based on race-ethnicity, class, and gender of asylum applicants that deploys power through regulation of a population considered less productive for US interests. Former president Trump considered female asylum seekers from Central America a fiscal burden.[13] In the case study analyzed in this chapter, I propose understanding the biopolitics of asylum as the several security *dispositifs* deployed by the Trump administration to exercise biopower as a regulatory power over the asylum claims and mobility of women from Central America escaping gender-based violence.

Biopower, Biopolitics, and Security *Dispositifs*

Understanding how biopolitics operates is fundamental to defining *biopower*. This term was coined by French philosopher Michel Foucault in the first volume of *The History of Sexuality* and *Security, Territory, Population*. While sovereign power refers to the right to decide life and death, biopower, an essential element of modern capitalism, marks the move from the sovereign power over death to the sovereign power over life.[14] Thus, power no longer exclusively worries about the security of the sovereign and the associated territory but rather about the security of the population.[15] The new role of the sovereign includes a governmental practice that involves the management of populations.[16] This new power over life is biopower, which is a technology of power used by modern states as a mechanism of government and those who govern a population.[17] Based on this notion of biopower, the population, nevertheless, is not the mere sum of individuals inhabiting a territory; it depends on a set of variables and new disciplines such as economic observation and demography. Thus, according to Foucault, the population refers to statistics such as the birth rate, migration, longevity, public health, mortality, employment rates, or housing used by governments to manage life but also to prevent insecurity in their territories.[18] Diverse techniques for achieving the control of populations mark the beginning of the biopower era, focusing on the individual body through surveillance, inspection, reporting, and separation/exclusion.[19] These interventions and regulatory controls are what Foucault called the *biopolitics of the population*.[20] Biopower thus ensures that the population is disciplined and regularized to serve the interests of the state.[21] Life itself has become the main reference object for security practices.[22] In sum, *biopower* is the power over a population, and it is materialized in society through biopolitics. Specifically, *biopolitics* refers to the tactics, *dispositifs*, and mechanisms deployed by a specific political system to manage and regulate populations. In the context under study, the regulation of asylum is a fundamental source of biopolitical analysis.

Two security *dispositifs* have distinguished modernity. A *dispositif* entails a set of social relationships involving a diverse ensemble of discourses, institutions, architectural forms, regulatory decisions, laws, administrative measures, and scientific statements.[23] Most importantly, a *dispositif* is understood as a discursive way of ordering things in a certain domain to make a course of action possible.[24] For instance, in the security domain, a *dispositif* involves discourses, policies, institutions, and laws responsible for regulating the population aimed at mitigating threats against the state and its territory. According to Michael Dillon, the first *dispositif* refers to *the geopolitics of security* that has defined its reference object around sovereign territoriality; this *dispositif* is the tool of sovereign power. *The geopolitics of security* deals with the mechanisms of war, diplomatic alliances, and subjective personal interests. The second *dispositif*, *the biopolitics of security*, deals with the problem of life in terms of population or, in more concrete terms, with the ways biopower is exercised.[25] *The biopolitics of security* is interested in the power/knowledge nexus within governmental technologies, which raises the contingency of a threat.[26] Since biopolitics is part of the security apparatus, the state of emergency is permanent in security policy.[27] Through the coexistence of geopolitics and biopolitics, society must be defended from those threats to the life of a population, because a vulnerable population could become a threat to the national security of the state.

Once contingency becomes the nucleus of security mechanisms, population mobility is regulated. This way of understanding security problems fosters the "biopolitics of contingency."[28] The contingent as risk, therefore, gives rise to a society at risk that must be regulated. Security problems are contained in speeches of danger, such as the discourse of US officials in the face of the massive asylum crisis of Central American women.

Intersectional Analysis of Defensive Asylum Applications

Although the regulation of asylum is a fundamental source of biopolitical analysis, it cannot be treated as a genderless experience. Furthermore, ignoring the intersectional interplay of gender with other dimensions of inequality in asylum is problematic. Intersectional feminism enhances our understanding of the diverse racial, class, and gendered experiences of female asylum seekers. Black feminist scholar Kimberlé Crenshaw, one of the founders of critical race theory in the US legal academy, introduced the term *intersectionality*.[29] This term analyzes the experiences of discrimination of several social groups, especially women of colour, and conceptualizes the relation between systems of oppression as they construct a person's multiple social locations in hierarchies of power and privilege.[30] Through the study of intersectionality, we can understand the interactions among gender, race, class, and other categories of difference "in individual lives, social practices, institutional arrangements and cultural ideologies and the outcomes of these interactions in terms of power."[31] Women of colour are discriminated against not only based on their gender but due to the intersection of their multiple identities. In the context under study, the biopolitics of asylum must be understood as the strategic rejection of female applicants based on their intersecting identities through the ensemble of security *dispositifs* aimed at excluding the subject of asylum. As a security *dispositif*, the biopolitics of asylum is reproduced through law, border enforcement, family separation, detention, and denial of asylum claims in immigration courts. Consequently, the US government regulates asylum seekers through the deployment of biopower, severely impacting women who are positioned in hierarchies of gender, race, ethnicity, and class.

The biopolitics of asylum shows its regulatory control through the division of affirmative and defensive procedures. Even though the United States is a signatory to numerous international agreements relating to nonrefoulement and has embedded them in several sections of the Immigration and Nationality Act (INA), it routinely deters, detains, and deports asylum seekers. Section 208 of the INA authorizes the granting of asylum. The grounds for granting asylum are the same as those for granting refugee status; however, there are some differences under US law. While an individual seeking asylum is already physically within the borders of the United States or seeking admission at a port of entry, a person must be outside the boundaries of the United States to apply for refugee status.[32] To apply for affirmative asylum, the person must be present in the United States and submit an asylum application within a year of their arrival. Many times, affirmative asylum seekers entered with a valid visa, such as a tourist visa, and overstayed.[33] In contrast, defensive asylum applicants usually do not possess a visa and express their intention to seek asylum at the port of entry or are otherwise put into removal proceedings by an asylum officer.[34] Thus, the experience of asylum seekers is not homogeneous; claimants' identities—based especially on their class but also their gender, race, and ethnicity—play a significant role.

The biopolitics of asylum targets low-income individuals who more often go through defensive asylum procedures. Many poor defensive applicants are not able to access resources to help with their asylum claims, while most affirmative asylum seekers have easier access to resources that increase their odds of a successful asylum claim. Unlike affirmative applicants, many defensive asylum applicants do not receive a clear explanation when their case is denied; they are just told that their application has failed to prove past or future persecution.[35] Affirmative applicants are usually middle class and know that presenting themselves at a port of entry could place them in a detention centre; defensive applicants have limited choices,[36] since they cannot apply for a visa in their home countries and overstay it in order to begin the affirmative process in the United States in the first place. In this chapter, I discuss the biopolitics of asylum using the case of defensive applicants. Through several interviews conducted with immigration attorneys and migrants' advocates, it was revealed that these women are generally low income, and some are from ethnic minorities in Honduras, Guatemala, and El Salvador. The interviews show the multiple forms in which the biopolitics of asylum regulates Latina women of colour through several punitive practices.

Central American victims of domestic violence are generally poor and can turn into a public charge, depending on the US government for financial support. Although the public charge ground of inadmissibility has been a part of US immigration law for more than a century, refugees and asylum seekers are not subject to this type of inadmissibility.[37] Nevertheless, attempts at removing domestic violence as a basis for political asylum was another security *dispositif* of the Trump administration to limit the granting of asylum to poor Central American female applicants who could potentially become public charges after adjusting their status as permanent residents. In June 2018, former attorney general Jeff Sessions issued a ruling instructing immigration judges to deny all asylum claims based on fear of domestic abuse or gang violence.[38] Consequently, the Department of Homeland Security issued guidance for asylum officers, declaring, "Few gang-based or domestic violence claims involving particular social groups defined by the members' vulnerability to harm may . . . pass the 'significant probability' test in credible fear screenings."[39] The aim of this guidance was to obstruct the first step in seeking asylum: the initial credible fear determination. However, US District Court judge Emmet Sullivan issued a permanent injunction on Sessions's order, stating it violated US immigration law.[40] The injunction functions to prohibit the government from applying unlawful portions of Sessions's ruling. Without the injunction, it would have effectively eliminated domestic or gang violence as a claim for asylum, making it even more difficult to win a claim and leaving many asylum-seeking victims of this form of violence—in particular, low-income Central American women—completely unprotected.

In the United States, gender asylum has been a controversial issue. The term *gender asylum* describes claims in which the form of persecution is unique to or disproportionately inflicted on women (e.g., female genital cutting, domestic violence, rape, or forced marriage). According to Karen Musalo, opponents of gender asylum claim that the 1951 Refugee Convention was never intended to protect victims of gendered persecution. First, they claim that the harms suffered by women often consist of acts tolerated by cultural norms; therefore, this has resulted in a reluctance to define them as persecution. Second, they affirm that nonstate actors such as husbands, fathers, or members of the applicant's extended community are the perpetrators of gendered harm; therefore, there has been resistance to accepting such claims within the refugee definition.[41] Under US law, it is required that the fear of persecution must extend to the entire country of origin. Consequently, a female applicant must do more than show a well-founded fear of persecution in a particular place within a country to meet the definition of a refugee; she must show that the threat of persecution exists for her countrywide. Defensive female applicants thus face biopower through the denial of their asylum claim. For example, some battered women may be denied asylum because they could have sought safety from the batterer by simply moving to another town in their country of origin. In this context, national protection takes precedence over international protection. In addition to the controversy around gender asylum and defensive asylum claims, the US government has exercised biopower over female applicants through several security *dispositifs* such as border enforcement, detention, and denial of asylum claims.

Border Enforcement

Female asylum seekers have become the target of the biopolitics of asylum through border enforcement and the family separation policy. From October 2018 to June 2019, 37,573 family units; 50,439 single adults; and 3,542 unaccompanied minors presenting themselves at ports of entry on the Southwest border were deemed inadmissible.[42] The Trump administration's policy of zero tolerance through US Customs and Border Protection (CBP) became part of numerous security *dispositifs*; this policy has frequently deterred asylum seekers from Central America and turned them away along the US southern border.[43] In Texas, CBP officers actively discourage asylum seekers at ports of entry, within a hundred miles of the border, and in the middle of international bridges, avoiding the provision of protection to those seeking asylum from violence and persecution.[44] Furthermore, under the "zero-tolerance" policy, US Immigration and Customs Enforcement (ICE) and US CBP have separated children from parents arriving at the border. Based on the idea of unauthorized entry, asylum seekers are treated as criminals: parents who cross the border are jailed, and the children of these parents are treated as unaccompanied minors and placed with guardians.[45] Family separation has increasingly become a deterrence strategy at the port of entry, limiting the capacity of families to access asylum and worsening the trauma of children and women who are fleeing violent circumstances.[46] On February 20, 2018, a woman from Honduras arrived at the Texas border with her eighteen-month-old son; she told border agents they were fleeing from political violence and needed to find refuge together. Despite this request, the agents ordered her to place her son in the back seat of a government vehicle, separating the mother from her son.[47] Chris Hall positions the policy of family separation biopolitically by framing it as an autoimmune process that relies on the perpetual maintenance of power structures, spatial control, and internal regulation.[48] Under the zero-tolerance policy, family separation became a measure that obviously rejects any attempt to incorporate the contaminating "illegal other."[49] The case described earlier illustrates the use of family separation as a tactic of surveillance, exclusion, and separation aimed at controlling entrance, criminalizing unwanted populations, and punishing female asylum seekers who try to save their lives and those of their children due to insecurity in their home countries. The testimony of an immigration attorney also demonstrates that the detention experience and the family separation policy promote further psychological harm to those women fleeing from violence, exacerbating the preexisting trauma of female detainees:

> I worked with probably around four hundred parents that were separated from their children. The effects of that separation and the effects of detention were so much more traumatic to the mothers than it was to the fathers. The fathers were upset, don't get me wrong. The mothers were absolutely lost. . . . Unable to function, unable to think, unable to eat, unable to sleep, unable to talk sometimes, unable to stand up. I had to hold one woman—like, literally put my arms under her shoulders and hold her up.[50]

In January 2019, the Trump administration expanded its biopower through two border enforcement initiatives aimed at making it harder for people of colour fleeing their homes to seek asylum in the United States: metering and Migrant Protection Protocols (MPP). Through metering, border agents check the papers of asylum seekers before they set foot on US territory. As metering spread across the border, the number of asylum seekers in Mexican border cities increased from approximately six thousand in November 2018, when the Honduran migrant caravan arrived in Tijuana, to nineteen thousand in May 2019.[51] Under the MPP, known informally as "Remain in Mexico," the Trump administration returned primarily Central American asylum seekers to ill-prepared and dangerous border towns in Mexico; they then have to wait in these towns until their US asylum court proceedings conclude, which could take months and even years. This policy puts low-income women of colour and other asylum seekers in a more precarious situation. First, in these Mexican border cities, they face barriers to receiving due process on their asylum claims. Second, they encounter a severe shortage of shelter space, leaving many asylum seekers on the streets. Third, they are also at risk of kidnapping, sexual assault, and violence.[52] As of June 24, 2019, the Mexican government reported that 15,079 people, mostly from Honduras, Guatemala, and El Salvador, returned to Ciudad Juárez, Mexicali, and Tijuana under the MPP program with instructions to appear months later in US immigration court across the border. This number includes at least 4,780 children with their parents and at least 13 pregnant women who may be especially vulnerable due to their medical condition, age, and gender.[53] By overwhelming the Mexican government, both metering and the MPP program have deployed the omnipresence of the state through the biopolitics of asylum, which relies on an institutionalized rejection of applicants based on their intersecting ethnic-racial, gender, and class identities and reimagines its territory beyond its traditional boundaries to deter/exclude a population considered undesirable by the United States' zero-tolerance policy.

Detention

Detention centres for asylum seekers are another expression of totalitarian biopolitics that goes hand in hand with border enforcement. Detention has been defined as "a practice of incarcerating noncitizens who are apprehended at ports of entry or within the nation's interior."[54]

Within the biopolitics of contingency, the detention of asylum seekers becomes the space of exception and the site of the reconfiguration of the human into the nonhuman. The biopolitics within the detention system erases the humanity of detainees,[55] in particular low-income, ethnic, racialized, and gendered others. Asylum seekers exemplify Giorgio Agamben's concept of the bare life of the *homo sacer*, since they only exist in legal and political domains by means of their exclusion; their human existence has no political or economic value.[56] The exceptionalism of sovereign power ensures that the detained asylum seeker remains excluded from the rights afforded to citizens. Detention punishes border crossers, deterring them from pursuing the asylum process and displaying both sovereign power and disciplinary power.[57] Detention, furthermore, ensures individuals will attend deportation hearings;

this procedure has become a key source of the biopolitics of asylum led by the US government. Deportation is the last step and goal of the biopolitics of asylum. Currently, detainees are incarcerated in three types of facilities: federal detention centres managed by ICE, privately contracted prison facilities, and state/municipal jails.[58] The population of detained immigrants has increased from approximately 5,000 in 1994, to over 34,000 in 2014,[59] to over 41,000 in the first 100 days of the Trump administration.[60] In 2018, 396,448 people were initially booked into an ICE detention facility.[61]

The fact that immigrant detention in Texas is a profitable business that relies on a bed quota affects women severely. The detention bed quota requires ICE to maintain thirty-four thousand beds occupied all the time.[62] The Trump administration has considered doubling the number of beds to over eighty thousand through the private contracting of detention facilities, adding another facility in South Texas.[63] The United States has 205 detention facilities.[64] Of the twenty-four Texas detention centres,[65] two have been dedicated as family detention centres and centres for unaccompanied minors: one in Karnes City (run by a private contractor, the GEO Group) and the other in Dilley (operated by for-profit corrections corporation CoreCivic). The facility in Dilley, Texas, alone took away $71.6 million in revenue, with women and children bringing in a larger profit, "likely because women and children do not require as many security mechanisms as men."[66] This form of understanding profit generation reinforces a patriarchal view of security within the detention system. As of August 2018, the South Texas Family Residential Centre in Dilley was holding 1,520 women and children ages one to seventeen, while the Karnes County Residential Centre was housing 630 fathers and their sons.[67] During 2019, in the detention centre in Karnes, federal officials have released families with notices to appear in court and used the facility to house easier-to-deport single adults.[68] This situation leaves Dilley as the only family detention centre in South Texas.

Due to the biopolitics of asylum, asylum seekers who present themselves at the Texas-Mexico border are placed in detention facilities while their attorneys gather all the evidence to establish a credible fear of persecution in their home country; these detentions frequently took place before the implementation of the Remain in Mexico policy. Under US law, asylum seekers who express fear of returning to their country of origin are interviewed to assess if they can pursue their asylum claims at immigration courts. The credible fear interview provides applicants with the opportunity to explain how they have been persecuted; however, asylum is not guaranteed. If the asylum claim is denied, applicants are subject to a final order of removal; they may remain in detention while the United States makes deportation arrangements. The process of relief from deportation takes months and even years if there are appeals.[69]

The gendered impacts of the biopolitics of asylum within the current detention system critically affect the possibility to create a strong credible fear statement. One attorney explained that one of the main problems he faces when trying to represent women is that they are unable to articulate their fear in the detention setting.[70] The length of the interviews and the pressure to give appropriate answers may contribute to asylum seekers with symptoms of post-traumatic stress disorder providing inconsistent testimony due to memory loss.[71] Women are also ashamed to describe everything that has happened to them in their home countries. Culturally, for Central American women, sensitive topics such as domestic violence and rape are generally difficult to discuss, especially with strangers in a foreign country.[72] Since detention centres do not offer the minimum levels of privacy, many women prefer not to tell their stories in front of their children. The detention setting thus worsens the trauma already suffered by women and affects the articulation of a successful asylum claim.

Detention centres in Texas, as a tool of the biopolitics of asylum, are plagued with poor-quality medical care for pregnant women. This poor medical care is an intentional form of exclusion and state control over a specific population. Viewing pregnant migrant women as threats to the host nation-state contributes to their framing as risky and undesired bodies. The reproductive bodies of noncitizen women thus become a site of management and exclusion to prevent "anchor babies."[73] Although ICE discouraged the detention of pregnant women, the Women's Refugee Commission reported a 35 percent increase in the detention of pregnant women during the first four months of the Trump administration.[74] Following a December 2017 policy change, ICE began to detain pregnant women in Texas despite the well-documented harmful effects of detention on both pregnant women and fetal development.[75] Several miscarriages have occurred in detention.[76] A Salvadoran woman who requested asylum in El Paso was detained at the port of entry. Even though she was pregnant, she was transferred to a detention centre. After her last transfer, she was diagnosed with placenta previa, which creates serious health risks to the unborn child and mother.[77]

Detention as a component of the biopolitics of asylum creates more insecurity for women. Although some women have experienced domestic violence in their home country, they also face physical, verbal, and sexual abuse in the host country. Research conducted by Freedom for Immigrants demonstrates the prevalence of sexual abuse, assault, and harassment in US immigration detention facilities and the lack of adequate government investigation of these cases.[78] The Department of Homeland Security–Office of the Inspector General (OIG) received 1,016 reports of sexual abuse filed by people in detention between May 2014 and July 2016; the OIG received on average more than one complaint of sexual abuse from people in detention per day during this time period. Freedom for Immigrants also found that the OIG investigated only 24 of those complaints, or 2.4 percent of the total.[79] Immigration attorneys commented on cases of rape of female asylum seekers who crossed the border and ended up in detention facilities. Their clients were sexually assaulted in either US Border Patrol or ICE custody. One attorney explained that having the first point of contact with a male in a uniform who has a lot of power is not an ideal situation for women; these women have been insulted, have been called racially derogatory names, and have been told that they have no rights.[80] Another attorney commented that one of her clients was sexually assaulted after she was locked in a broom closet that the officer knew was out of range of security cameras. Despite this abuse of power, he only lost his job and was given a six-month sentence.[81] A shelter director pointed out that asylum seekers should not be jailed, but if they are going to be, only female guards should take care of female asylum seekers.[82] Relying on the detention of female asylum seekers, biopower is exercised to sustain classed, racialized, and gendered systems of oppression.

The use of detention centres in the biopolitics of asylum is not a practice that originated with the Trump administration. Since 1896, immigration imprisonment has been declared constitutionally permissible, and individuals can be detained while the government decides whether they can remain in the United States.[83] Detention emerged on both coasts: Ellis Island in New York and Angel Island in San Francisco Bay. Since then, Republicans and Democrats have relied on the use of detention centres to deter migrants and asylum seekers. In the 1980s, the Reagan administration ordered the Immigration and Naturalization Service (INS) to detain Cubans and Haitians who were fleeing totalitarian regimes and accommodate them at the Krome Avenue Detention Center in Miami; this facility remains operational today.[84]

South Texas also became the epicentre of the immigration detention system, imprisoning Central Americans fleeing massive human rights violations led by US-supported dictatorships in the region during the Cold War. The INS denied 97 percent of asylum petitions by Salvadorans and 99 percent by Guatemalans.[85] In 2014, thousands of women with children and unaccompanied minors from Central America fled to the United States. As a result, in 2014, the Obama administration revived the family detention system to keep together detained immigrant women and children, sometimes for several months;[86] the South Texas Family Residential Centre was built in Dilley, Texas, and became the largest family detention centre in the country. By the last months of the Obama administration, ICE held 40,000 people daily; this number rose under Trump, surpassing 42,000 daily in 2018.[87] While the Obama administration detained families together, the Trump administration promoted a family separation policy as a means of population control through deterrence mechanisms. As of July 2018, families accounted for 9,258 of the US Border Patrol's 31,303 arrests, or 29.5 percent.[88] Data released by the federal government in 2018 shows that every day, 15,852 people are detained in Texas; this state has the largest number of people in US immigration detention.[89] The US government thus regularizes the mobility of asylum seekers by deterring them through detention as another security *dispositif* of the biopolitics of asylum. Although, as a candidate President Biden offered to put an end to prolonged detention and the use of for-profit immigration detention centres, his administration has continued the detention policy, jailing thousands of asylum seekers in remote facilities.

Detention of asylum seekers is not limited to the US-Mexico border. Several scholars and advocates have questioned Canada's benign and welcoming reputation regarding refugees.[90] Like its neighbour, Canada's restrictive measures and use of detention centres have also proved controversial. In 2012, Canada amended the Immigration and Refugee Protection Act, including the Protecting Canada's Immigration System Act and the Balanced Refugee Reform Act. These changes consolidated the securitization of the Canadian Refugee System by the Conservative government of Stephen Harper (2006–15), resulting in violations of asylum seekers' human rights.[91] This "2012 refugee reform" applies to in-land asylum seekers and entails numerous restrictive measures such as increased immigration detention, reduced procedural guarantees, and expedited refugee claim hearings that leave no time for preparation of those claims.[92] By criminalizing asylum seekers, this reform enabled the Canada Border Services Agency (CBSA) to detain an average of 7,215 individuals per year in the period from 2012 to 2017; each individual spent an average of 19.5 days in these detention centres.[93] These prisons mark asylum seekers as an "undesirable" population that must be regulated.[94]

Denial of Asylum Claims

In what follows, the role of the immigration court is explained to demonstrate how the denial of asylum claims of low-income Central American women is another security *dispositif* displayed by the biopolitics of asylum to exclude and regulate this population, worsening the insecurity of female applicants by turning away survivors of gender-based violence.

Access to legal representation is crucial in winning asylum cases. Regrettably, data from the Transactional Records Access Clearinghouse reveal the percentage of asylum seekers who are unable to access legal counsel increased remarkably, from 13.6 percent in 2007 to 20.6 percent in 2017.[95] Moreover, the Trump administration forced immigration court judges to impose punitive bonds on asylum seekers.[96] Since these bonds are set too high to be paid, this measure compels asylum seekers with limited financial resources to self-deport.

The Department of Justice has prosecuted more people who come to the United States looking for protection, creating a backlog in immigration courts. Between October 2017 and April 2018, the US Department of Homeland Security referred approximately thirty thousand apprehended migrants for prosecution under title 8, section 1325 of the US Code. Due to the massive backlog in immigration judges' dockets, there were 140,027 cases pending in Texas through June 2019.[97] This situation prolongs the length of the detention of asylum seekers. The Department of Justice has implemented the use of videoconferences for hearings to address the backlog in immigration courts, but this does not address the main problems of the court system. An immigration judge finds that the entire system is problematic due to the way the current immigration court is set up. She claims that the court system is stationed in the Department of Justice, which is a law enforcement agency headed by a chief federal prosecutor.[98] For this judge, this situation undermines the integrity of the court and uses it as a political messaging tool. To send a message consistent with the administration's latest law enforcement policies, the judges are now faced with quotas and deadlines; their livelihood is put on the line if they do not complete a certain arbitrary number of cases in a specific period.[99] Certainly, the politicization of the immigration courts aligns with the biopolitics of asylum. Quotas and deadlines reflect an increase in the denial of claims, controlling which population deserves to enter US territory.

Another important aspect of the biopolitics of asylum is the expedited removal of asylum seekers who arrive at a port of entry, thereby denying them the opportunity for a successful asylum claim. According to one attorney,

> The overwhelming majority of people, even those claiming asylum . . . are turned away at the border. . . . Even though they have legitimate asylum claims, most of those people are put in what is called expedited removal, which means they don't really have a chance to make a claim. These . . . people . . . sometimes have almost twenty-four hours to prepare an asylum case. They can never get relevant evidence from their country related to their particular situation . . . while people who are put into the full procedure get months if not years to prepare their case. Lawyers can ask for medical records, for police records from their home countries . . . can search information about that country, and . . . can make a coherent argument to the immigration officials. As an immigration lawyer, I recognize that it is almost impossible to be successful in an expedited removal, and for me that is a denial of a due process.[100]

Expedited removals, as a dispositive of the biopolitics of asylum, violate the nonrefoulement principle, permitting the rapid deportation of female asylum seekers who may have a credible fear of returning to their home countries due to insecurity conditions.

By denying legal representation for female applicants, the biopolitics of asylum keeps them vulnerable and guarantees deportation. Unlike criminal courts, the constitutional right to legal counsel is not guaranteed in immigration proceedings.[101] Although most attorneys interviewed in this study have a private practice, they are also pro-bono lawyers who volunteer to provide this service and can only take a few cases. A director of a shelter for asylum seekers explains how the lack of legal representation contributes to the deportation of applicants who do not have a work permit and therefore cannot afford to pay for a lawyer:

> It's very difficult to win asylum without a lawyer. It is unrealistic that somebody arriving at our border can afford to hire a lawyer.

You are just conceding them to deportation by not giving them legal representation. . . . Asylum seekers are not given any support from the government while they are in proceedings, and that makes them very vulnerable. . . . They cannot work legally; they must work in a kind of undocumented setting. It takes many months to get a work permit. . . . In general, the main rule is that you have to apply for asylum, turn in your application, which means that you have to find somebody that can help you, and you have to submit it. And then you wait 150 days, so that's another five months, and then you can apply for [a] work permit, and that takes between four and six months. So really, it will take you at least a year for the average person to get a work permit.[102]

Denial rates of asylum claims are consistently high in Texas. With a 98.8 percent denial rate, El Paso has the second-highest denial rate in the country. Other immigration courts in Texas, such as in San Antonio, have immigration judges with very high denial rates (96.4 percent or more). In contrast, Harlingen, which is comparable to El Paso due to its location at the Mexico-Texas border, has a relatively low denial rate, between 47.5 percent and 64.5 percent.[103] Asylum denial rates rose during the Trump administration. For fiscal year 2018, the overall approval rate was 26 percent as of February 2018.[104] In June of that year, denials climbed due to decisions announced by former attorney general sessions that harshly limited the grounds on which immigration judges could grant asylum. Central American women and children fleeing gangs and domestic violence were no longer deemed asylum candidates.[105] As a result of the biopolitics of asylum, female applicants have been deported to countries where physical and sexual violence are permitted, femicide rates are among the highest in the world, and impunity is not properly addressed.

Conclusion

Discussing the concept of biopower and observing how it has been deployed within the biopolitics of asylum to regularize women's mobility adds to the analysis of biopolitics as a tool used to jeopardize the right of international protection of female asylum seekers. This right is constantly violated through several mechanisms of exclusion, separation, and surveillance employed by the US government to decide who can or cannot remain within US territory. In this chapter, these mechanisms have been called security *dispositifs*. As a result of the biopolitics of asylum under the Trump administration, these *dispositifs* have been carried out as deterrence practices, such as border enforcement, family separation, detention, and denial of women's asylum claims at immigration courts. Examining female applicants as targets of the biopolitics of asylum in combination with intersectional feminism permits us to better comprehend the way the US government views them as an undesirable population. Furthermore, viewing these women as a risk to US society has justified the deployment of several security *dispositifs* to control the mobility of low-income female asylum applicants from Central America. The chapter examines how the security apparatus composed of border security agents and guards in detention centres worsened the security conditions of these women. The biopolitics of asylum ensures that female applicants are kept vulnerable owing to their intersecting identities based on class, gender, ethnicity, and race. In this vein, female applicants detained for long periods or who have been forced to remain in Mexico have been deported to countries where impunity and femicide rates are among the highest in the world.

The criminalization of female asylum seekers in Texas goes beyond a local consideration. This case study highlights that the story of the inhumane treatment of these asylum seekers at ports of entry and detention centres in the United States is not new and is not limited to its borders. This chapter examined the fact that the use of detention centres did not originate with the Trump administration and that Canada's use of such centres has also proved controversial. Unfortunately, the case study presented in this chapter illustrates the success of biopower and how the implementation of the biopolitics of asylum has become an accepted security *dispositif* that will remain in future administrations.

Acknowledgements

This research was carried out with the help of the Internal Faculty Research Grant Program from St. Mary's University, San Antonio.

Notes

Some of the empirical information included in this chapter served in the analysis presented in Claudia Donoso, "Securitisation of Female Asylum Seekers and Healthcare in Detention Centres in Texas," *International Journal of Migration and Border Studies* 6, no. 3 (2020): 186–205.

1. Permission to proceed with this study was granted in September 2018 by the ethics review board at St. Mary's University (my home institution), which determined that the planned use of interview material satisfied federal regulations regarding the protection of human subjects, specifically 45 CFR 46.101(b)(2).

2. Suzanne Gamboa, "Sexual, Gender Violence Driving Central American Youths to Flee Their Countries"; Anastasia Moloney, "Why 'Terrorized' Members of Central America's LGBTQ Community Are Fleeing"; Victoria Sanford, "From Genocide to Feminicide: Impunity and Human Rights in Twenty-First Century Guatemala," 104–22.

3. Diana Russell, "Introduction: The Politics of Femicide," 3.

4. David Carey and M. Gabriela Torres. "Precursors to Femicide: Guatemalan Women in a Vortex of Violence," 142–64, https://doi.org/10.1017/s0023879100011146; Sanford, "From Genocide to Feminicide."

5. Julia E. Fragoso and Cynthia Bejarano. "The Disarticulation of Justice: Precarious Life and Cross-Border Feminicides in the Paso Del Norte Region," 43–70, https://doi.org/10.1057/9780230112919_3; Shae Garwood, "Working to Death: Gender, Labour, and Violence in Ciudad Juarez, Mexico," 1–23; Lourdes Godínez Leal, "Combating Impunity and Femicide in Ciudad Juárez," 31–33, https://doi.org/10.1080/10714839.2008.11725408.

6. Amnesty International, *Amnesty International 2017/18 Report. The State of the World's Human Rights.*

7. USAID, *Guatemala Gender Analysis Final Report.*

8. Ana Leticia Aguilar, "Femicidio . . . La pena Capital por ser Mujer."

9. Sanford, "From Genocide to Feminicide," 113. According to the Guatemalan National Statistics Institute (2018), some 848 femicides were reported between 2014 and 2017.

10. Marina Prieto-Carrón, Marilyn Thomson, and Mandy Macdonald, "No More Killings! Women Respond to Femicides in Central America," 26.

11. Organization of American States (OAS), *IACHR Has Concluded Its Visit to Honduras and Presents Its Preliminary Observations.*

12. Organization of American States (OAS), *Conclusions and Observations on the IACHR's Working Visit to El Salvador.*

13. Madeline Buiano and Susan Ferriss, "Data Defies Trump's Claims That Refugees and Asylees Burden Taxpayers."

14. Benjamin Muller, "Globalization, Security, Paradox: Towards a Refugee Biopolitics," 52. See also Michel Foucault, *The History of Sexuality*, vol. 1, *An Introduction*, 135.

15. Michel Foucault, *Security, Territory, Population: Lectures at the Collège de France, 1977–1978*, 65.

16. Foucault, *History of Sexuality*, 71–74.

17. Foucault, *Security, Territory, Population*, 66.

18. Foucault, *Security, Territory, Population*, 70–71; Foucault, *History of Sexuality*, 140.

19. Michel Foucault, "Right of Death and Power over Life," 262.

20. Foucault, *History of Sexuality*, 139.

21. Michel Foucault, *"Society Must Be Defended,"* 242, 246–47.

22. Brad Evans, "Foucault's Legacy: Security, War and Violence in the 21st Century," 413.

23. Ariadna Estévez, "The Biopolitics of Asylum Law in Texas: The Case of Mexicans Fleeing Drug Violence in Juárez"; Staf Callewaert, "Foucault's Concept of Dispositif."

24. Callewaert. "Foucault's Concept of Dispositif," 30.

25. Michael Dillon, "Governing Terror: The State of Emergency of Bio-political Emergence," 10.

26. Dillon, "Governing Terror," 10–11.

27. Michael Dillon and Luis Lobo-Guerrero, "Biopolitics of Security in the 21st Century," 266.

28. Dillon, "Governing Terror," 8–9.

29. Kimberlé Crenshaw, "Demarginalizing the Intersection of Race and Sex: A Black Feminist Critique of Antidiscrimination Doctrine, Feminist Theory and Antiracist Politics."

30. Anna Carastathis, "The Concept of Intersectionality in Feminist Theory." See also Hae Yeon Choo and Myra Marx Ferree, "Practicing Intersectionality in Sociological Research: A Critical Analysis of Inclusions, Interactions, and Institutions in the Study of Inequalities."

31. Kathy Davis, "Intersectionality as Buzzword: A Sociology of Science Perspective on What Makes a Feminist Theory Successful," 68.

32. US Citizenship and Immigration Services (USCIS), *Refugees and Asylum*; Dan Cadman, "Asylum in the United States: How a Finely Tuned System of Checks and Balances Has Been Effectively Dismantled."

33. US Citizenship and Immigration Services (USCIS), *Obtaining Asylum in the United States*.

34. Ibid.

35. Estévez, "Biopolitics of Asylum Law," 64–65.

36. Estévez, "Biopolitics of Asylum Law," 66.

37. US Citizenship and Immigration Services (USCIS), *Public Charge Fact Sheet*.

38. Katie Benner and Caitlin Dickerson, "Sessions Says Domestic and Gang Violence Are Not Grounds for Asylum," *New York Times*, June 11, 2018,

https://www.nytimes.com/2018/06/11/us/politics/sessions-domestic-violence -asylum.html.

39. US Department of Homeland Security, "U.S. Citizenship and Immigration Services, Policy Memorandum, Guidance for Processing Reasonable Fear, Credible Fear, Asylum, and Refugee Claims in Accordance with Matter of A-B-."

40. Alan Gomez, "Federal Judge Blocks Another Attempt by Trump to Limit Asylum," *USA Today*, December 19, 2018, https://www.usatoday.com/story/ news/world/2018/12/19/second-judge-blocks-attempt-trump-limit-asylum -migrant-caravan-immigration-border/2066608002/.

41. Karen Musalo, "A Short History of Gender Asylum in the United States: Resistance and Ambivalence May Very Slowly Be Inching Towards Recognition of Women's Claims," 46–63.

42. US Customs and Border Protection, *Southwest Border Migration FY 2019*.

43. Karolina Walters, "Asylum Seekers Are Being Systematically Turned Away at the U.S.-Mexico Border."

44. Hope Border Institute, *Sealing the Border: The Criminalization of Asylum Seekers in the Trump Era*; Aaron Montes, "Try Later: It's Getting Tougher for Migrants to Claim Asylum at U.S. Ports of Entry."

45. Adam Isacson, "Jailing All Border Crossers and Separating Families Would Break U.S. Courts, Ports, and Prisons. (It's Cruel, Too.)"

46. Hope Border Institute, *Sealing the Border*.

47. Caitlin Dickerson, "Hundreds of Immigrant Children Have Been Taken from Parents at U.S. Border," *New York Times*, April 20, 2018, https://www.nytimes .com/2018/04/20/us/immigrant-children-separation-ice.html.

48. Chris Hall, "(Auto)immunity, Racism, and Crisis: From the Biopolitical to the Allopolitical," 83.

49. Hall, "(Auto)immunity," 86.

50. Interview with immigration attorney PF, 2018.

51. Savitri Arvey and Steph Leutert, "Thousands of Asylum-Seekers Left Waiting at the US-Mexico Border."

52. Human Rights Watch, "'We Can't Help You Here': US Returns of Asylum Seekers to Mexico."

53. Human Rights Watch, "'We Can't Help You Here.'"

54. David Hernández, "Pursuant to Deportation: Latinos and Immigrant Detention," 203.

55. Lana Zannettino, "From Auschwitz to Mandatory Detention: Biopolitics, Race, and Human Rights in the Australian Refugee Camp," 1–26.

56. Estévez, "Biopolitics of Asylum Law," 62.

57. Sara Riva, "Across the Border and into the Cold: *Hieleras* and the Punishment of Asylum-Seeking Central American Women in the United States," 309–26.

58. Hernández, "Pursuant to Deportation."

59. Detention Watch Network, *Immigration Detention 101*.

60. US Department of Homeland Security, *ICE ERO Immigration Arrests Climb Nearly 40%*.

61. US Immigration and Customs Enforcement (ICE), *Fiscal Year 2018 ICE Enforcement and Removal Operations Report*.

62. Hope Border Institute, *Sealing the Border*.

63. Madison Pauly, "The Private Prison Industry Is Licking Its Chops over Trump's Deportation Plans."

64. Detention Watch Network, *Immigration Detention 101*.

65. US Immigration and Customs Enforcement (ICE), *Detention Facility Locator*.

66. Interview with Laura Litcher in Smith, "Here's the Biggest Immigration Issue That Trump Isn't Talking About."

67. Weissert, "Texas Lockup Is Epicenter of Family Immigration Detention."

68. Nick Miroff and Maria Sacchetti, "U.S. Weighs Plan to Phase Out Family Detention at Texas Facility, despite Migration Surge," *Washington Post*, March 14, 2019, https://www.washingtonpost.com/immigration/us-weighs -plan-to-phase-out-family-detention-at-texas-facility-despite-migration -surge/2019/03/14/c240cf6a-467d-11e9-aaf8-4512a6fe3439_story.html?utm _term=.88f8eade39c1.

69. Nina Rabin, "Unseen Prisoners: Women in Immigration Detention Facilities in Arizona," 699.

70. Interview with attorney BB, 2018.

71. Adrianne Aron, "Applications of Psychology to Assessment of Refugees Seeking Political Asylum," 85–86.

72. Interview with shelter director in Laredo, 2018.

73. The term *anchor baby* refers to a child born to a noncitizen mother in a country; this child has birthright citizenship. According to the Fourteenth Amendment to the US Constitution and the Immigration and Nationality Act (INA), US citizenship is granted automatically to any person born within US territory.

74. Women's Refugee Commission, *Joint Complaint on ICE Detention and Treatment of Pregnant Women*.

75. Human Rights First, *Ailing Justice: Texas. Soaring Immigration Detention, Shrinking Due Process*, June 14, 2018, https://www.humanrightsfirst.org/ resource/ailing-justice-texas-soaring-immigration-detention-shrinking-due -process.

76. Interview with representative of Detention Watch Network, April 2019.

77. Hope Border Institute, *Sealing the Border*.

78. Freedom for Immigrants, *Widespread Sexual Assault*, 2018, https://www
.freedomforimmigrants.org/sexual-assault.

79. Freedom for Immigrants, *Widespread Sexual Assault*.

80. Interview with attorney SD, 2018.

81. Interview with attorney PF, 2018.

82. Interview with director of shelter NO, 2018.

83. César Cuauhtémoc García Hernández, *Migrating to Prison: America's
Obsession with Locking Up Immigrants*.

84. García Hernández, *Migrating to Prison*.

85. García Hernández, *Migrating to Prison*.

86. Laura Smith, "Here's the Biggest Immigration Issue That Trump Isn't Talking
About."

87. García Hernández, *Migrating to Prison*.

88. Will Weissert, "Texas Lockup."

89. Freedom for Immigrants, *Detention by the Numbers*, 2018, https://www
.freedomforimmigrants.org/detention-statistics.

90. George Melnyk and Christina Parker, eds., *Finding Refuge in Canada:
Narratives of Dislocation*; Petra Molnar and Stephanie J. Silverman, "Canada
Needs to Get Out of the Immigration Detention Business."

91. Idil Atak et al., "The Securitisation of Canada's Refugee System: Reviewing the
Unintended Consequences of the 2012 Reform," 1–24.

92. Atak et al., "Securitisation."

93. Molnar and Silverman, "Canada Needs to Get Out."

94. Delphine Nakache, "Détention des demandeurs d'asile au Canada: Des
logiques pénales et administratives convergentes."

95. TRAC Immigration, *Asylum Representation Rates Have Fallen amid Rising
Denial Rates*.

96. Hope Border Institute, *Sealing the Border*.

97. TRAC Immigration, *Immigration Court Backlog Tool Pending Cases and
Length of Wait by Nationality, State, Court, and Hearing Location*, 2019, https://
trac.syr.edu/phptools/immigration/court_backlog/.

98. Interview with judge KK, March 2019.

99. Interview with judge KK.

100. Interview with attorney MR, 2018.

101. Ingrid Eagly and Steven Shafer, "Access to Counsel in Immigration Court."

102. Interview with director of shelter NO, December 2018.

103. TRAC Immigration, *Asylum Representation Rates*.

104. US Department of Homeland Security, *Annual Report 2018 Citizenship and Immigration Services Ombudsman*.

105. TRAC Immigration, *Asylum Decisions and Denials Jump in 2018*, https://trac .syr.edu/immigration/reports/539/.

Bibliography

Aron, Adrianne. "Applications of Psychology to Assessment of Refugees Seeking Political Asylum." *Applied Psychology: An International Review* 41, no 1 (1992): 77–91.

Aguilar, Ana Leticia. "Femicidio . . . La pena Capital por ser Mujer." July 14, 2005, https://americalatinagenera.org/violencia-contra-las-mujeres/femicidio-la-pena -capital-por-ser-mujer/.

Amnesty International. *Amnesty International 2017/18 Report. The State of the World's Human Rights*, February 22, 2018. https://www.amnesty.org/en/ documents/pol10/6700/2018/en/.

Arvey, Savitri, and Steph Leutert. "Thousands of Asylum-Seekers Left Waiting at the US-Mexico Border." *Conversation*, June 17, 2019. https://theconversation.com/ thousands-of-asylum-seekers-left-waiting-at-the-us-mexico-border-118367.

Atak, Idil, Graham Hudson, and Delphine Nakache. "The Securitisation of Canada's Refugee System: Reviewing the Unintended Consequences of the 2012 Reform." *Refugee Survey Quarterly* 37, no 1 (2018): 1–24. http://dx.doi.org/10.2139/ssrn.2977986.

Benner, Katie, and Caitlin Dickerson. "Sessions Says Domestic and Gang Violence Are Not Grounds for Asylum." *New York Times*, June 11, 2018. https://www .nytimes.com/2018/06/11/us/politics/sessions-domestic-violence-asylum.html.

Buiano, Madeline, and Susan Ferriss. "Data Defies Trump's Claims That Refugees and Asylees Burden Taxpayers." Center for Public Integrity, May 8, 2019. https:// publicintegrity.org/inequality-poverty-opportunity/immigration/data-defies -trump-claims-that-refugees-and-asylees-are-a-taxpayer-burden/.

Cadman, Dan. "Asylum in the United States: How a Finely Tuned System of Checks and Balances Has Been Effectively Dismantled." Center for Immigration Studies, March 26, 2014. https://cis.org/Report/Asylum-United-States.

Callewaert, Staf. "Foucault's Concept of Dispositif." *Praktiske Grunde: Nordisk tidsskrift for kultur- og samfundsvidenskab*, nos. 1–2 (2017): 29–52. http:// praktiskegrunde.dk/2017/praktiskegrunde(2017-1+2f)callewaert.pdf.

Carastathis, Anna. "The Concept of Intersectionality in Feminist Theory." *Philosophy Compass* 9, no 5. (2014): 304–14.

Carey, David, and M. Gabriela Torres. "Precursors to Femicide: Guatemalan Women in a Vortex of Violence." *Latin American Research Review* 45, no. 3 (2010): 142–64. https://doi.org/10.1017/s0023879100011146.

Choo, Hae Yeon, and Myra Marx Ferree. "Practicing Intersectionality in Sociological Research: A Critical Analysis of Inclusions, Interactions, and Institutions in the Study of Inequalities." *Sociological Theory* 28, no. 2 (2010): 129–49.

Crenshaw, Kimberlé. "Demarginalizing the Intersection of Race and Sex: A Black Feminist Critique of Antidiscrimination Doctrine, Feminist Theory and Antiracist Politics." *University of Chicago Legal Forum* 140 (1989): 139–67.

Davis, Kathy. "Intersectionality as Buzzword: A Sociology of Science Perspective on What Makes a Feminist Theory Successful." *Feminist Theory* 9, no. 1 (2008): 67–85.

Detention Watch Network. *Immigration Detention 101*, October 10, 2017. https://www.detentionwatchnetwork.org/issues/detention-101.

Dickerson, Caitlin. "Hundreds of Immigrant Children Have Been Taken from Parents at U.S. Border." *New York Times*, April 20, 2018. https://www.nytimes.com/2018/04/20/us/immigrant-children-separation-ice.html.

Dillon, Michael. "Governing Terror: The State of Emergency of Bio-political Emergence." *International Political Sociology* 1, no 1 (2007): 7–28.

Dillon, Michael, and Luis Lobo-Guerrero. "Biopolitics of Security in the 21st Century." *Review of International Studies* 34, no 2 (2008): 265–92.

Eagly, Ingrid, and Steven Shafer. "Access to Counsel in Immigration Court." *American Immigration Council*, September 28, 2016. https://www.americanimmigrationcouncil.org/research/access-counsel-immigration-court.

Estévez, Ariadna. "The Biopolitics of Asylum Law in Texas: The Case of Mexicans Fleeing Drug Violence in Juárez." *Norteamérica* 8, supplement (2013): 55–81.

Evans, Brad. "Foucault's Legacy: Security, War and Violence in the 21st Century." *Security Dialogue* 41, no. 4 (2010): 413–33.

Foucault, Michel. *The History of Sexuality*. Vol. 1, *An Introduction*. Translated by Robert Hurley. London: Penguin, 1990.

Foucault, Michel. "Right of Death and Power over Life." In *The Foucault Reader*, edited by Paul Rabinow, 258–72. New York: Pantheon Books, 1984.

Foucault, Michel. *Security, Territory, Population: Lectures at the Collège de France, 1977–1978*. Edited by Michel Senellart. Translated by Graham Burchell. New York: Picador, 2007.

Foucault, Michel. *"Society Must Be Defended": Lectures at the Collège de France, 1975–1976*. Edited by Mauro Bertani and Alessandro Fontana. Translated by David Macey. New York: Picador, 2003.

Fragoso, Julia E., and Cynthia Bejarano. "The Disarticulation of Justice: Precarious Life and Cross-Border Feminicides in the Paso Del Norte Region." In *Cities and Citizenship at the U.S.-Mexico Border*, edited by Kathleen Staudt, César M.

Fuentes, and Julia E. Monárrez Fragoso, 43–70. New York: Palgrave Macmillan, 2010. https://doi.org/10.1057/9780230112919_3.

Freedom for Immigrants. *Detention by the Numbers*, April 12, 2018. https://www
.freedomforimmigrants.org/detention-statistics.

Freedom for Immigrants. *Widespread Sexual Assault*, April 12, 2018. https://www
.freedomforimmigrants.org/sexual-assault.

Gamboa, Suzanne. "Sexual, Gender Violence Driving Central American Youths to Flee Their Countries." NBC News, May 4, 2017. https://www.nbcnews.com/news/latino/sexual-gender-violence-driving-central-american-youths-flee-their-countries-n754886.

García Hernández, César Cuauhtémoc. *Migrating to Prison: America's Obsession with Locking Up Immigrants*. New York: New Press, 2019.

Garwood, Shae. "Working to Death: Gender, Labour, and Violence in Ciudad Juarez, Mexico." *Journal of Peace, Conflict and Development* 2, no. 2 (2002): 1–23.

Gomez, Alan. "Federal Judge Blocks Another Attempt by Trump to Limit Asylum." *USA Today*, December 19, 2018. https://www.usatoday.com/story/news/world/2018/12/19/second-judge-blocks-attempt-trump-limit-asylum-migrant-caravan-immigration-border/2066608002/.

Hall, Chris. "(Auto)immunity, Racism, and Crisis: From the Biopolitical to the Allopolitical." *SubStance* 48, no. 3 (2019): 82–100.

Hernández, David. "Pursuant to Deportation: Latinos and Immigrant Detention." In *Governing Immigration through Crime: A Reader*, edited by Julie A. Dowling and Jonathan Xavier Inda, 199–215. Stanford: Stanford University Press, 2013.

Hope Border Institute. *Sealing the Border: The Criminalization of Asylum Seekers in the Trump Era*, January 2018. https://docs.wixstatic.com/ugd/e07ba9_909b9230ae734e179cda4574ef4b6dbb.pdf.

Human Rights First. *Ailing Justice: Texas. Soaring Immigration Detention, Shrinking Due Process*, June 14, 2018. https://www.humanrightsfirst.org/resource/ailing-justice-texas-soaring-immigration-detention-shrinking-due-process.

Human Rights Watch. "'We Can't Help You Here': US Returns of Asylum Seekers to Mexico." July 2, 2019. https://www.hrw.org/report/2019/07/02/we-cant-help-you-here/us-returns-asylum-seekers-mexico.

Isacson, Adam. "Jailing All Border Crossers and Separating Families Would Break U.S. Courts, Ports, and Prisons. (It's Cruel, Too.)" *WOLA Advocacy for Human Rights in the Americas*, May 15, 2018. http://web.archive.org/web/20220409224921/https://www.wola.org/analysis/jailing-border-crossers-separating-families-break-u-s-courts-ports-prisons-cruel/.

Leal, Lourdes Godínez. "Combating Impunity and Femicide in Ciudad Juárez." *NACLA Report on the Americas* 41, no. 3 (2008): 31–33. https://doi.org/10.1080/10714839.2008.11725408.

Melnyk, George, and Christina Parker, eds. *Finding Refuge in Canada: Narratives of Dislocation*. Edmonton: Athabasca University Press, 2021.

Miroff, Nick, and Maria Sacchetti. "U.S. Weighs Plan to Phase Out Family Detention at Texas Facility, despite Migration Surge." *Washington Post*, March 14, 2019. https://www.washingtonpost.com/immigration/us-weighs-plan-to-phase-out -family-detention-at-texas-facility-despite-migration-surge/2019/03/14/c240cf6a -467d-11e9-aaf8-4512a6fe3439_story.html?utm_term=.88f8eade39c1.

Molnar, Petra, and Stephanie J. Silverman. "Canada Needs to Get Out of the Immigration Detention Business." CBC News, July 5, 2018. https://www.cbc.ca/ news/opinion/immigration-detention-1.4733897.

Moloney, Anastasia. "Why 'Terrorized' Members of Central America's LGBTQ Community Are Fleeing." Huffpost, November 29, 2017. https:// www.huffingtonpost.com/entry/central-america-lgbtq-community_us _5a1ef3c9e4b0d52b8dc22e9a.

Montes, Aaron. "Try Later: It's Getting Tougher for Migrants to Claim Asylum at U.S. Ports of Entry." NBC News, June 23, 2018. https://www.nbcnews.com/ storyline/immigration-border-crisis/try-later-it-s-getting-tougher-migrants -claim-asylum-u-n885861.

Muller, Benjamin. "Globalization, Security, Paradox: Towards a Refugee Biopolitics." *Refuge* 22, no. 1 (2004): 49–57.

Musalo, Karen. "A Short History of Gender Asylum in the United States: Resistance and Ambivalence May Very Slowly Be Inching Towards Recognition of Women's Claims." *Refugee Survey Quarterly* 29, no. 2 (2010): 46–63.

Nakache, Delphine. "Détention des demandeurs d'asile au Canada: Des logiques pénales et administratives convergentes." *Criminologie* 46, no. 1 (2013): 83–105. https://www.erudit.org/en/journals/crimino/2013-v46-n1-crimino0551/ 1015294ar/.

Organization of American States (OAS). *Conclusions and Observations on the IACHR's Working Visit to El Salvador*, January 29, 2018. https://www.oas.org/en/ iachr/media_center/PReleases/2018/011A.asp.

Organization of American States (OAS). *IACHR Has Concluded Its Visit to Honduras and Presents Its Preliminary Observations*, August 3, 2018. http://www .oas.org/en/iachr/media_center/PReleases/2018/171.asp.

Pauly, Madison. "The Private Prison Industry Is Licking Its Chops over Trump's Deportation Plans." *Mother Jones*, February 21, 2017. https://www.motherjones .com/politics/2017/02/trumps-immigration-detention-center-expansion/.

Prieto-Carrón, Marina, Marilyn Thomson, and Mandy Macdonald. "No More Killings! Women Respond to Femicides in Central America." *Gender and Development* 15, no. 1 (2007): 25–40.

Rabin, Nina. "Unseen Prisoners: Women in Immigration Detention Facilities in Arizona." *Georgetown Immigration Law Journal* 23, no. 4 (2009): 695–763.

Riva, Sara. "Across the Border and into the Cold: *Hieleras* and the Punishment of Asylum-Seeking Central American Women in the United States." *Citizenship Studies* 21, no. 3 (2017): 309–26.

Russell, Diana. "Introduction: The Politics of Femicide." In *Femicide in Global Perspective*, edited by Diana Russell and Roberta Harmes, 3–11 New York: Teacher College Press, 2001.

Sanford, Victoria. "From Genocide to Feminicide: Impunity and Human Rights in Twenty-First Century Guatemala." *Journal of Human Rights* 7, no. 2 (2008): 104–22.

Smith, Laura. "Here's the Biggest Immigration Issue That Trump Isn't Talking About." *Mother Jones*, January 12, 2017. https://www.motherjones.com/politics/2017/01/family-detention-immigration-refugees-texas-dilley/.

TRAC Immigration. *Asylum Decisions and Denials Jump in 2018*, November 29, 2018. https://trac.syr.edu/immigration/reports/539/.

TRAC Immigration. *Asylum Representation Rates Have Fallen amid Rising Denial Rates*, November 28, 2017. http://trac.syr.edu/immigration/reports/491/.

TRAC Immigration. *Immigration Court Backlog Tool Pending Cases and Length of Wait by Nationality, State, Court, and Hearing Location*, May 20, 2017. https://trac.syr.edu/phptools/immigration/court_backlog/.

USAID. *Guatemala Gender Analysis Final Report*, September 14, 2018. https://banyanglobal.com/wp-content/uploads/2018/10/USAID-Guatemala-Gender-Analysis-Final-Report.pdf.

US Citizenship and Immigration Services (USCIS). *Obtaining Asylum in the United States*, October 19, 2015. https://www.uscis.gov/humanitarian/refugees-and-asylum/asylum/obtaining-asylum-united-states.

US Citizenship and Immigration Services (USCIS). *Public Charge Fact Sheet*, May 25, 2020. http://web.archive.org/web/20221127225921/https://www.uscis.gov/archive/public-charge-fact-sheet.

US Citizenship and Immigration Services (USCIS). *Refugees and Asylum*, December 11, 2015. https://www.uscis.gov/humanitarian/refugees-asylum.

US Customs and Border Protection. *Southwest Border Migration FY 2019*, March 5, 2019. https://www.cbp.gov/newsroom/stats/sw-border-migration.

US Department of Homeland Security. *Annual Report 2018 Citizenship and Immigration Services Ombudsman*, June 28, 2018. https://www.dhs.gov/sites/default/files/publications/cisomb/cisomb_2018-annual-report-to-congress.pdf.

US Department of Homeland Security. *ICE ERO Immigration Arrests Climb Nearly 40%*, May 17, 2017. https://www.ice.gov/features/100-days.

US Department of Homeland Security. "U.S. Citizenship and Immigration Services, Policy Memorandum, Guidance for Processing Reasonable Fear, Credible Fear, Asylum, and Refugee Claims in Accordance with Matter of A-B-." July 11, 2018. https://www.uscis.gov/sites/default/files/document/memos/2018-06-18-PM-602 -0162-USCIS-Memorandum-Matter-of-A-B_Redacted_12-19-201.pdf.

US Immigration and Customs Enforcement (ICE). *Detention Facility Locator*, 2018. https://www.ice.gov/detention-facilities.

US Immigration and Customs Enforcement (ICE). *Fiscal Year 2018 ICE Enforcement and Removal Operations Report*, December 17, 2018. https://www.ice.gov/features/ ERO-2018.

Walters, Karolina. "Asylum Seekers Are Being Systematically Turned Away at the U.S.-Mexico Border." *American Immigration Council*, November 15, 2017. http:// immigrationimpact.com/2017/11/15/asylum-seekers-turned-away-border/.

Weissert, Will. "Texas Lockup Is Epicenter of Family Immigration Detention." August 10, 2018. https://apnews.com/ba773477c52c49f3a046fc6c9ad47011.

Women's Refugee Commission. *Joint Complaint on ICE Detention and Treatment of Pregnant Women*, September 26, 2017. https://www.womensrefugeecommission .org/rights/resources/1524-joint-complaint-ice-detention-treatment-of-pregnant -women.

Zannettino, Lana. "From Auschwitz to Mandatory Detention: Biopolitics, Race, and Human Rights in the Australian Refugee Camp." *International Journal of Human Rights* 16, no. 7 (2012): 1–26. https://doi.org/10.1080/13642987.2012.664136.

8 Experiences at the New Canadian-US Frontier

"I Just Assume That No Laws Exist . . ."

Evan Light, Sarah Naumes, and Aliya Amarshi

National borders are in flux, with the United States government enforcing norms that include parsing social media accounts and imposing biometric documentation regimes. Our research represents the state of affairs preceding the COVID-19 pandemic, the fallout of which may include the imposition of biometric systems that enter the genetic realm.[1] Human migration and travel systems are no longer simply the business of flesh, blood, and bureaucracy but have been integrated into the transnational digital infrastructure of big data and algorithmic governance.[2] Borders consist of walls and fences, officers and vehicles, weapons and visions, roads and traffic control, and devices for digital registration, identification, tracking, and tracing, all relying on data centres, protocols, and microdecisions.[3] Border control is an intervention magnifying the scale of all that passes before it, serving as a point of entry and exit, arrival and departure, or interminable stasis. Through the New Preclearance Act, which replaced Canada's Air Transport Preclearance Agreement in 2019, the US border exists both virtually and physically through its manifestation in several airports in the country with plans to extend this system to rail, land, and marine travel.[4] Similarly, the European Union's borders have been extended as far as the Mediterranean and central Africa through migration control and management systems.[5]

When we cross an international border, whether virtual or physical, the experience is fundamentally communicational. We are asked questions and

provide answers; we are prompted to complete forms and provide fingerprints, retina scans, and photographs, and we comply. We are compelled to
surrender our computers or smartphones with little recourse. In 2017, over
one hundred million border crossings between the United States and Canada
were recorded.[6] What is concerning is that "at the borders, CBSA officers
have an even wider range of powers than police. They can stop travellers for
questioning, take breath and blood samples, and search, detain, and arrest
non-citizens without a warrant."[7] These processes occur in the absence of any
independent civilian oversight or neutral reporting.[8] The result is the creation
of a legal space—"the border"—in which all who enter are subject to policies and laws governing their experience that are unclear and ever changing.
In every instance of crossing the Canada-US border, we are processed and
documented according to a set of laws and policies that are not self-evident.
While laws and some policies are public information, it is fair to say that as
border crossers, most of us are not experts on the legal apparatus to which
we submit ourselves. Instead, we surrender ourselves to border authorities
who have control over our bodies and belongings. Canadian border authorities have immense power, yet they lack public oversight.[9] One of the most
difficult issues to navigate when maneuvering in the terrain of border policy is
its partially visible nature. This chapter presents a research plan and preliminary results for making visible—and at times *divining*—Canadian border policy.

Despite the vast scale of cross-border human circulation between Canada and the United States, only limited research has been conducted into
the experiences of those crossing the border. Research has focused on small
groups of people or certain geographic locations, on the working practices
of border officers, or on the technology employed both at official border
crossings and in continual border surveillance.[10] Other work has examined
border-crossing mechanisms and their roles in and effects on economic life.[11]
Authors such as Benjamin J. Muller have questioned the extent to which
Canadian-American collaboration on border security has threatened Canadian sovereignty.[12] Through these approaches, the border is understood
to be a biopolitical manifestation of post-9/11 national security priorities.
The border appears as the discrete mechanization of a system premised on
marrying the flesh and blood of individuals crossing imaginary lines with
immeasurable quantities of data, feeding opaque decision-making processes.
The effects of this system on the individuals who are subject to it appear at
times in focused narratives—for instance, the ways that young Muslim men

experience security at the Canada-US border.[13] However, given the scale of mobility at this border, it is important that we conduct research capable of capturing the broad diversity of individuals who cross this border and their experiences. This text lays out a plan to do so, analyses the results of a small pilot study, and identifies obstacles to the execution of this research.

The Larger Beast

Our collaborative project, Border Probes, consists of two independent but complementary research projects. Border Walk / Border Talk is a long-term project, the pilot of which is explored in this chapter. It aims to discern policies carried out by Canadian Border Services Agency (CBSA) officers through the experiences of individuals crossing the Canada-US border into Canada. By *publicizing surveillance infrastructure and policy, we* seek to render transparent the surveillance capabilities and concomitant legal frameworks at land crossings and airport preclearance facilities. The border exists in its physical form and has been extended through systems of surveillance and documentation as well as spatially through the creation of a network of preclearance areas in nine Canadian airports. This research examines experiences of border crossings, partly through the data that flow to and from the border and are used to make decisions. The first project documents border surveillance technologies at work through access-to-information requests, interviews with former and current border security personnel, and examination of public records. In the second project, we plan to use an open-source system for detecting cell phone surveillance to probe for surveillance infrastructure at land crossings and airports.[14] These two projects will combine to construct maps of data collection and flow, on which we will model speculative policies in the absence of freely available ones. Based on our research, and in the absence of transparent official policy, we ask, What are the policies and practices at work at the Canada-US border, and what effects do they have on us?

Our Research Participants

The research outlined in this chapter is part of a larger study that aims to catalogue and make sense of people's experiences at the increasingly precarious Canada-US border using different methodological means. For this study segment, the research team conducted eleven in-depth, semistructured interviews with members of the York University community who had crossed the Canada-US border (by car or air) between January 20, 2017, and February 2018. This first date, which marked the inauguration of US president Donald Trump, was chosen to explore whether border practices may have changed in stride with other shifts in policy enacted by the new president. We work within a one-year time frame for feasibility reasons. Our decision to focus on the experiences of York University community members was a way for us to limit recruitment to a manageable population in the project's pilot stage. Participants were recruited through ads posted in university departmental email lists and newsletters, social media, and flyers posted in buildings on campus.

Our sample consisted of six women and five men. Of these participants, nine were white, and two self-identified as racialized. Both racialized participants were of South Asian descent, and one was Muslim. Regarding citizenship, nine informants were Canadian citizens, one carried dual Canadian and US citizenship, and one was an Indian citizen. Participants included a mix of undergraduate, master's, and PhD students. As with many qualitative studies, while our sample is not representative, the data provide an entry point to understand how the largely opaque practices of border security forces impact those who journey between Canada and the United States. Thus, our study aimed not to offer conclusive results about the current status of the Canada-US border but rather to engage in an initial interrogation, or pilot study, of how the border is either changing or remaining the same. As such, we chose in-depth, semistructured interviews to obtain rich narrative accounts of how people experience and navigate the changing practices and procedures they encounter at the border. The limited context of our study and the small number of participants allowed us to participate in more thorough conversations in a manner that would not have been possible had we elected to use a method that did not involve such close engagement with research participants (e.g., an isolated survey). The informational similarities that we noted in the sentiments described by participants undoubtedly indicate a need for further study of the changing nature of the Canada-US border. Further research is particularly needed around the differences in experience between racialized border crossers and those who are white—something that our study was not able to satisfactorily explore.

Informed by feminist methodological insights, our own positionalities as researchers impacted the field site, and as such, we shared, when appropriate, how our own embodied experiences of gender, race, and citizenship have played out in our border-crossing experiences.[15] Such an exercise in self-reflexive sharing can dismantle hierarchies between the researcher and participant. It can deepen the rapport between both parties—allowing for more enriching and illuminating knowledge sharing and production. Given that our sample was made up of undergraduate and graduate students in critical fields such as sociology, political science, and gender studies, we had the advantage of engaging with participants whose narratives carried a thoughtfulness and self-reflection that further enhanced our research.

Interviews took place between November 2017 and February 2018. Each interview differed in length—ranging from fifteen minutes to more than two hours. Participants were asked to recount their experiences at the Canada-US border, including how they would characterize their treatment by border authorities; what types of questions they were asked; whether explanations were provided for the legal processes and procedures to which they were subject; and what personal information was extracted from them. Specifically, they were asked if their personal electronic devices were examined and if any biometric data (e.g., retina scans, fingerprints) were collected. Informants were also asked to reflect on any differences they have encountered in their crossing experiences in the last several years—such as upon 9/11 and the inauguration of Donald Trump. Finally, we asked questions about the measures, if any, that participants were taking to ensure their digital privacy when crossing the border. Interviews were recorded, transcribed, and coded thematically. Thematic coding identifies commonalities in participant narratives, integrating existing codes around a central theme.[16]

Three Discoveries

Our research yielded three significant findings that merit further interrogation from both scholars and activist groups:

1.   Donald Trump's election may have had a chilling effect on border crossings into the United States from Canada, exacerbating post-9/11 travel concerns.
2.   While many border crossers have a heightened awareness of digital privacy and surveillance issues, there is a lack of knowledge surrounding cell phone encryption techniques.
3.   Laws and protocols at the Canada-US border are opaque.

By exploring these three findings in detail, we illuminate an important dimension of Canada-US border crossings wherein that line is exposed as an expanding temporal and physical space.

When an individual crosses the Canada-US border, they reference their own previous experiences and broader social and cultural sentiments. This framing has resulted in a nuanced emotional space that is expanding—or has already expanded—beyond the confines of a physical crossing point.

The Impact of Donald Trump's Election

For many of our informants, crossing the border is marked by anxiety and anticipation. While Trump's election contributed to these sentiments, five of the eleven participants indicated that crossing the Canada-US border had a chilling effect *prior* to Trump's inauguration. When these five participants referenced a temporal event, it tended to be 9/11—a point when Canada-US border crossings changed dramatically.[17]

Both participants who self-identified as racialized indicated that the Canada-US border has had a long-standing unsettling effect on them. This has led to significant considerations about whether and how to cross the border and how to physically present oneself. One participant who identified as Muslim described being encouraged by his father to shave his beard in advance of border crossings. He said,

> If I remember when I had my visa interview, it's a funny story because he was, like, adamant that I shave otherwise I'm not getting a visa if I look like an Islamic extremist according to him. And I told him, I don't want to do it, but eventually just the idea that not being about to go to grad school because of something as stupid as this, I sort of caved, and I did shave. And when I came to my visa interview, the person interviewing me was wearing the hijab.

This statement is significant in that it reflects the fear of Islamophobia that permeates border spaces as well as the burden that is placed on racialized individuals to conform to Western standards of appearance as a means of easing their passage. Interestingly, it also highlights how racialized people can be recruited to carry out discriminatory practices and policies against people who share similar backgrounds.

Two participants who indicated that crossing the Canada-US border had a deleterious effect before Donald Trump's election described how that sense has been exacerbated since January 20, 2017. Six interviewees, including these two participants, described a chilling effect post–January 20, 2017.

Only two participants expressed that crossing the Canada-US border has not been an uncomfortable or unpleasant experience for them. Both of these interviewees were white, and one described circumstances in which crossing the Canada-US border had unfortunate consequences for friends and family after the inauguration of Donald Trump.

The extent to which self-censorship and chilling were expressed in interviews varied. One participant stated, "I generally try not to go in and out of the country too much." This statement illuminates how border crossers may self-select out of engaging with the Canada-US border to protect against potentially negative encounters or invasions of privacy. This participant also indicated that they perceived that Trump's election emboldened xenophobic questioning by American authorities at the border.

One participant described deleting contents on their electronic devices before crossing the border. Again, this indicates a level of self-censorship at the Canada-US border—one that is not explicitly enforced by authorities but occurs nonetheless. Another participant, a white male, described dressing in a suit and shaving (to present a "cleaner" appearance), bringing mail as evidence of their address, avoiding explicit discussions of political motivations for travel—in this case, the Women's March—and turning off their cell phone when crossing the border. This participant viewed the Canada-US border as a space with unclear authority and laws. In another, a different participant— a white woman—noted a chilling effect at the border and discussed avoiding being the driver when crossing the border because of concerns about looking too "paranoid" to border authorities. Again, this indicates a lack of clarity surrounding authority and laws, in addition to exemplifying the atmosphere of fear and anxiety that border spaces hold.

Specifically regarding the post–January 20, 2017, context, a white male participant stated, "After Trump, I feel like the rules have changed." This was echoed by a white female interviewee who made a similar statement, but in reference to the experiences of visible minorities. A white male participant accounted for extra travel time because of stories circulating in the media about border-crossing experiences but did not notice a significant difference in protocol. Another white female interviewee explained that a family member who was born in Sudan but who is a Canadian citizen cancelled a trip to the United States after Trump issued Executive Order 13769, labeled the "Muslim ban." In another case, a racialized female participant described "mapping" documents and justifications for travel ahead of crossing the border.

While Trump's election may have had a potential chilling effect on the Canada-US border, it is clear from our interviews that border crossers have had concerns since at least 9/11 in many circumstances. This is not shocking, given how border security shifted after that date. Furthermore, although our research intended to capture the post–January 20, 2017, context, we noted that it was difficult for participants to contemplate the Canada-US border within a discrete temporality. Each previous encounter by participants themselves, in conjunction with stories from friends, family, and acquaintances, painted a picture of what to expect at the border. In many cases, while interviewing, even though we expressed clear parameters about our time frame for interviewees, we had to ask for clarification about when certain experiences began to arise. This indicates to us that the totality of border experiences and narratives frame what border crossers can expect. Further, border experiences have been marked by fear for an extended period.

Ignorance of Cell Phone Encryption Techniques

Of the eleven participants interviewed, eight indicated that they either had not encrypted their cellular telephone or were unaware of what constitutes encryption. Of the remaining three participants, one was not asked in their interview whether they encrypt their cell phone, one encrypts as part of workplace protocol, and one had an unclear answer. This is notable given that those who participated in the interview process often indicated the seemingly unchecked power of border authorities and concerns regarding privacy and surveillance. It is also remarkable because our participant pool was composed entirely of university students with elevated access to encryption techniques and information about the rationale for protecting personal data.

In 2018, the British Columbia Civil Liberties Association (BCCLA) published an *Electronic Devices Privacy Handbook* with the express intent of explaining what one's rights are at the Canada-US border and how to manage one's electronic devices at the border to safeguard one's privacy.[18] The handbook explains full-disk encryption, which is available on most smartphones and portable computers, as a method that "essentially scrambles the contents of your electronic device. The data is unlocked with a passphrase."[19] Smartphones running the Android operating system have had full-disk encryption enabled by default since 2015.[20] Most Apple mobile devices have full-disk encryption enabled by default as well.[21] Encryption is useless, though, if a logged-in smartphone or laptop is, for instance, given to border authorities.

In one case, when asked whether their phone was encrypted, one white male participant stated, "It is because I turned it on. It's one of the options in the phone just to encrypt all the contents and everything like that." Taking a different approach to privacy, one racialized male participant stated, "I'm not sure what encrypted means, but I make it a point to not store any important information on my phone." A white female participant admitted, "I do not know. I mean, I know my email is, but I don't know if the phone itself is. Do you mean just like passwords and stuff like that? . . . Or not passwords, but phone numbers and logs and details like that?" Another white female participant laughed and said, "Um, I don't know what that means. I think that the BlackBerry was. The BlackBerry had some feature where if you put in the wrong password ten times, it will erase everything on your phone." Another racialized female participant simply said, "I don't think so." Finally, a white male interviewee expressed that the phone was encrypted through biometrics. They stated, "The password on my phone uses my biometrics—it uses my fingerprint."

While encryption can, in more extreme cases, be bypassed,[22] it is a tool that border crossers can use to hinder unwanted invasions of privacy. Although this was before January 20, 2017, the cell phone of one of our interview participants—a white woman—had been examined twice by US authorities. When we asked whether they had ever refused to allow the authorities to examine their phone, the participant stated, "No, that would be a very bad move. I mean, now it's a little different because I am a permanent resident, so maybe I have, like, a right to be in Canada, but especially when you're on a visa, like, you can be refused entry at any time, right? So, if they ask you to do ten jumping jacks, you're going to do eleven, right?"

While encryption might be an effective means by which border crossers may resist surveillance efforts, the question, however, remains as to how border authorities respond to encrypted devices. Might they see encryption as grounds for suspicion rather than the exercise of one's right to privacy? Indeed, the instincts of these individuals are well founded. According to the BCCLA's analysis of CBSA policies concerning digital devices at the border, the consequences of refusing to provide access to one's digital device can be severe and unpredictable. They may include having one's device seized for an unspecified amount of time (possibly months) for forensic analysis or being arrested for impeding the work of a border officer.[23] In 2019, a grand total of 207,822,527 travellers were processed at the border. Of these, 27,405 had digital devices examined, and of these examined devices, 10,860 resulted in the discovery of customs or immigration-related offenses. CBSA only began tracking the frequency with which its officers searched digital devices in November 2017.[24]

Poorly communicated border policies shift the rights of individuals, making it increasingly difficult for border crossers to navigate and seek recourse. For example, the aforementioned participant is aware that if they were to refuse authorities access to their device, their ability to cross the border might also be refused without remedy. While the participant credits their lack of permanent resident status as a possible explanation for why they might be refused, recent developments in border policy under the Preclearance Act stipulate that even citizens of a country are no longer accorded the freedom to refuse searches and invasive procedures by claiming that they would like to change their mind and turn back.[25] Rather, refusal to go through with security measures may result in border officials holding travellers for further detainment and interrogation at the hands of their own country's border guards. For example, a Canadian border crosser who refuses a search by US authorities may now be detained and interrogated by Canadian border authorities who interpret such a refusal as grounds for suspicion. This troubling development further entrenches border crossers within a regime of questionable legality, in which one's arrival at the border forfeits their right to make choices around the policies and procedures that are imposed on them—now not only in the case that they want to make their flight but even in cases in which they would prefer to turn back.

Invisible Laws and Arbitrary Protocols

In their experiences crossing the Canada-US border since January 20, 2017, all eleven research participants indicated that the legal processes and procedures that border agents followed were never explained. When we asked whether legal processes and procedures were clearly presented, we were frequently met with scoffs and laughter, as if to indicate the absurdity of the idea that a border agent would make clear the laws under which they are functioning. A few research participants described text on customs forms or posters hanging at the Canada-US border or in the airport indicating some laws, policies, or procedures. There were no verbal discussions about border laws or policies. In one instance, a white male research participant described being detained in secondary screening. Once he was allowed to leave, the participant asked why they were detained, and the border officer said, "I can't divulge that."

In perhaps the most illuminating statement of our interviews, when asked whether border officials had explained the legal authority under which they were operating, one white female participant stated, "I just assume that no laws exist at the border." This answer frames a general sentiment that the border exists as an exceptional space wherein border crossers have little to no recourse for actions taken by authorities. The border operates in a permanent state of exception.[26] The same participant stated at a different point in the interview, "I just assume, I don't know, they could do whatever they want, right?"

These statements are particularly troubling considering the general sentiment we encountered that border practices disproportionately impact racialized individuals. The chilling effect that we noted in many interviews creates an uneven atmosphere for opacity at the border wherein certain individuals can pass through without drawing attention to themselves and others feel as though they are the subject of scrutiny and surveillance.

Expressing a sentiment of concern about how previous correspondence could be an issue at the border, one white female participant claimed, "You don't know what they're allowed to do and what they're allowed to look at, and you worry, like, is some ancient text message gonna, like, be read a certain way and they'll be like, 'Oh, we gotta search your entire car now'? Um, I'd say I never used to worry about it, but definitely within the last like seven years. Yeah, I don't know what they're allowed to do or what they're allowed to look at on my phone."

Conclusion

> . . . headed, I fear, toward a most useless place. The Waiting Place . . .
> . . . for people just waiting.
> Waiting for a train to go
> or a bus to come, or the rain to go
> or the phone to ring, or the snow to snow

or waiting around for a Yes or No
or waiting for their hair to grow.
Everyone is just waiting.[27]

Time is, as Dr. Seuss points out, a political instrument of a varied sort. It may regulate our lives in a most natural way or one that is contrived, confining, or seemingly arbitrary. In the discretely regulated border spaces we are concerned about, time is of the utmost political value, whereby our fundamental political identities are defined temporally.[28] *How long have you lived at this address? How long have you been a permanent resident? How long have you been abroad?* The answers to such questions—not uncommon ones to experience while crossing the border—and other unidentified information lead to us being treated in certain ways. The deceptively simple questions at the heart of our research are "*How?*" and "*Why?*" The degree to which the state apparatus safeguards the answers to these questions calls for radically new ways of doing border research, capable of gathering, parsing, and analyzing the experiences of millions of border crossers. Without an arms-length oversight body that would engage in such work, we propose such oversight is possible in the academic realm in collaboration with civil society.

Although this study was conducted in a limiting setting, our findings identify important themes that warrant further exploration into how the Canada-US border is shifting both in a post-9/11 context and after the inauguration and tenure of Donald Trump. Special attention must be given to the racialized aspects of border crossing, something that this chapter was not able to fully explore due to our overwhelmingly white data set. Future studies will undoubtedly also have to account for how the border has and continues to shift in a world that is adapting to the real and constructed threats of the COVID-19 pandemic.

Additionally, as we look forward to how this research might unfold, we aim to incorporate the filing of access-to-information requests on the part of research participants, seeking access to CBSA's documentation of each border-crossing experience. While our initial methodological model included this, our efforts to adopt this approach have proven, perhaps predictably, difficult. The access-to-information apparatus should, by design, insulate those who request information—or about whom information is requested—from the apparatus that is being queried.[29] However, civil liberties experts with whom we consulted disagree. Key to the successful design and execution of the project we propose here is the ability to conduct this work without bringing harm to our subjects, ensuring that a willingness to partake in critical research on border policy through sharing one's experiences does not lead to one being "flagged" at the border. This obstacle speaks to the need for government to ensure border spaces are no longer perceived as states of exception, a need for oversight and transparency around policies and expectations, and a rehumanization of a political space within which politics and practices of dehumanization have become embedded.[30]

Notes

1. Miranda Bryant, "'Are You Immune?': The New Class System That Could Shape the Covid-19 World."
2. Matthew Longo, *The Politics of Borders: Sovereignty, Security, and the Citizen After 9/11.*
3. Corey Johnson et al., "Interventions on Rethinking 'the Border' in Border Studies," 61–69, https://doi.org/10.1016/j.polgeo.2011.01.002; Élisabeth Vallet, *Borders, Fences and Walls: State of Insecurity?*
4. Legislative Services Branch, "Preclearance in Canada Regulations"; Parliament of Canada, "House Government Bill C-23 (42–1): An Act Respecting the Preclearance of Persons and Goods in Canada and the United States," C-23 (2017); Harry J. Chang, "The Government of Canada Implements Its New Preclearance Act."
5. Louise Amoore, "Biometric Borders: Governing Mobilities in the War on Terror," 336–51; Dennis Broeders, "The New Digital Borders of Europe: EU Databases and the Surveillance of Irregular Migrants," 71–92; Forschungsgruppe, "Transit Migration"; Sabine Hess et al., *Der lange Sommer der Migration: Grenzregime III*; Irma Van der Ploeg, "The Body as Data in the Age of Information."
6. Bureau of Transportation Statistics, Data Tables and Query Tool, Border Crossing Entry Data: Monthly Data, 2004, https://data.bts.gov/stories/s/Tables -Query-Tool/6rt4-smhh.
7. British Columbia Civil Liberties Association (BCCLA), *Oversight at the Border: A Model for Independent Accountability at the Canada Border Services Agency*, 4.
8. Dale Smith, "Oversight at the Border."
9. BCCLA, *Oversight at the Border*; Vicky Mochama, "Canadian Border Services Agency Lacks Oversight, but That's Only Part of the Problem"; Josh Paterson and Lorne Waldman, "Paterson and Waldman: Canada Border Services

Needs Proper Oversight"; Dale Smith, "Border Agency Oversight Bill Stalls in Parliament."

10. Baljt Nagra and Paula Maurutto, "Crossing Borders and Managing Racialized Identities: Experiences of Security and Surveillance among Young Canadian Muslims," 165–94; Jane Helleiner, "Canadian Border Resident Experience of the 'Smartening' Border at Niagara," 87–103,; Reg Whitaker, "Securing the 'Ontario-Vermont Border,'" 53–70; Vic Satzewich, *Points of Entry: How Canada's Immigration Officers Decide Who Gets In*; Anna Pratt, "Between a Hunch and a Hard Place: Making Suspicion Reasonable at the Canadian Border," 461–80; Karine Côté-Boucher, "Technologies, déqualification et luttes d'influence chez les professionnels de la sécurité frontalière," 127–51, https://doi.org/10.7202/1026731ar; Özgün E. Topak et al., "From Smart Borders to Perimeter Security: The Expansion of Digital Surveillance at the Canadian Borders," 880–99; Longo, *Politics of Borders*; Karine Cote-Boucher, "The Diffuse Border: Intelligence-Sharing, Control and Confinement along Canada's Smart Border."

11. Karine Côté-Boucher, "Risky Business? Border Preclearance and the Securing of Economic Life in North America," 37–67; Geoffrey Hale, "Politics, People and Passports: Contesting Security, Travel and Trade on the US-Canadian Border," 27–69; Christopher Sands, "Toward a New Frontier: Improving the U.S.-Canadian Border."

12. Benjamin J. Muller, "The Day the Border Died? The Canadian Border as Checkpoint in an Age of Hemispheric Security and Surveillance," 297–318.

13. Nagra and Maurutto, "Crossing Borders."

14. Border Probes, "Stingray Stingers."

15. Sharlene Nagy Hesse-Biber, "The Practice of Feminist In-Depth Interviewing," 110–48.

16. Johnny Saldaña, *The Coding Manual for Qualitative Researchers*.

17. Mark B. Salter, "Passports, Mobility, and Security: How Smart Can the Border Be?" 71; Buster C. Ogbuagu, "Constructing America's 'New Blacks': Post 9/11 Social Policies and Their Impacts on and Implications for the Lived Experiences of Muslims, Arabs, and Others," 470; Mathew Coleman and Austin Kocher, "Detention, Deportation, Devolution and Immigrant Incapacitation in the US, Post 9/11," 230.

18. British Columbia Civil Liberties Association and CIPPIC, "Electronic Devices Privacy Handbook: A Guide to Your Rights at the Border."

19. British Columbia Civil Liberties Association and CIPPIC, 46.

20. Jerry Hildenbrand, "Enable Encryption on Your Android."

21. Electronic Frontier Foundation, "How to: Encrypt Your iPhone."

22. Danny Yadron, Spencer Ackerman, and Sam Thielman, "Inside the FBI's Encryption Battle with Apple."
23. British Columbia Civil Liberties Association and CIPPIC, "Electronic Devices Privacy Handbook," 29–30.
24. Government of Canada, Canada Border Services Agency, "Examining Digital Devices at the Canadian Border."
25. Chang, "Government of Canada."
26. Giorgio Agamben, *State of Exception.*
27. Dr. Seuss, *Oh, the Places You'll Go!*
28. Elizabeth F. Cohen, *The Political Value of Time: Citizenship, Duration, and Democratic Justice,* 97–108.
29. Kevin Walby and Mike Larsen, "Getting at the Live Archive: On Access to Information Research in Canada," 623–33.
30. Nisha Kapoor, *Deport Deprive Extradite: 21st Century State Extremism,* 23–50.

Bibliography

Agamben, Giorgio. *State of Exception.* Chicago: University of Chicago Press, 2005.

Amoore, Louise. "Biometric Borders: Governing Mobilities in the War on Terror." *Political Geography* 25, no. 3 (March 1, 2006): 336–51. https://doi.org/10.1016/j.polgeo.2006.02.001.

Border Probes. "Stingray Stingers." *Border Probes* (blog). Accessed February 21, 2020. https://borderprobes.glendon.yorku.ca/stingray-stingers/.

British Columbia Civil Liberties Association (BCCLA). *Oversight at the Border: A Model for Independent Accountability at the Canada Border Services Agency.* Vancouver: British Columbia Civil Liberties Association, June 2017. https://bccla.org/wp-content/uploads/2017/06/FINAL-for-web-BCCLA-CBSA-Oversight.pdf.

British Columbia Civil Liberties Association and CIPPIC. "Electronic Devices Privacy Handbook: A Guide to Your Rights at the Border." British Columbia Civil Liberties Association and CIPPIC, n.d. https://bccla.org/our_work/electronic-devices-privacy-handbook-a-guide-to-your-rights-at-the-border/.

Broeders, Dennis. "The New Digital Borders of Europe: EU Databases and the Surveillance of Irregular Migrants." *International Sociology* 22, no. 1 (January 1, 2007): 71–92. https://doi.org/10.1177/0268580907070126.

Bryant, Miranda. "'Are You Immune?': The New Class System That Could Shape the Covid-19 World." *Guardian*, June 10, 2020. http://www.theguardian.com/us-news/2020/jun/10/are-you-immune-the-new-class-system-that-could-shape-the-covid-19-world.

Bureau of Transportation Statistics. "Border Crossing/Entry Data." January 10, 2019. https://www.bts.gov/content/border-crossingentry-data.

Chang, Harry J. "The Government of Canada Implements Its New Preclearance Act." *Dentons*, September 3, 2019. https://www.dentons.com/en/insights/ alerts/2019/september/3/the-government-of-canada-implements-its-new -preclearance-act.

Cohen, Elizabeth F. *The Political Value of Time: Citizenship, Duration, and Democratic Justice*. Cambridge: Cambridge University Press, 2018.

Coleman, Mathew, and Austin Kocher. "Detention, Deportation, Devolution and Immigrant Incapacitation in the US, Post 9/11." *Geographical Journal* 177, no. 3 (September 1, 2011): 228–37. https://doi.org/10.1111/j.1475-4959.2011 .00424.x.

Côté-Boucher, Karine. "The Diffuse Border: Intelligence-Sharing, Control and Confinement along Canada's Smart Border." *Surveillance & Society* 5, no. 2 (2008). https://doi.org/10.24908/ss.v5i2.3432.

Côté-Boucher, Karine. "Risky Business? Border Preclearance and the Securing of Economic Life in North America." In *Neoliberalism and Everyday Life*, edited by Susan Braedley and Meg Luxton, 37–67. Montréal: McGill-Queen's University Press, 2010.

Côté-Boucher, Karine. "Technologies, déqualification et luttes d'influence chez les professionnels de la sécurité frontalière." *Criminologie* 47, no. 2 (2014): 127–51. https://doi.org/10.7202/1026731ar.

Electronic Frontier Foundation. "How to: Encrypt Your iPhone." Surveillance Self-Defense, September 17, 2014. https://ssd.eff.org/en/module/how-encrypt-your -iphone.

Forschungsgruppe. "Transit Migration." In *Turbulente Ränder: Neue Perspektiven Auf Migration an Den Grenzen Europas*, 87–106 Bielefeld: transcript, 2007.

Government of Canada, Canada Border Services Agency. "Examining Digital Devices at the Canadian Border." December 3, 2019. https://cbsa-asfc.gc.ca/travel -voyage/edd-ean-eng.html#08.

Government of Canada, Transport Canada. "Transportation in Canada 2017." Annual report. Ottawa: Transport Canada, June 21, 2018. https://www.tc.gc.ca/ eng/policy/transportation-canada-2017.html.

Hale, Geoffrey. "Politics, People and Passports: Contesting Security, Travel and Trade on the US-Canadian Border." *Geopolitics* 16, no. 1 (January 31, 2011): 27–69. https://doi.org/10.1080/14650045.2010.493768.

Helleiner, Jane. "Canadian Border Resident Experience of the 'Smartening' Border at Niagara." *Journal of Borderlands Studies* 25, nos. 3–4 (September 1, 2010): 87–103. https://doi.org/10.1080/08865655.2010.9695773.

Hess, Sabine, Bernd Kasparek, Stefanie Kron, Mathias Rodatz, Maria Schwertl, and Simon Sontowski. *Der lange Sommer der Migration: Grenzregime III*. 1st ed. Berlin: Assoziation A, 2016.

Hesse-Biber, Sharlene Nagy. "The Practice of Feminist In-Depth Interviewing." In *Feminist Research Practice*, edited by Sharlene Nagy Hesse-Biber and Patricia Lina Leavy, 110–48. Thousand Oaks, CA: SAGE, 2007.

Hildenbrand, Jerry. "Enable Encryption on Your Android." Android Central, February 26, 2016. https://www.androidcentral.com/how-enable-encryption -android.

Johnson, Corey, Reece Jones, Anssi Paasi, Louise Amoore, Alison Mountz, Mark Salter, and Chris Rumford. "Interventions on Rethinking 'the Border' in Border Studies." *Political Geography* 30, no. 2 (February 1, 2011): 61–69. https://doi.org/10 .1016/j.polgeo.2011.01.002.

Kapoor, Nisha. *Deport Deprive Extradite: 21st Century State Extremism*. London: Verso, 2018.

Law Times. "Border Agency Oversight Bill Stalls in Parliament." *Law Times*, January 9, 2017. https://www.lawtimesnews.com/article/border-agency-oversight -bill-stalls-in-parliament-13075/.

Legislative Services Branch. "Preclearance in Canada Regulations." August 15, 2019. https://laws.justice.gc.ca/eng/regulations/SOR-2019-183/index.html.

Longo, Matthew. *The Politics of Borders: Sovereignty, Security, and the Citizen After 9/11*. Cambridge: Cambridge University Press, 2018.

Mochama, Vicky. "Canadian Border Services Agency Lacks Oversight, but That's Only Part of the Problem." *Toronto Star*, June 28, 2018. https://www.thestar.com/ opinion/2018/06/27/canadian-border-services-agency-lacks-oversight-but-thats -only-part-of-the-problem.html.

Muller, Benjamin J. "The Day the Border Died? The Canadian Border as Checkpoint in an Age of Hemispheric Security and Surveillance." In *National Security, Surveillance and Terror: Canada and Australia in Comparative Perspective*, edited by Randy K. Lippert, Kevin Walby, Ian Warren, and Darren Palmer, 297–318. Crime Prevention and Security Management. Cham: Springer International, 2016. https://doi.org/10.1007/978-3-319-43243-4_13.

Nagra, Baljt, and Paula Maurutto. "Crossing Borders and Managing Racialized Identities: Experiences of Security and Surveillance among Young Canadian Muslims." *Canadian Journal of Sociology* 41, no. 2 (June 30, 2016): 165–94. https:// doi.org/10.29173/cjs23031.

Ogbuagu, Buster C. "Constructing America's 'New Blacks': Post 9/11 Social Policies and Their Impacts on and Implications for the Lived Experiences of Muslims, Arabs, and Others." *Mediterranean Journal of Social Sciences* 4, no. 1 (2013): 469–80.

Parliament of Canada. House Government Bill C-23 (42–1): An Act Respecting the Preclearance of Persons and Goods in Canada and the United States, C-23 (2017). https://www.parl.ca/LegisInfo/BillDetails.aspx?billId=8362244&Language=E& Mode=1.

Paterson, Josh, and Lorne Waldman. "Paterson and Waldman: Canada Border Services Needs Proper Oversight," *Ottawa Citizen*, September 10, 2018. https://ottawacitizen.com/opinion/columnists/paterson-and-waldman-latest -death-in-canada-border-services-custody-shows-independent-oversight -needed.

Pratt, Anna. "Between a Hunch and a Hard Place: Making Suspicion Reasonable at the Canadian Border." *Social & Legal Studies* 19, no. 4 (December 1, 2010): 461–80. https://doi.org/10.1177/0964663910378434.

Saldaña, Johnny. *The Coding Manual for Qualitative Researchers.* 2nd ed. Los Angeles: SAGE, 2013.

Salter, Mark B. "Passports, Mobility, and Security: How Smart Can the Border Be?" *International Studies Perspectives* 5, no. 1 (February 1, 2004): 71–91. https://doi .org/10.1111/j.1528-3577.2004.00158.x.

Sands, Christopher. "Toward a New Frontier: Improving the U.S.-Canadian Border." Brookings Institute, March 2009. https://www.brookings.edu/wp-content/ uploads/2012/04/20090325_sands.pdf.

Satzewich, Vic. *Points of Entry: How Canada's Immigration Officers Decide Who Gets In*. Vancouver: UBC Press, 2015.

Seuss, Dr. [Theodor Seuss Geisel]. *Oh, the Places You'll Go!* New York: Random House Books for Young Readers, 1990.

Smith, Dale. "Oversight at the Border." *CBA / ABC National*, Canadian Bar Association, January 28, 2020. http://nationalmagazine.ca/en-ca/articles/law/hot -topics-in-law/2020/oversight-at-the-border.

Topak, Özgün E., Ciara Bracken-Roche, Alana Saulnier, and David Lyon. "From Smart Borders to Perimeter Security: The Expansion of Digital Surveillance at the Canadian Borders." *Geopolitics* 20, no. 4 (October 2, 2015): 880–99. https://doi .org/10.1080/14650045.2015.1085024.

Vallet, Élisabeth. *Borders, Fences and Walls: State of Insecurity?* Farnham, UK: Ashgate, 2014.

Van der Ploeg, Irma. "The Body as Data in the Age of Information." In *Routledge Handbook of Surveillance Studies*, edited by David Lyon and Kevin D. Haggerty, 176–83. London: Routledge, 2012.

Walby, Kevin, and Mike Larsen. "Getting at the Live Archive: On Access to Information Research in Canada." *Canadian Journal of Law and Society* 26, no. 3 (December 2011): 623–33. https://doi.org/10.3138/cjls.26.3.623.

Whitaker, Reg. "Securing the 'Ontario-Vermont Border.'" *International Journal* 60, no. 1 (March 1, 2005): 53–70. https://doi.org/10.1177/002070200506000105.

Yadron, Danny, Spencer Ackerman, and Sam Thielman. "Inside the FBI's Encryption Battle with Apple." *Guardian*, February 18, 2016, sec. Technology. https://www.theguardian.com/technology/2016/feb/17/inside-the-fbis-encryption -battle-with-apple.

Afterword: On Being Unsettled

Discomfort and Noninnocence in Border Studies

Anne McNevin

En route to the conference from which this volume emerges, I flew for the first time from New York to Butte, Montana; on to Lethbridge, Alberta; and over the Great Plains. These were the names the pilot used in his explanation of the route we would take—names that corresponded to the maps with which I was familiar. From the air, I was struck by the sheer expanse of flatness as far as the eye could see, by the patchwork grid that parceled this land into neat geometric lots, and by its apparent totality. Nothing appeared to separate square from square: no variation, no wild or unruly patches of earth, no hints of what this land might have been before its division in this way. The visual completeness of seeming domestication was breathtaking, at least for this viewer who, granted, had little sense of where or how to look for less obvious traces of difference and survival.

I was, of course, flying over lines that cross lands that are named, inhabited, and occupied in very different ways: as Blackfoot territory, as the United States and Canada, as North America and Turtle Island, to name only English-language variants. I was staring out the window at the beauty and ingenuity of lands steeped in violence and regeneration. What struck me as distinctive in its flat uniformity seemed also to capture the peculiar effects of universalization as a technique of erasure. And my immediate sense of this place, filtered through my own ill-attunement to the forms of life and land below, was wrapped up with the habits of mind and body through which erasures persist.

This volume engages critically with lines, borders, and lands from the perspective of an academic enterprise, itself implicated in the drawing of epistemological lines that divide and devalue, strike through and erase. Not least in this respect, this volume is the outcome of a conference that was uncomfortable. It should have been uncomfortable, because its academic format reflected one of the many divides between what or who is deemed authoritative and what or who is not. The title of the conference, "The Line Crossed Us," refers most explicitly to the nineteenth-century annexation of Mexican territory by the United States—a process through which many people marked by forms of racial and colonial difference and living in what we now know as Texas came to be seen as alien to the place that was their home. From their perspective and from that of subsequent generations, when "the line crossed us," it produced forms of nonbelonging and, later, criminality that were otherwise nonsensical. Implicitly, however, the conference title also refers to the lines that cross and constitute knowledge-producing practices in ways that intersect with concrete border lines. Disciplinary knowledge, transmitted and honed in conferences of this kind, has long served to generate and justify borders through which we come to know such things as "international relations" as something that happens between pregiven states and through which we come to distinguish "ethnography" from "history" in ways that determine what counts as evidence in land rights claims and what belongs in which museum.

Discomfort may therefore be a fitting feeling in the face of the task that we, as contributors to this volume, have set for ourselves. Feminist scholars have argued as much, noting that discomfort, like other affects too often dismissed as impediments or irrelevant to research methodologies, has productive effects: "'turn[ing] us on' or 'turn[ing] us off' to certain lines of thinking, conceptualizing, knowing and making sense."[1] At the conference itself, I felt uncomfortable delivering an address in a place I was not from and had little knowledge of, on a topic that would resonate in untold ways with those in the audience for whom the borders over which I had flown and about which I spoke were lived on an everyday basis as lines that crossed their particular bodies in painful, debilitating ways. I feel uncomfortable now, as I write this afterword—a genre that implies a summation from a hindsight perspective on the whole. Such perspectives are always partial and risk more occlusion than illumination when expressed without humility, or with the kind of humility that emanates from a position of power that is enhanced by virtue signaling. This double-edged humility is often at work in attempts to dislodge the givenness of borders, including in acknowledgements of unceded lands by non-Indigenous people that have now become commonplace, even formulaic, in certain settler-colonial contexts (though notably less so in the United States). Endorsed by audiences and institutions that are deeply implicated in contemporary colonial conditions, such rituals are as insufficient as they are sincerely felt. I count my own intervention in these pages as part of this discomforting mix of reflexivity and privilege. The value of this volume is that it calls out these tensions even as it traces and performs the borders and conventions in question. This messy business keeps us focused on what is at stake, more answerable to our claims, and exposed in our inconsistencies. This is the discomfort that rightly attends a critical colonial encounter.

It is with these productive tensions in mind that the contributions to this volume raised ongoing questions for me. What does it mean to engage borders as objects of inquiry with and without reference to the First Nation lands crossed by those borders? If, as Evan Light, Sarah Naumes, and Aliya Amarshi argue in chapter 8, the US-Canada border is a manifestation of "post-9/11 security priorities," is it not also a manifestation of settler-colonial dispossession? If school-age children in Finland narrate the loss of Finnish territory to Russia in terms of a "phantom limb," as Chloe Wells describes in chapter 3, how does this square with the forms of loss experienced by Sámi peoples initiated by earlier rounds of cartographic division? What do we fail to understand about post-9/11 security priorities or "the 'geo-bodies' of nation-states" when we fail to interrogate how they are conditioned by ongoing colonial relations?

It is jarring to read those chapters directly concerned with lines that cross peoples singled out for colonial erasure alongside those that investigate, without colonial context, policing technologies enforcing those lines against newly marked intruders and usurpers. But this reaction is also because the volume as a whole challenges the notion that inquiry into borders—critical or otherwise—is an innocent endeavor. The ways in which questions are posed and answered order knowledge in such a way as to give some experiences more weight than others and to designate relevance unevenly. That these effects unsettle the reader is one measure of the volume's success. Another is the extent to which what or who has been cast aside as finished or irrelevant is brought to light with the kinds of affective sensitivities that produce what Ramón Resendiz and Rosalva Resendiz call in chapter 1—following Ann Stoler, Ariella Aisha Azoulay, and others—a decolonial archive.

If part of this volume's value lies in its juxtaposition of chapters concerned with different aspects of borders, it also lies in contributions that bring different kinds of border regimes into dialogue with one another. Ryan Hall, for example, draws attention to Lakota, Dakota, and Blackfoot people, displaced by the so-called Indian Wars of the nineteenth century, whose movement from the United States to Canadian territory marked them as refugees even though they had not always left their own lands. What is at stake in conceptualizing this kind of border crossing in terms of refugeehood? What possibilities are signalled by this formulation, including for the kinds of coalitions able to resist the reassertion of national borders and ethno-national privilege in local and global contexts? As Hall notes, "Seeing Indigenous people (whose identity is generally defined by their connection to specific homelands) in the same terms as refugees (whose identity is defined by their lack of place) can . . . feel counterintuitive." While Indigenous people sometimes express affinity with displaced peoples, identifying as refugees in their own lands,[2] others displaced within their own cities and states have resisted the trope of refugeehood precisely because it is suggestive of nonbelonging. This was the case, for example, when African Americans displaced by Hurricane Katrina in 2005 insisted that they were not refugees but citizens.[3] They were responding to the racialized production of refugeehood as a pejorative status—a process that has accelerated since the end of the Cold War. If Western bloc states had once received a slow drip of refugees whose escape from communist countries could be exploited for political advantage, the politicization of more recent arrivals from what has become the Global South has been far more virulent. In the case of the Blackfoot in the nineteenth century, Hall notes that the trope of refugeehood may well have been strategically deployed by the Blackfoot themselves in order to compel negotiation of a treaty with Canadian authorities. The example is a reminder of the ways in which those crossing borders, then as now, must navigate the political terrain in which their movements are read and how they deploy a range of tactics from refusal to reappropriation.

For Hall, the designation of the Blackfoot as refugees makes more sense if we understand Indigenous peoples as "transnational actors" and treaties as "transnational events." Here, Hall is challenging the border regimes—juridical, material, and representational—that shape associations with refugees and Indigenous peoples alike. Indigenous peoples have always moved across and through different First Nation territories only later colonized by settlers. Casting such movements as domestic rather than transnational is a bordering practice that serves to reinforce the naturalness of the nation-state and, in this case, of Canada and the United States as the obvious geopolitical identities constituting most of North America. Understanding Indigenous peoples as "transnational actors" *before and after* settlement decentres state borders as the only relevant marker of transnational mobility. Hall's contribution is most compelling when the space and time of transnational action with which he is concerned are extended in this way.

Since the codification of refugee status under international law in the mid-twentieth century, the transnational dimension of refugeehood has been linked exclusively to state borders such that one can only be a refugee in legal terms if a state border is crossed in the process of displacement. This is why, for displaced African Americans in the twenty-first century, the ascription of refugeehood was taken to undermine the value of their citizenship: one simply could not be a fully endowed citizen and a refugee at once. Hence another way of reading Hall's attention to Indigenous refugees is as a provocation that challenges the reduction of refugeehood to a technical form under international law. In this reading, refugees are produced not only by exile but also by embodied and affective experiences of dispossession, exclusion, and erasure, even if a person remains, as it were, in place. Such an account of refugeehood provides an opening to consider the experiences of different groups of people (Indigenous, migrant, and racialized citizens) in relation to each other and in relation to border regimes and forms of sovereign power that pit those groups against each other in a zero-sum game for proprietary control over territory.[4] This is not to suggest an equivalence in the forms of loss at stake but rather to emphasize that border regimes generate forms of violence in cross-cutting and intersectional ways and that broad coalitions might be built to resist those dynamics and to forge alternative futures.

Resisting the limits of a strictly legal account of refugeehood seems ever more important as international and domestic law increasingly becomes a means through which displaced people are denied anything approaching an intuitive notion of refuge. This is the trend that Claudia Donoso examines in chapter 7 in her account of the legal challenges to gender-based violence and gang violence as legitimate grounds for credible asylum claims in the context of the Texas side of the US-Mexico border. We could equally point to legal maneuvers deployed by European and Australian states to reduce opportunities to seek asylum and punish those who do and increasingly to prosecute those attempting to rescue migrants at sea for crimes related to people-smuggling.[5] In all these cases, ever-narrowing and perversely deployed definitions of "genuine" refugee status harden attending borders between forced/voluntary, political/economic, and licit/illicit migration and therefore between deserving/undeserving and legalized/criminalized migrants. The result is a legal regime that produces illegitimacy among its target population and has become more focused on policing and excluding than providing the refuge for which the regime was ostensibly created.

Partly because of this interplay between concrete borders and the cuts of human difference that rationalize their uneven policing, critical border scholars have tended to de-emphasize the special status of refugees in favour of a more generic category of migrant. Such perspectives refuse the notion that migration can be mapped in crude binary terms of agency and force despite the dramatically different conditions that shape the contexts in which one decides to migrate and the chances one has of success. More than semantic, these interventions take seriously the productive dimension of language. As Stephan Scheel has put it, taking refugees and asylum seekers as "given realities waiting to be researched"—even in sympathetic ways—risks reproducing residual forms of humanitarian paternalism and methodological nationalism and takes as given the norms of the liberal international order that are decidedly illiberal when it comes to freedom of movement.[6] Doing so then predetermines the scope of the affective and geopolitical frames in which cross-border mobility is referenced.

In order to maintain critical distance from prevailing categories and conventions, the impulse is often to generate new conceptual vocabularies. Equally revealing, however, are the terms in which those positioned on the sharp side of borders identify themselves and how longer-standing subject forms are reclaimed and reconfigured in the process. For example, refugees who have been subject to long-term incarceration by the Australian government in the course of their claims to asylum have continued to insist that they *are* refugees and that what it means to be a refugee is something fundamentally human, irreducible to the imprimatur of international law, humanitarian forms of objectification, or imagined forms of innocence.[7] The claim "We are human" that attends migrant struggles in camps, in cages, and on border-lines around the world is likewise a resignification of humanity itself.[8] The disjuncture between the claim's common sense and the forms of inhumanity visited on migrants compelled to state the obvious shows the ways in which universal rights, including those under refugee law, have proven insufficient to deliver substantive forms of mobility justice.[9]

If habits of mind pursued to examine borders make a difference to the politics at stake, so too do habits of body engaged at the literal point of border crossing. In this regard, the chapter by Evan Light, Sarah Naumes, and Aliya Amarshi draws attention to the ease with which border crossers acquiesce to data surveillance and incursions on their privacy as they hand over unencrypted mobile devices for inspection by airport border guards. These routine inspections that rely on voluntary compliance become part of the rituals (like passport checks, body scans, and questioning) through which borders, border authorities, and their assumed powers come to be normalized in the course of everyday mobility. "As border crossers," Light, Naumes and Amarshi contend, "most of us are not experts on the legal apparatus to which we submit ourselves." Many of us are also not experts in the historical and conceptual reframing that underwrites that legal apparatus, or if we are, we choose to ignore it at the point of border crossing. Who wants to hear a lecture on the line that crossed us when everyone is tired and just trying to get through customs? Yet these rituals of crossing, in this case, from the United States into Canada normalize those identities and make it harder to imagine and recognize other relations to land, law, and collective political life—both those that exist already and those yet to be forged, including on the basis of transformed accounts of what it means to be a refugee or, indeed, to be human.

I have spent almost two decades engaged in research and writing on borders, particularly those borders policed against refugees, asylum seekers, undocumented people, and others whose mobility is criminalized. I have been slow to recognize the laws, authorities, and administrative categories I have taken for granted as starting points for critique and the ways in which that givenness serves to reproduce an apparatus of control. Disputes framed in terms of rights to enter and exit and under what conditions too often elide fundamental questions about the particular kinds of subjects around which universal human rights have been shaped in exclusionary terms and whether such rights, even if applied uniformly and humanely, might still entail enduring injustices. Disputes framed in terms of borders that might be opened or closed too often assume that bounded territory under sovereign control is the given spatial reference point for questions of mobility. Other ways of knowing land and its relationship to more-than-human worlds are dismissed in the process and further distanced from what comes to stand for political realities that shape the parameters of the possible. Such habits of mind that were always based on the habits of certain bodies now seem just as potent to me as the border-crossing rituals that Light, Naumes, and Amarshi rightly associate with the mundane ways in which structural violence is authorized and reproduced.

This combination of material and epistemic violence is, after all, what has produced the apparent extinction of the Sinixt people that Lori Barkley, Marilyn James, and Lou Stone describe in chapter 5. In this case, extinction is pursued via knowledge production and knowledge erasure as well as by overt forms of disappearance: by the wiping of territories from maps along with Native nomenclature for those lands, by the noninvitation of Sinixt delegates to the relevant arbitrations over land claims, by the nonreference to Sinixt people in acknowledgements of First Nation lands, by the designation of Sinixt people as "nonresident aliens," and by the ongoing cultural resonance of the social Darwinist idea of peoples unsuited for survival. The authors insist on the noninnocence of academic, white, settler, and Indigenous discourses that strategically or uncritically perpetuate forms of presence and absence that are written into the maps we take for granted, the language we use, the forms of status we recognize, and the rituals of acknowledgement we endorse.

Against this background, the aesthetic, conceptual, and methodological strategies pursued in several chapters of this volume provide helpful orientations for critical inquiry. In their intervention, Leslie Gross-Wyrtzen and Heather Parrish argue for an interdisciplinary method built on both recognition and critique of the political, material, and epistemological "lines that cross us." Their contribution reflects on the process through which a collaborative artwork emerged, with each installation of the piece representing a unique "cutting together-apart"[10] of the intersecting borders—disciplinary, institutional, colonial, and more—through which borders themselves are accorded particular ontologies. The piece assembled for the conference consisted of strikingly ethereal paper columns of colour and light drawn from the material stuff of borders yet suggestive of other permutations and reconfigured possibilities. The paper columns were cut apart literally even as they formed a moving whole, fluttering intermittently as they caught drafts of air in the gallery space. The piece prompted reflection on the seduction and appeal of what is also violent and divisive, the parallel presence of generative and destructive forces in lines that are drawn in different ways, with different effects on and in particular bodies and places.

The process described by Gross-Wyrtzen and Parrish—incorporating modes of exploration, conversation, and invitation—is an attempt to open up the range of reactions and perspectives entailed in generating knowledge about borders. By contrast, the methodological commitments described in chapter 1 by Ramón Resendiz and Rosalva Resendiz in the production of their documentary film *El Muro | The Wall* centre the experiences and the perspectives of Indigenous activists who struggled for acknowledgement in negotiations over compensation for title holders whose lands were slated for intersection by the US-Mexico border wall. Drawing a hard line between colonizer and colonized, Resendiz and Resendiz chose from the outset of their process to refuse "any face time" to any "agent aligned with or sympathetic to the colonial/imperial goals of [Customs and Border Patrol] or the [US Department of Homeland Security]" and to give a platform only to those whom their main protagonist vetted as allies to the cause of Indigenous land rights. While I am sympathetic to this margin-to-centre approach and recognize its value in the "redress [of] asymmetric colonial injustices," I am less convinced by wholesale distinctions between those on one side of border justice and those on the other, especially in a context in which those recruited to police the US-Mexico border as agents of government are frequently drawn from poor communities of colour policed by the very structures they are enticed to defend.[11] More generally, I take seriously the concerns raised by Barkley, James, and Stone in relation to disputes between different First Nation peoples that while such disputes are conditioned by ongoing colonial injustices, identifying rightfulness in any scenario does not always map onto clear-cut lines between innocence and guilt.

If borders are messy, the impulse to engage them from nonbinary perspectives of interconnection and entanglement, whether in the queer or quantum terms that Murphy explores in his chapter, does not in and of itself signal a move in decolonizing directions. Fuzzy borderlines that ebb and flow in response to strategic imperatives have long been deployed by states and empires, for instance, as part of uneven, exceptional, and imperial forms of rule. Treaties that established the principle of sovereignty among European powers also established ambiguous legal and spatial identities in the form of extraterritoriality.[12] Today, states push their borders offshore, onto islands, and into the high seas in order to evade domestic and international laws that would challenge the containment and imprisonment of people on the move or people moved forcibly to the jurisdictions in question. These deliberately ambiguous carceral geographies turn refugees into illegal aliens and prisoners of war into enemy combatants with a legal sleight of hand.[13] The kinds of quantum metaphors that Murphy pursues *can* provide a fresh and better grasp on the spatial and temporal disjunctures that exhibit certain kinds of continuity in border policing over time. Studies of this kind can help us understand how bordering technologies actually work, including for purposes of colonization, and how the rhetoric of borders as two clear sides of a fixed borderline is *part* of those technologies rather than a once-was reality under contemporary assault.

The urgency of finding creative ways to articulate and appreciate these spatial and temporal complexities has only been compounded in the time between our physical presence at the conference in Lethbridge and the publication of this volume in the aftermath of the COVID-19 pandemic. If the pandemic focused the attention of those slow to acknowledge all manner of global interdependencies, it also precipitated a defensive mobilization of national borders, both materially and symbolically, almost as a reflex response. The pandemic revealed the relative absence of alternative space-time registers through which to respond to contagion in ways that do not simply assume the legitimacy and inevitability of prevailing borders and exceptional powers as well as their ability to preserve what remains a fantasy of impermeability. The uneven distribution of deaths, infections, and economic fallout generated by the pandemic also brought into stark relief another kind of border, or global colour line, no less pervasive than the national borders across and within which it functions but much less frequently called upon as a cartographic reference point from which to perceive other enduring and morphing forms of (racist) contagion.[14] As much as borders morph in form, they also stay stuck on enduring cuts of difference hiding in plain sight. The global and local configurations of those cuts and their attachments to specific combinations of nationalism, authoritarianism, neoliberalism, colonialism, patriarchy, and capitalism are the borders we face today. Whether and how we move through them depends on who and where we are; whether and how we transform them remains to be seen. The theory and practices required to do so, from freedom of movement to survival, demand our attention in the meantime.

Acknowledgements

I thank the editors and contributors to this volume for inviting me to be part of a collective and unsettling undertaking to think in new ways about the lines that cross us and to learn with and from one another.

Notes

1. Rachelle Chadwick, "On the Politics of Discomfort," 559; see also Sara Ahmed, *Living a Feminist Life*, 123.
2. Victoria Grieves, "The Seven Pillars of Aboriginal Exception to the Australian State: Camps, Refugees, Biopolitics and the Northern Territory Emergency Response (NTER)."
3. Jesse Jackson in John M. Broder, "Amid Criticism of Federal Efforts, Charges of Racism Are Lodged."
4. Aileen Moreton-Robinson, *The White Possessive: Property, Power, and Indigenous Sovereignty.*
5. Daniel Ghezelbash, *Refuge Lost: Asylum Law in an Interdependent World*; Martina Tazzioli, "Crimes of Solidarity: Migration and Containment through Rescue," 4–10.
6. Stephan Scheel, *Autonomy of Migration? Appropriation of Mobility within Biometric Border Regimes*, 218.
7. Behrouz Boochani, *No Friend but the Mountains: Writing from Manus Prison.*
8. Sandro Mezzadra, "Proliferating Borders in the Battlefield of Migration: Rethinking Freedom of Movement."
9. Ulrike Krause, "Colonial Roots of the 1951 Refugee Convention and Its Effects on the Global Refugee Regime"; Lucy Mayblin, *Asylum After Empire: Colonial Legacies in the Politics of Seeking Asylum.*
10. Karen Barad, "Diffracting Diffraction: Cutting Together-Apart," 168–87.
11. David Cortez, "Latinxs in La Migra: Why They Join and Why It Matters."
12. John Gerard Ruggie, "Territoriality and Beyond: Problematizing Modernity in International Relations," 139–74.
13. Deirdre Conlon and Nancy Hiemstra, "Mobility and Materialization of the Carceral: Examining Immigration and Immigration Detention," 100–114; Ruth Wilson Gilmore, "Abolition Geography and the Problem of Innocence," 223–40; Alison Mountz, "The Enforcement Archipelago: Detention, Haunting, and Asylum on Islands," 118–28.
14. Though see Marilyn Lake and Henry Reynolds, *Drawing the Global Colour Line: White Men's Countries and the International Challenge of Racial Equality.*

Bibliography

Ahmed, Sara. *Living a Feminist Life*. Durham, NC: Duke University Press, 2017.

Azoulay, Ariella Aïsha. *Potential History: Unlearning Imperialism*. London: Verso, 2019.

Barad, Karen. "Diffracting Diffraction: Cutting Together-Apart." *Parallax* 20, no. 3 (2004): 168–87.

Boochani, Behrouz. *No Friend but the Mountains: Writing from Manus Prison*. Sydney: Pan Macmillan Australia, 2018.

Broder, John M. "Amid Criticism of Federal Efforts, Charges of Racism Are Lodged." *New York Times*, September 5, 2005. https://www.nytimes.com/2005/09/05/us/nationalspecial/amid-criticism-of-federal-efforts-charges-of-racism-are.html. Accessed 13 Mar 2019.

Chadwick, Rachelle. "On the Politics of Discomfort." *Feminist Theory* 22, no. 4 (2021): 556–74.

Conlon, Deirdre, and Nancy Hiemstra. "Mobility and Materialization of the Carceral: Examining Immigration and Immigration Detention." In *Carceral Mobilities: Interrogating Movement in Incarceration*, edited by J. Turner and K. Peters, 100–114. London: Routledge, 2017.

Cortez, David. "Latinxs in La Migra: Why They Join and Why It Matters." *Political Research Quarterly* 74, no. 3 (2020): 688–702.

Ghezelbash, Daniel. *Refuge Lost: Asylum Law in an Interdependent World*. Cambridge: Cambridge University Press, 2018.

Gilmore, Ruth Wilson. "Abolition Geography and the Problem of Innocence." In *Futures of Black Radicalism*, edited by G. T. Johnson and A. Lubin, 223–40. London: Verso, 2017.

Grieves, Victoria. "The Seven Pillars of Aboriginal Exception to the Australian State: Camps, Refugees, Biopolitics and the Northern Territory Emergency Response (NTER)." In *"And There'll Be No Dancing": Perspectives on Policies Impacting Indigenous Australia since 2007*, edited by E. Baehr and B. Schidt-Haberkamp, 87–109. Newcastle upon Tyne: Cambridge Scholars, 2017.

Krause, Ulrike. "Colonial Roots of the 1951 Refugee Convention and Its Effects on the Global Refugee Regime." *Journal of International Relations and Development* 24, no. 3 (2021): 599–626.

Lake, Marilyn, and Henry Reynolds. *Drawing the Global Colour Line: White Men's Countries and the International Challenge of Racial Equality*. Cambridge: Cambridge University Press, 2008.

Mayblin, Lucy. *Asylum After Empire: Colonial Legacies in the Politics of Seeking Asylum*. London: Rowman and Littlefield, 2017.

Mezzadra, Sandro. "Proliferating Borders in the Battlefield of Migration: Rethinking Freedom of Movement." In *Liquid Borders: Migration as Resistance*, edited by M. Moraña, 17–26. New York: Routledge, 2021.

Moreton-Robinson, Aileen. *The White Possessive: Property, Power, and Indigenous Sovereignty*. Minneapolis: University of Minnesota Press, 2015.

Mountz, Alison. "The Enforcement Archipelago: Detention, Haunting, and Asylum on Islands." *Political Geography* 30 (2011): 118–28.

Ruggie, John Gerard. "Territoriality and Beyond: Problematizing Modernity in International Relations." *International Organization* 47, no. 1 (1993): 139–74.

Scheel, Stephan. *Autonomy of Migration? Appropriation of Mobility within Biometric Border Regimes*. London: Routledge, 2019.

Stoler, Ann Laura. *Duress: Imperial Durabilities in Our Times*. Durham, NC: Duke University Press, 2016.

Tazzioli, Martina. "Crimes of Solidarity: Migration and Containment through Rescue." *Radical Philosophy* 2, no. 1 (2018): 4–10.

Contributors

Aliya Amarshi holds a PhD in sociology from York University, where she studied the relationship between progressive social movements and political emotions. Her postdoctoral research has focused on the barriers faced by new immigrants in the Canadian labour market as well as the impacts of social oppression on the mental health of racialized Canadians. She is currently a practicing Gestalt psychotherapist involved in efforts to make explicit the link between social trauma and mental health.

Lori Barkley is a settler, political anthropologist, educator, and activist living in the heart of unceded Sinixt təmxʷúlaʔxʷ in what is called British Columbia, Canada. After teaching in the BC postsecondary sector for over twenty-five years, Barkley left academic teaching to work on Sinixt resurgence, working with NGOs, settler governments, museums, environmental organizations and anyone who will listen. She is co-author of several academic publications and has given many public talks on Sinixt in Canada.

Claudia Donoso received her PhD in interdisciplinary studies from the University of British Columbia. The title of her dissertation was "Feminist Critical Human Security: Women's (In) Security and Smuggling on Ecuador's Borders." This research was carried out with a grant from the International Development Research Centre (IDRC), Canada. She is chair and associate professor in the Department of International Studies and Global Affairs at St. Mary's University in San Antonio, Texas. Her research interests involve critical security studies, intersectional feminism, border studies, human security in communities in the Global South, and Latin American politics and security. Her most recent work has appeared in the *Journal of Borderlands Studies* and the *International Journal of Migration and Border Studies*.

Leslie Gross-Wyrtzen is a lecturer in the MacMillan Center for International Studies at Yale University. She is a feminist geographer whose work focuses on the relationship among borders, race, and political economy between Africa and Europe. Gross-Wyrtzen received her PhD in geography from Clark University in 2019. Her first book project, *Bordering Blackness: Race and the Political Economy of Migration*, draws on ethnographic research among West and Central African migrants moving through or contained within Morocco and was funded by the National Science Foundation and Fulbright-Hays. She has also published peer-reviewed articles in the *Journal of North African Studies, Environment and Planning D: Society and Space, Geoforum,* and *ACME: An International Journal for Critical Geographies.*

Ryan Hall is an associate professor of Native American studies and history at Colgate University. He is the author of *Beneath the Backbone of the World: Blackfoot People and the North American Borderlands, 1720–1877* (University of North Carolina Press, 2020) as well as articles in the *Journal of the Civil War Era,* the *Western Historical Quarterly,* the *Pacific Historical Review,* the *Pacific Northwest Quarterly,* and *Agricultural History.* He received his PhD from Yale University in 2015 and lives in Hamilton, New York.

Marilyn James (MEd Simon Fraser University) is a Smum iem matriarch appointed by Sinixt elders to uphold Sinixt protocols and laws in Sinixt tmxʷúlaʔxʷ (homeland) under the laws of whuplakʼn and Smum iem. Her work includes the repatriation of sixty-four ancestral remains from museums and collections back to their rightful places in Nkʕáwxtən (Vallican, BC). Appointed spokesperson for the Sinixt Nation in Canada (1990–2013), her work as Smum iem matriarch and Sinixt knowledge-keeper is ongoing. James is an accomplished storyteller of traditional and contemporary Sinixt stories and works extensively in the field of curriculum development. Co-author of *Not Extinct: Keeping the Sinixt Way* (Maa Press, 2021), she is an ardent advocate for her ancestors, the land, and the water of Sinixt təmxʷúlaʔxʷ.

Evan Light is an associate professor in the Faculty of Information at University of Toronto. He actively runs the Social Sciences and Humanities Research Council and British Academy–funded Deobfuscating State Surveillance in Canada project, which aims to document the surveillance capabilities of the Canadian state from municipal to federal. Light also maintains an archive of the Edward Snowden files and an off-line Snowden Archive-in-a-Box, which has travelled the globe as an art installation.

Paul McKenzie-Jones is a settler associate professor of Indigenous Studies at the University of Lethbridge and an external research affiliate with the Purai Global Indigenous and Diaspora Research Center of the University of Newcastle, Australia. He is committed to working in solidarity with Indigenous Peoples across the globe through research, teaching, and advocacy. He is the author of *Clyde Warrior: Tradition, Community, and Red Power* (OU Press, 2015). His current research projects focus on Indigenous intellectual, political, and cultural resistance to, and at, the Canada-US border since 1924 and global transnational Indigenous environmental, cultural, and political resistance since the 1960s.

Sheila McManus is a professor of history and one-third of the Lethbridge Border Studies Group. They are the author of *The Line Which Separates: Race, Gender, and the Making of the Alberta-Montana Borderlands*, co-published by the University of Nebraska Press and University of Alberta Press in 2005; *Choices and Chances: A History of Women in the U.S. West*, published by Harlan Davidson (now Wiley) in 2010; and *Both Sides Now: Writing the Edges of the North American West* (Texas A&M, 2022). They also co-edited *One Step over the Line: Toward a History of Women in the North American Wests*, co-published by Athabasca University Press and the University of Alberta Press in 2008.

Anne McNevin is an associate professor of politics at The New School. She is the author of *Contesting Citizenship: Irregular Migrants and New Frontiers of the Political* and numerous journal articles on the transformation of citizenship, sovereignty, migration, and mobility. Her recent publications examine aspects of time and temporality in relation to borders. She is working on a new book, *Worldmaking and Border Politics*, that aims to bring a world beyond bordered states into the realm of serious political consideration.

Michael P. A. Murphy is the Buchanan Postdoctoral Fellow in Canadian Democracy at Queen's University and a former Digital Policy Hub Fellow at the Centre for International Governance Innovation. He is the author of *Quantum Social Theory for Critical International Relations Theorists* (2021),

Weak Utopianism in Education (2024), over forty peer-reviewed articles, and numerous book reviews and chapters, receiving over 2000 citations.

Sarah Naumes is a PhD candidate (ABD) in the Department of Politics at York University. Her doctoral research on US Army veteran resilience led to a multiyear lawsuit in federal court, which resulted in the distribution of previously undisclosed government documents (see *Naumes v. Dep't of the Army*). She is employed at Columbia University, where she works with principal investigators to strategically secure large-scale extramural funding.

Heather Parrish is an assistant professor and program head of printmaking in the School of Art, Art History, and Design at the University of Iowa. She is a multidisciplinary artist with an ongoing interest in the mutually creative relationship between inhabitant and environment and the dynamic relation-alities enacted across boundaries. Recent solo exhibitions include *Seeing Out the Other Eye—a View through Waller Creek* at Flatbed Center for Contemporary Printmaking, Austin, Texas; *Precipitate, with the Scope collective* at Open Source Gallery, Brooklyn, New York; *Homing* at the Snite Museum of Art, Notre Dame, Indiana; and numerous other exhibitions. Collaboration is integral to her practice, including ongoing projects *Border Work* with political geographer Leslie Gross-Wyrtzen and *Scope* with biologist Elizabeth Hénaff and acoustic engineer Léonard Roussel.

Ramón Resendiz is a Chicanx documentary filmmaker and media anthropologist from the south Texas US-Mexico borderlands. Resendiz is currently a Post Doctoral Fellow at the Center for Research on Race and Ethnicity in Society at Indiana University Bloomington who will be taking a position in the Anthropology Department at the University of Oregon. He holds a PhD in media, culture, and communication from New York University and a master of communication from the Native Voices Documentary Media Program at University of Washington. His research interrogates the material and imaginary intersections of national borders, memory, visual culture, systemic violence, and settler colonialism. His book project, *Archival Resistance: Countervisual Documentary Media on the Margins of the U.S.*, investigates the historic violence, erasures, and undocumentation of critical Latinx Indigeneities in the national constructions of Texas, Mexico, and the United States. He critically studies how settler-colonial nation-states are visualized by archival institutions across the south Texas/US and northern Mexico border landscapes and the ways visual documentary producers contest and render these erasures visible. His filmography includes an array of collaborative community-based documentaries regarding immigration, social justice, human rights issues, Indigenous resistance, and the evidentiary. Chief of these is *El Muro | The Wall* (2017), a feature-length documentary film project co-produced with the Lipan Apache Band of Texas Tribal Board. His films have been screened across film festivals, community screenings, and academic conferences.

Rosalva Resendiz holds a PhD in sociology/social (dis)organization theory from Texas Woman's University. She is currently an associate professor in the Department of Criminal Justice at the University of Texas Rio Grande Valley, previously known as the University of Texas–Pan American. Resendiz identifies as Chicanx Indigenous mestiza, focusing on social justice, critical criminology, critical race theory, decoloniality, postcolonial studies, Chicana feminism, Mexican American / border studies, and organized crime. Most recently, she co-edited *Criminology Throughout History: Critical Readings* (2021) and *Gender, Crime, and Justice: Critical and Feminist Perspectives* (2021). She also has a co-authored book chapter in *BIPOC Alliances: Building Communities and Curricula* (2022): "Reclaiming Our Indigeneity: Deconstructing Settler Myths within Our Family."

Lou Stone is an Autonomous Sngaykstskx (Sinixt) activist and former five-term Inchelium Representative of the Colville Business Council, governing body of the Colville Confederated Tribes in the United States. He resides within Sngaykstskx tmxʷúlaʔxʷ (territory) in Washington State. He is an undergraduate from Western Washington University and has a master's of social work from Portland State University in community organizing and planning. Stone commits extensive time to advocate social justice and decolonizing principles that seek to restore justice for Sngaykstskx and other Indigenous peoples and education for ongoing settler-colonizer relations.

Chloe Wells studied at the University of Eastern Finland and completed her PhD in human geography at the end of 2020 with the publication of her thesis monograph *Vyborg Is Y/ours: Meanings and Memories of a Borderland City Amongst Young People in Finland*. Wells's work crossed academic borders, combining concepts from the disciplines of human geography, border studies, and memory studies. Wells now works outside academia, but her fascination with borders, and with Finland, continues.

Julie Young is an associate professor and Canada Research Chair (Tier 2) in Critical Border Studies in the Department of Geography and Environment at the University of Lethbridge, Alberta, Canada. Much of her research to date has focused on how migrants and advocates in Canada-US and Mexico-Guatemala border communities interact with and challenge those borders. Young is co-editor, with Susan McGrath, of the open-access book *Mobilizing Global Knowledge: Refugee Research in an Age of Displacement* (University of Calgary Press, 2019).